D1229395

Maine Lighthouses

Documentation of Their Past

Maine Lighthouses
Documentation of Their Past

J. Candace Clifford

Mary Louise Clifford

Cypress Communications

Alexandria, Virginia

2005

Printed in the United States of America by Kirby Lithographic Company, Inc., Arlington, Virginia

10   9   8   7   6   5   4   3   2   1

ISBN 0-9636412-6-3

Front cover: *Mount Desert Rock Light Station, designed by Alexander Parris and according to a letter written by Parris to Stephen Pleasonton dated May 21, 1850 (National Archives Record Group 26, Entry 17C), was built by J. W. Coburn in 1847. (Courtesy U.S. Coast Guard)*

Back cover: *Architectural rendering entitled "Side Elevation of the Light House and Keepers Dwellings proposed for Erection on Petit Menan Island, Me." Under the title block, it appears that the First District Inspector W. B. Franklin signed off on the plans on November 13, 1854, and that they were approved and construction authorized by the U.S. Light-House Board on December 4, 1854. (Drawing found in National Archives Record Group 26)*

Title page: *Architectural rendering of 1850 Monhegan Island light tower. A letter from Alexander Parris to Stephen Pleasonton dated May 21, 1850, found in National Archives Record Group 26, Entry 17C, indicates that Parris designed this tower. Reflectors were used in the lantern before a Fresnel lens was installed in 1856.*

Designed, produced, published, and distributed by Cypress Communications, 35 E. Rosemont Avenue, Alexandria, VA 22301; <jcclifford@earthlink.net>

Acknowledgements

The staff at the National Archives in Washington, D.C., was extremely helpful in assisting Candace in locating much of the material in this volume. A special thanks to Charles Johnson in the maritime reference section of the National Archives for his numerous searches in the stacks to find the exact volumes or boxes that Candace needed. In addition we would like to acknowledge archivists Becky Livingston, Susan Abbott, Kim McKeithan, Stephanie Richmond, and Rick Peuser as well as the technicians who pulled endless carts of material.

The majority of photos used in this volume came from the U.S. Coast Guard Historian's Office in Washington, D.C. We appreciate the hospitality and assistance of Robert Browning, Scott Price, and Chris Havern in that office.

Also many thanks to Candace's gracious hosts while visiting lighthouses in Maine: Anne Webster and Troy Wallace; Dave and Pat Gamage; Ken Black; and Scott Drombrowski. And additional thanks to Dave Gamage; Ken Black, Shore Village Museum; Dana Smith, St. George Historical Society; Nathan Lipfert, Maine Maritime Museum; Dolly Snow Bicknell; and Jeremy D'Entremont for contributing photos.

We are ever grateful to Susannah Livingston, our fantastic copyeditor.

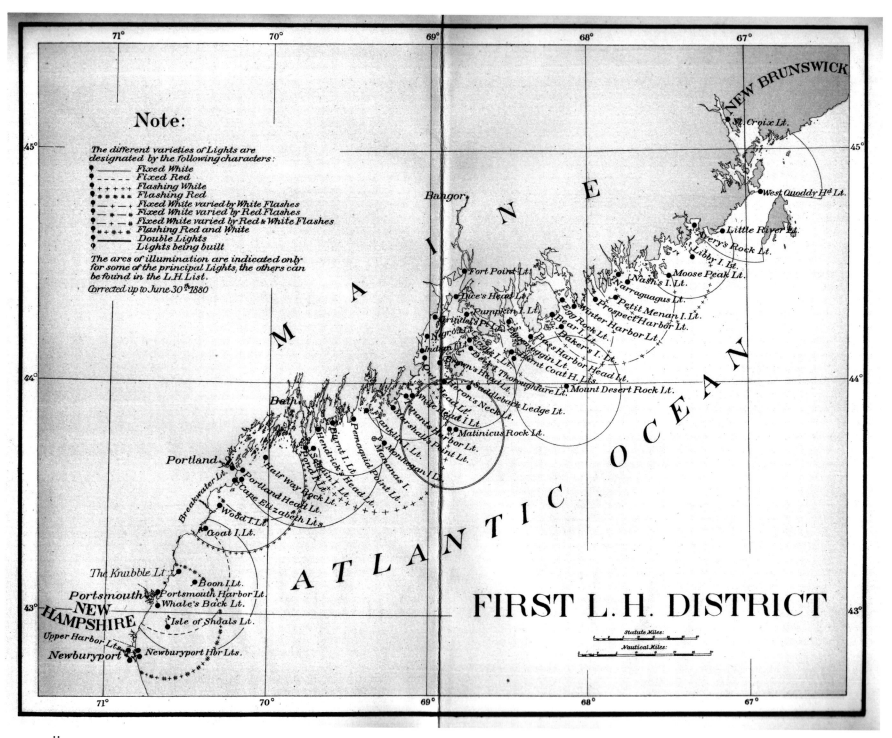

FIRST L. H. DISTRICT

ii

Contents

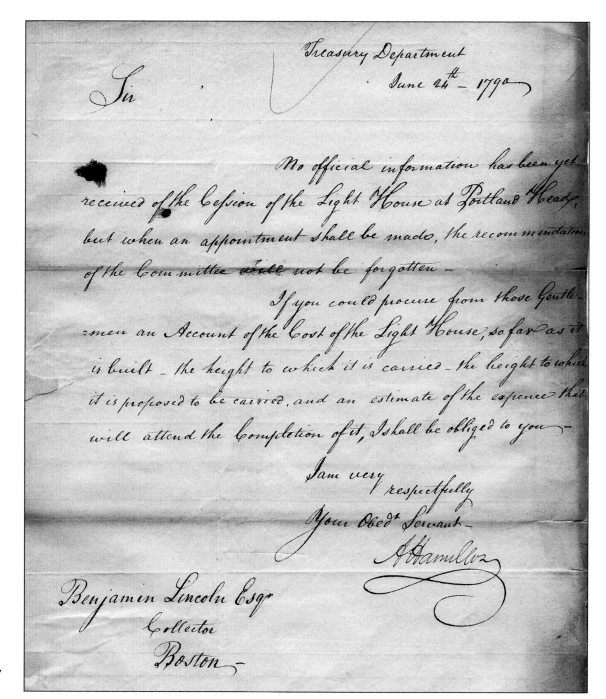

Example of an original document found at the National Archives in Waltham, Massachusetts.

Foreword

Maine Lighthouses: Documentation of Their Past is based almost entirely on primary sources.

Every lighthouse extant today exists within a realm of stories—recollections of past keepers and their children; tales of fierce storms, shipwrecks, and daring rescues of seamen; feature stories about keepers in local newspapers; obituaries of keepers; histories published by local historical societies. These are all secondary sources, unless they were written down by the participants themselves.

People living in a lighthouse neighborhood tell these stories and authors write them down, but few of them access original source material which outlines the choosing of the site, the construction the lighthouse, the appointment of a keeper, the upkeep of the station as the decades slid by. Most of this information is contained in records deposited in the National Archives; in letters of the customs collectors who superintended lighthouses in their districts in the first half of the nineteenth century and their instructions from the administration in Washington; in annual reports published by the U.S. Light-House Board after 1852; in journals kept by lighthouse keepers after 1872; in letters from lighthouse engineers who selected sites and oversaw construction and inspectors who checked on all the lighthouses and their keepers in their districts; and in the files of the U.S. Bureau of Lighthouses, which administered lighthouses until the U.S. Coast Guard took over in 1939. The records of the Coast Guard's stewardship of lighthouses are mixed in with those of the Coast Guard's many other duties and are less easy to access, and so this book closes as the Coast Guard assumes responsibility for the nation's light stations.

Throughout the first century and a half of American lighthouses, all documents were laboriously written by hand. (The typewriter was not invented until 1874.) Federal government officials had clerks who either copied drafts or wrote them as dictated. They mailed one copy, having made a second copy for the files. Customs collectors, who supervised the early lighthouses, may have had a clerk or they may have written their own letters. Keepers generally wrote their own letters, and these invariably revealed the extent of the keeper's education.

Historic photographs provide details that written records cannot. The first photographic survey of lighthouses was undertaken by an employee of the Light-House Board around 1859. Many of these images show keepers living a Spartan existence in rough rural settings. The various lighthouse agencies, including today's Coast Guard, continued photographing lighthouses. The majority of the photographs used in this volume are from the collection housed at the U.S. Coast Guard Historian's Office in Washington, D.C.

Most textual documentation relating to lighthouses and their administration has been gathered into Record Group 26 (RG 26) in the National Archives headquarters in Washington, D.C. (Photos and plans are housed at Archives II in College Park, Maryland.) RG 26 is divided into entries organized by the type of correspondent for distinct time periods or geographical areas. For example, the correspondence of the customs collectors in Entry 17C is filed according to the town in which the customs office was located. Copies of correspondence from Stephen Pleasonton, who supervised lighthouse matters in the Treasury Department from 1820 to 1852, are recorded in volumes in Entry 18. Keepers' journals or logbooks are found, arranged by lighthouse, in Entry 80. Some records are contained in bound volumes with indexes; much loose correspondence, however, is gathered into packages tied with ribbons and fitted into boxes. One member of our writer duo is a very enthusiastic researcher, mining the archives for the gems sought by historians working in the field. The records of the lighthouses in Maine presented in this book have been culled as part of that process.

Each letter chosen was reproduced by digital camera or photocopy, and was read and transcribed. Our transcriptions of these letters are exactly as they were written. Style and handwriting varied from clerk to clerk. If some of the quoted prose looks quaint, bear in mind the clerks who copied or wrote these letters and whose spelling, punctuation, and capitalization reflected the particular school each attended or even the particular teacher who taught him grammar. No common rules for grammatical style existed in the nineteenth century. Even the Government Printing Office, established in 1860, did not publish a style manual until 1894.

In the early days only a few light lists and circulars were typeset. Once the U.S. Light-House Board took over in 1852, annual reports, light lists, and employee instructions were typeset and published on a regular basis. Correspondence produced after the invention of the typewriter in 1874 is much easier to read.

The rich maritime heritage of the United States is abundantly apparent in the history of Maine. Many settlers and later residents of Maine relied on the sea for their livelihood. Ships were vital to the fishing, granite, lime, lumber, and shipbuilding industries that thrived in Maine's early coastal communities. Later, numerous steamships carried passengers in Maine's growing tourist trade. Some 67 light stations with resident keepers were built to aid shipping along Maine's rocky coastline between 1791, when the light at Portland Head was lit, and 1910, when the last traditional lighthouse was lit at Whitlocks Mill.

PART I. Early Lighthouse Administration and Construction

Early lighthouse administration

When our republic was founded, sailing ships traveled up and down the coast, turning into the rivers, bays, and harbors or out across the Atlantic, transporting lumber, fish, and other goods. New England was the dominant hub of commerce and industry. Ship owners and captains needed aids to help them navigate the rocky coastline and the numerous offshore shoals and islands. During the colonial period, 12 lighthouses had been built to meet this need, paid for either by lottery or by fees levied on the ships using a harbor.[1]

In 1789 the new federal government took over the colonial lighthouses, with the president personally approving all decisions regarding their administration.[2] In 1791 Treasury Secretary Alexander Hamilton would have conferred with President Washington on the appointment of a keeper for the just-completed Portland Head Light.

Although major decisions were made at the federal level, clearly some local federal official was needed on the spot to supervise operation, maintenance, and new construction of lighthouses. Because each major port on the eastern seaboard had a Collector of Customs responsible for collecting the revenues that supported the new republic, those officials were given the additional responsibility of superintending lighthouses in their districts. They reported to the Commissioner of the Revenue in the Treasury Department, to whom Hamilton assigned responsibility for lighthouses from 1792 to 1802.

Between 1802 and 1813—during the Jefferson and part of the Madison administration—Secretary of the Treasury Albert Gallatin personally directed lighthouse activities, with those duties transferred back to the commissioner between 1813 and 1820. In 1820 President Monroe by executive order transferred "care and superintendence of the lighthouse

establishment" to the Fifth Auditor of the Treasury, a position established by Congress in 1817 to deal with the business of a rapidly growing nation. When Stephen Pleasonton[3] took over the Lighthouse Establishment in 1820, the United States had 55 lighthouses, eight of them located in what would that same year become the state of Maine. During Pleasonton's 32-year administration the number of lighthouses and lightships increased to 325[4]; 35[5] of these were in Maine.

The local collectors of customs were charged with selecting sites and purchasing land on which to build new lighthouses. They also oversaw the contractors who erected the new towers and related structures, and authorized repairs of existing stations.[6] While Maine was still part of Massachusetts, the collector in Boston oversaw all lighthouses in Maine. Revolutionary War General Benjamin Lincoln, former Secretary of War, held this post from 1791 to 1809. Henry Dearborn replaced

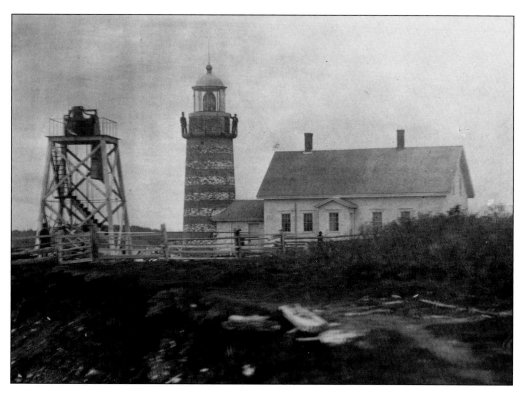

Located inshore of a dangerous ledge of rocks on the Bay of Fundy near Lubec, Maine, West Quoddy Head Light was the easternmost light station in the United States. President Thomas Jefferson ordered its establishment in 1808 to guide burgeoning coastal shipping along a rockbound coast. (National Archives photo # 26-LG-4-78A)

Independent State, they feel a desire that the superintending care and authority above mentioned should *now* be exercised by *one of their own citizens*. They therefore hope and respectfully request that Mr. Ilsley may be appointed.[8]

On June 7, 1820, Isaac Ilsley began his new duties. His first action was to advertise for placing a fog bell near the lighthouse on West Quoddy Head.[9] Ilsley held the position until John Chandler replaced him on February 9, 1833. Chandler was succeeded by John Anderson on March 8, 1837. Anderson served until 1848. Luther Jewett assumed the post a few years later.[10]

him on February 11, 1809, and served until 1812. Dearborn's son Henry Alexander Scammell Dearborn replaced his father as collector and served from 1812 until 1830.[7]

When Maine became a state in 1820, it was recommended that

the care and superintendence of Light Houses, Buoys . . . in Maine might be usefully transferred from the Collector of the Port of Boston, Charlestown, to Isaac Ilsley, Esq., Collector of the Customs for the Port of Portland. His character as a prompt, faithful, and intelligent officer is well known, and as *Maine* is now an

Lighthouse construction

Because lighthouses were needed in isolated locations, their construction was often difficult to supervise. Most collectors had no expertise in building any kind of structure and rarely visited the stations. Instead, they relied heavily on reports from keepers (although communicating with them could also be difficult), and from those contractors who delivered oil and other supplies. The captains of the local revenue cutters sometimes visited the lighthouses, providing Pleasonton with reports on conditions at the stations and the effectiveness of their lights in aiding navigation. Winslow Lewis, a canny lighthouse entrepreneur,[11] won a contract to "supply lamps, wick burners, and tube glasses"[12] to all lighthouses, and was often called upon to make repairs where needed. He frequently provided reports on his visits to the stations.

The early lighthouses were built of materials that were readily available: wood and rubblestone. Because wooden towers burned or deteriorated faster than masonry in the harsh marine environment, no early examples survive in Maine.

Generally built on a foundation of natural rock, the New England masonry towers used rubblestone split from the adjacent ledges or cliffs or collected on the beach. The cracks between the stones were filled with a lime and sand mortar. The masonry towers varied in height from 20 to 50 feet; the walls were usually three feet thick at the base, tapering to two feet in thickness at the top. A brick dome was placed on the top of the tower and an iron and glass lantern (which shielded the lamps) was attached to the tower by imbedding the lower ends of its iron angle-posts into the masonry walls.[13]

After the Revolution, the candles used in colonial times were replaced by flat-wick lamps burning whale oil. Early models smoked dreadfully, clouding the lantern glass and blackening the ceiling. Keepers were enthusiastic about a

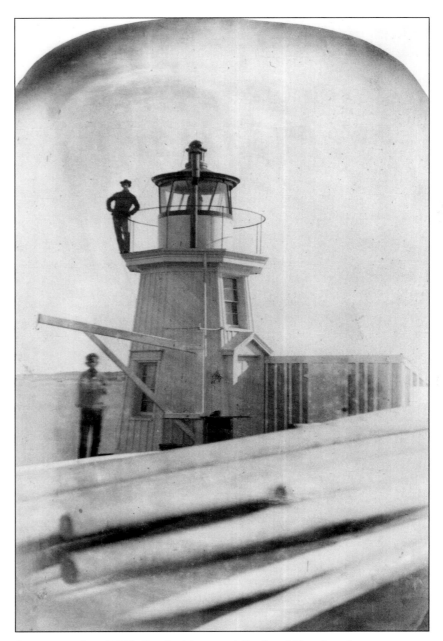

Constructed in 1855, the first tower at Portland Breakwater was an example of wood construction. (Ca. 1859 photo courtesy of U.S. Coast Guard)

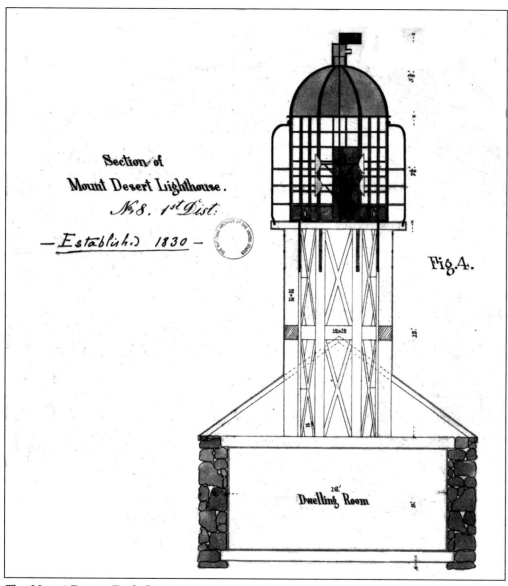

Section of
Mount Desert Lighthouse.
№ 8. 1st Dist:
— Establish.) 1830 —

Fig.4.

12x12

12x12

Dwelling Room

The Mount Desert Rock Station was established 20 miles off the coast of Maine in 1830. The original tower shown here was reported in 1831 to have been badly built: "the material is all bad—the mortar in particular is made with salt water sand & mixed with salt water, if you analyze it you can see no Lime whatever . . . the dwelling House in bad order—leaks much—and smoaks badly."[14] (National Archives drawing in RG 26)

newer whale oil lamp with a hollow, circular wick that gave off much less acrid smoke. The lamps were hung on a chandelier in front of parabolic reflectors that magnified the light. (Two different versions were named for their inventors, Ami Argand in Europe and Winslow Lewis in the United States.)[15] In 1835, Collector Chandler reported that in Maine, "the lamps, I believe, with one exception, are those of Winslow Lewis's patent,[16] with the addition of Black's patent heaters."[17]

When deteriorating towers were torn down, the materials were often recycled for use in newer towers or other structures on the station. In addition to a tower and dwelling, early nineteenth-century stations might include a garden site, a place to store whale oil, a system to provide water, and maybe a chicken house and shelter for a milk cow. The simple keeper's quarters generally had wood or rubblestone walls, shingled roofs, and brick chimneys. The first floor was divided into three rooms, while the second or attic floor contained three small chambers. Cylindrical wooden tanks secured with iron hoops were located in the cellar to collect rainwater from the roof. Wells offering spring water were not common. Some keepers on offshore stations had the onerous task of sailing to the mainland with casks for carrying fresh water to their station.[21]

PART I. Early Lighthouse Construction and Administration

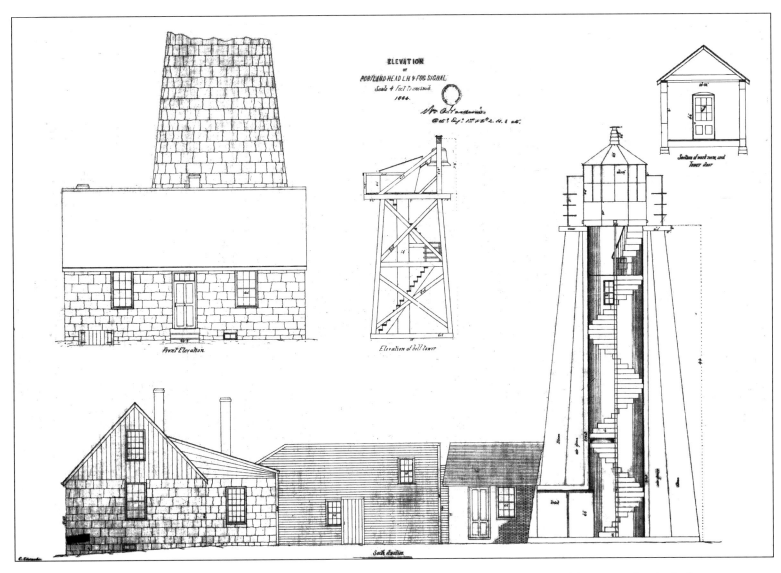

ELEVATION
of
PORTLAND HEAD L.H. & FOG SIGNAL.
Scale 4 Feet to one inch.
1864.

Front Elevation.

Elevation of bell tower.

Section of work room and Tower door.

Maine's oldest lighthouse, Portland Head, was begun by the Commonwealth of Massachusetts and completed under the federal government in 1791. In 1809 Keeper Barzillai Delano reported that

The difficulty in getting from the dwelling House to light House is very great, by reason of the passage being very steep & rocky & in addition to this is often frozen over in the Winter season, by reason of the sea washing over it. I therefore beg your permission to build a Shed at the expense of the States from one building to the other, about Sixty feet in length, Six feet in width & seven feet high, for a passage way, which I think is really necessary & will get it done as cheap as possible.[18]

The covered passageway is shown in this 1864 drawing. (National Archives drawing in RG 26)

Lanterns were gradually improved in the first half of the century. Early lanterns used thick sashes and small panes in order that "the Lanterns might not blow away in the time of severe storms."[19] The early tower at Mount Desert Rock, shown here, is an example. By 1843, however, Pleasonton reported, based on experience, "that it does not require half the quantity of sash formerly used, & that we may dispense with half at least, & enlarge the panes any size, . . . sometimes 24 by 18 and sometimes 3 ft. by 2 ft."[20] As the old lanterns became corroded and worn out, they were replaced with this newer design, which permitted wider dispersion of light. (National Archives drawing in RG 26)

Maine's earliest lighthouse: Portland Head

On January 17, 1791, Secretary of the Treasury Alexander Hamilton wrote to Collector Benjamin Lincoln, Superintendent of Lighthouses in Boston:

> You will find enclosed the President's commission for Mr. Joseph Greenleaf as keeper of the light house of Portland. It will be necessary that an agreement be made with him for compensation for this service, to be subjected for approbation to the President of the United States. Also that you make provision for the requisite supplies of oil, wicks, etc. in the same form.[22]

Early correspondence focused on defects in Portland Head's construction. Some thought was given to building an outer wall to enclose the original tower, but on July 19, 1797, Commissioner of the Revenue Tench Coxe wrote that

> Nothing, however, but the pointing and wash . . . appears advisable till the thickness, goodness, badness, etc. of the stone, mortar, stonework, manner of laying, etc. has been examined and noted by the Inspectors. . . . Will you be pleased to have the pointing inside and out with the best mortar effected and to direct the seams to be first picked with an instrument, and the white wash to be put on at the proper moment.[23]

In 1809, Keeper Barzillai Delano reported to Collector Henry Dearborn, Superintendent of Lighthouses in Boston:

> The Light House leaks very badly, which has been the case for some years past. Gen'l Lincoln had it new pointed about ten years since from the top to the bottom to prevent its leaking, but it did not answer the purpose only for a short time; its being situated so near the sea that it is continually washing in upon it & has destroyed the pointing & cracked the building considerably. Gen'l Lincoln proposed to have it Boarded on the outside in order to make it tight, which if you should conclude to have done, please to write me & I will let you know what the expence will be.

> The other buildings do not want much repairing; a few nails only are wanting. The work I can do myself.

> The Lanthorn is Seven feet high & six feet in diameter. There is only one lamp in the lanthorn which holds about twelve Galls. of Oil & has twenty tubes for the wicks. . . .[24]

Lighthouse entrepreneur Winslow Lewis submitted his views to Secretary of the Treasury Albert Gallatin on November 14, 1812:

> Portland Head Light house is a stone building standing on an eminence 50 feet above the level of the sea. The tower is 72 feet from the foundation to the lantern. It appears that when this Light house was built that 50 feet of it was built of the best materials, done in a workmanlike manner. Some difference then

PART I. Early Lighthouse Construction and Administration

The tower at Portland Head was heightened and shortened several times during its first century of service. The final modification to the tower height was completed in 1885, when it was raised to stand 101 feet above sea level. (National Archives photo # 26-LG-4-79)

Maine Lighthouses: Documentation of Their Past

arose among the contractors. The finishing was undertaken by another sett of men, who carried up the last 22 feet in the most slighty manner possible, on which they put a lantern of only 5 feet diameter. This Lantern was built different from anything of the kind I ever met with, being made wholly with copper, without any iron, the posts being formed of Copper Tubes. . . . The building is decidedly too high. I should recommend taking of[f] 20 feet. This would take of[f] all that part that was so badly done at first & give a sufficient deck for a lantern of ten feet diameter. The building then would be substantial & they would have a light equal to the importance of the situation of it.[25]

Secretary Gallatin accepted Lewis's proposal and authorized Collector Dearborn to advertise a contract "for cutting down and putting a new Lantern to the Light House next Summer, agreeably to Mr. Lewis's recommendation."[26] A new keeper's dwelling was completed at Portland Head by Henry Dyer in 1816 for $1,175.[27]

The light itself was improved in 1821. On August 31, Collector Ilsley wrote Pleasonton:

By my Annual return of the state of Light Houses in Maine for the year 1820, in the column of Remarks you were informed of the frequent complaints of the Light on Portland Head, that the cause of complaint was that the Light is too small for the Lantern, and that Mr.

Lewis recommended the addition of four or five Lamps and reflectors; the cost of which he estimated at 500 Dollars.

The Light House on Portland Head is of more importance than any other on this coast. It has a large Lantern capable of receiving an additional number of lamps, . . . or as Mr. Lewis has lately proposed, to remove the whole of the apparatus with the lamps and reflectors from Portland light to the Light Houses building at Kennebeck or Boothbay, and make a complete new set with fifteen 16-inch reflectors, with lamps for the Portland Light House. . . .

I am of opinion that something should be done to make the Portland Light more brilliant and discoverable at a greater distance; probably the addition or alteration above proposed will have the desired effect. Mr. Lewis is confident that it will.[28]

Other early towers
Seguin Island

The second lighthouse built in what would become the State of Maine was on Seguin Island, near the mouth of the Kennebec River. On June 3, 1794, Commissioner of the Revenue Tench Coxe instructed Collector Benjamin Lincoln, Superintendent of Lighthouses in Boston:

. . . steps [should] be taken to fix upon the most eligible spot for the actual site and to run out the ten acres, so as . . . to

include the most profitable land & . . . a convenient Landing. It is possible that the stone, wood, and timber on the land may be objects worthy of attention for present use in the building or for fuel, repairs, fencing, etc. As there are several Ports in the district of main which will be more or less accommodated by this building, it will be proper that the Collector of the Customs, Merchants & others in each, be apprized of the time when the measures shall be taken to fix upon the site. It is understood there is a considerable desire in favor of each end of the Island tho' it is supposed not to contain twenty acres of land. Every part of it is presumed to be firm & free from quick sands.[29]

Coxe listed all the facts that should be determined before the building could be planned: the best spot for the building; the elevation above the sea at high water and at low water; the composition of the soil and its suitability for grain, grass, fruit, and vegetables; the kinds, sizes, and quantity of wood and timber growing on the location; the kind and quantity of building stone; economical sources of building materials; and the respective contract costs for a building of stone, brick, or wood.[31]

Coxe also instructed General Lincoln that if there were competing views of the best location for the light, he should obtain in writing "the ideas of those who may be for & against the several

The keeper of the Seguin Island Light, John Polerecsky, wrote on November 11, 1796,

I Receivd 25 barrells of oil . . .. It took four stout men to Cary one barell to the house, and the Same four men and Myself to lift the barell on the top of the Cisterns to empty them, being Six foott high. If I could afford to keep a pair of steers or a horse, I could Save all that trouble & expence in taking the oil on the shore to the house in half this time, but I should run my Self in debt, ... I have but one Cow here for my family and one tun of haye I purchased for her, delivered to the house, Cost me 20 dolars and so it is with all the necessaries of life till I Cann Raise them. Therefor hope you will be so obliging as to have My Salary Raised to 300 dollars. . . .[30]

The rocky terrain is shown here in a ca. 1889 photo of the second lighthouse on Sequin Island. (Photo by H.G. Peabody courtesy of U.S. Coast Guard)

situations. The under named gentlemen have been mentioned by General Dearborn of the House of Representatives as persons suitable to be consulted on the subject."[32]

The only proposal for building the lighthouse was submitted by General Henry Dearborn, who would later serve as the Collector of Customs and Superintendent of Lighthouses in Boston.[33] Commissioner Coxe attributed the lack of response to the advertisements to "the paucity of workmen equal in skill and capital to such works in North Carolina & Maine & to the profitable business in adjacent scenes which the ablest workmen in the great towns at this time have, creating a disinclination to go for employment far from home."[34] The Commissioner contrasted this with the many offers for the proposed lighthouse at Montauk on Long Island in New York.

The plans for a lighthouse on Seguin Island, the first offshore station in Maine, were simple. Coxe asked for a wooden lighthouse that included "a costly and firm stone foundation, if necessary, a stone cellar to the house, a capacious and secure oil vault." He also required "the light House to be wider & higher, of course stouter, and the lantern is to be of the first rate."[35] The lantern proposed for Seguin was to be the same size as that proposed for the lighthouses

at Montauk, New York, and Cape Hatteras, North Carolina—both important coastal lights.[36] The original specifications were not strictly adhered to, as a deep foundation was found impractical in the hard rock.

On October 12, 1796, Dearborn reported to Commissioner Coxe:

On the tenth inst. I completed the light house, dwelling house, oil vaults & cisterns, and had the oil arrived with wicks and rods or chanes for hanging the lamps, it might have been lighted on the night of the tenth inst. but no oil had arrived when I left the Island the day before yesterday. . . . Carey[37] visited the Island a few days before the whole was completed, he advised . . . building a small barn which I have done, I have likewise been at some expense in preparing a large rock with a ring bolt through it with a long chane to secure a boat in the harbour, no slip has been made.[38]

Major John Polerecsky had received the keeper appointment the previous March so that he could make preparations for gardening and farming on the island, although his salary was not to commence until the lighthouse was finished and he began his duties as keeper.[39] Lighting was delayed by lack of oil, wicks, and chains or rods for hanging the lamps.

Keeper Polerecsky was paid to clear the land surrounding the station to reduce the risk of fire and to provide

land for grazing and possible cultivation.[40] Polerecsky reported other necessary alterations to the collector. Commissioner Coxe wrote to Henry Dearborn on August 14, 1797:

Information has been received by the superintendent of the Light Houses in Massachusetts from the Keeper of that on Seguin Island that no well has been sunk there. This being plainly within the terms of your contract, and being absolutely necessary it is an unexpected circumstance that it is not completed. . . .

It is also understood from the Keeper "that the electrical [lightning] rods want altering" without which there is supposed to be danger of shattering or setting fire to the building. . . .

It is likewise represented that the lantern does not pass off its smoke. From this it is doubted whether there are enough ventilators, or whether there are any or at least enough of air pipes in the floor, or of aperture in the lower part of the sides of it."[41]

Dearborn replied to Coxe on August 30, 1797:

This day received yours of the 14th instant enclosed in a letter from Genrl. Lincoln—in answer to the complaint about a well. I was at considerable expence in digging in several places on the Island with a view of ascertaining when a durable well could be obtained; one of which places was within about three rods of the house, and after what I thought a fair experiment, determined on

PART I. Early Lighthouse Construction and Administration

Because the wooden lighthouse on Whitehead Island had badly deteriorated, in 1852 a 41-foot conical tower (shown here ca. 1859) was constructed and a Jones fog bell hung in a scaffold. In 1855 a third-order lens replaced the lamps and reflectors in the tower. (Courtesy of U.S. Coast Guard)

stoning it & fixed it for use. This well was Sunk in October 1795. We used the water for all my workmen and oxen thro' the whole course of the summer and fall. In August and September we had a severe drought, but there was no want of water. It was therefore presumed that the well would be sufficient for all the purposes it was intended for, and I have never heard of any want of water . . . . As to the electrical conductors, there was no other deficiency but the want of a very small alteration in the lower short joint, which was not crooked exactly conformably to the make of the rock or foundation, but they are as perfectly safe as any conductors could be. . . . I have been informed by several of our Coasters that the Seguin light can be seen farther than any other light in New England.[42]

Although the lantern, constructed by a Mr. Wheeler,[43] was reportedly one of the best in the United States, the small wooden tower supporting it soon deteriorated and had to be replaced in 1819.

Whitehead Island

After Seguin, the next lighthouse built on the Maine coast was on Whitehead Island. In March 1798, sea captains petitioned for a lighthouse there to guide ships, both foreign and domestic, to and from Penobscot Bay, stating

. . . That the entrance to this Bay, which is now extremely hazardous, might be made safe and free from danger by the erection of a Light House on a place called White Head, twenty leagues eastward of Seguin, and about two leagues and a half S. West from Thomaston Harbour. That there are about two hundred vessels, from fifty to one hundred and twenty tons, which are employed in the coasting business and which pass through said Bay as often as once a week during nine months in the year, and that not one of these vessels can enter the Bay in safety without the Light which is here prayed for.[44]

On August 30, 1803, Commissioner William Miller reported to the Secretary of the Treasury:

> Gen'l Lincoln informs me that he has visited Whitehead and fixed on a Site for the Light House and Keeper's Dwelling: The former will stand upon a Rock near the Channel, about 20 feet from high water mark in the fullest tides. The Dwelling will be near to it, in the wood which is to be fallen and burnt prior to the erection of the Building, in order to avoid accident of the adjacent woods, should it at any time take fire.[45]

Although Collector Lincoln reported complaints about the leaky condition of the wooden lighthouse at Seguin, the Treasury Department decided not to build a more substantial stone tower on Whitehead. The Department justified the decision by stating that the lighthouse at Whitehead was "considered merely a harbor light" as opposed to a coastal one. (The Jefferson administration seemed more concerned with economy than maritime safety.) In 1803, Benjamin Beal and Duncan W. Thaxter of Hingham, Massachusetts, received the contract to erect a wooden lighthouse for $2,150. Ellis Dowlf was appointed keeper at an annual salary of $200 in June 1804.[46]

Franklin Island Lighthouse, near the mouth of the St. George River, was constructed in 1806 for a sum of $3,150. President Jefferson appointed John Lowell as the first keeper on January 28, 1807.[47] The 1839 Light List recorded that it had 10 lamps with 14-inch reflectors and stood 50 feet above the high watermark. The replacement tower shown here was first lit in 1855. (Courtesy of U.S. Coast Guard)

Franklin Island, West Quoddy Head, and Wood Island

Beal and Thaxter, the same contractors who built the Whitehead Island Lighthouse, won contracts to construct lighthouses on Franklin Island near the mouth of the St. George River (1806), on Wood Island at the Saco River mouth (1807), and at West Quoddy (Passamaquoddy) Head on the Bay of Fundy (1808).[48]

In 1813, when Thomas Dexter, the first keeper at West Quoddy Head, resigned, his closing inventory of the property at the station included

PART I. Early Lighthouse Construction and Administration

5 Blank form[s] of Annual Returns, & one fill[ed] up for direction

8 ditto for Quarterly Accounts, including Duplicates

1 Printed Letter of March 5, 1813– Instructions

1 W. Lewis Book, Instruction to Manage Patent Lamps

1 Letter authorizing the Purchase of Coal for Light House

1 Light House Dimensions as per Annual Return

1 Dwelling House . . . wanting repairs . . .

1 Oil Vault Contain[ing] 5 Oil Butts or Tubs unoccupied (out of repair)

1 Small Row Boat—Much out of Repair Having Neither Oars, Painter or Sails

1 Hoisting Machine with Two Block and Tackle Full—Wanting Hooks & Thimbles

Schedule of Sundry Articles to Keep in Repair to Cleanse & furnish Lewis Patent Lamps in Order, Excepting the difficency of some Used & Consumed for the Purpose.[49]

Dexter's replacement, Peter Godfrey, ran into difficulties during the War of 1812. On April 8, 1815, L. Trescott reported from the Custom House at Passamaquoddy:

The Keeper of the Light House at West Quoddy head has made me the following representation:

"That there is not more than 10 days oil in the vault, that the British Comman-dant at Eastport claims the Controul of the Light House until the British Troops leave Castine, that he had been promised by the said Commandant that his Sallarey should be paid by the British Goverment & had received orders for his pay (which had not been realized) to the first of the present month, [and] that being verry poor & a large family to support he asks liberty to draw on the superintendant for his sallarey & hopes considering his situation the Goverment of the United States will indulge him in allowing him a part of his pay sence the first of October last."[50]

By the1830s, all of the wooden lighthouses built by Beal and Thaxter had deteriorated so much that they had to be replaced. A new lighthouse at West Quoddy was completed under a contract with Joseph Berry for $2,350. Its ten lamps were lit on August 1, 1831.[51] Ezekiel D. Demuth was contracted to build a lighthouse and dwelling on Franklin Island for $2,364; Jonathan Knight and Joseph Berry were contracted to build a boathouse and slip at the same station for $400.[52] Its ten lamps were lit up on August 25, 1831.[53] Berry also completed the new lighthouse and dwelling at Whitehead

The whitewashed 1858 stone tower shown here was the third tower on Wood Island. (Photo ca. 1859 courtesy of U.S. Coast Guard)

and hung and put into operation a fog bell for $3,000.[54] The 10 lamps at Whitehead were lit on September 5, 1831.[55] Collector Chandler petitioned for a new lighthouse on Wood Island in 1835, indicating that the old one was "rotten" and "the tower rocks so that it is impossible to keep it shored up."[56]

Disaster on Libby Island

In mid-August 1822, Stephen Pleasonton accepted the lowest bid, $2,850, for constructing the lighthouse on Libby Island. Benjamin Beal and Quincy Bicknell had submitted the bid. Winslow Lewis was contracted to fit up the tower with a lighting apparatus and associated supplies for $800. Pleasonton had given Collector and Superintendent of Lighthouses Isaac Ilsley some latitude in the design of the new tower, indicating that the material should be stone and that the dwelling should be similar to the others built under the collector's direction. Pleasonton cautioned Ilsley, however, to stay within the amount appropriated.[57]

The tower was constructed quickly ahead of the approaching cold season. On October 31, 1822, Ilsley requested that a keeper be appointed, indicating that the tower would be ready in 10 or 15 days.[58] In less than six months the following report was submitted to Collector Ilsley:

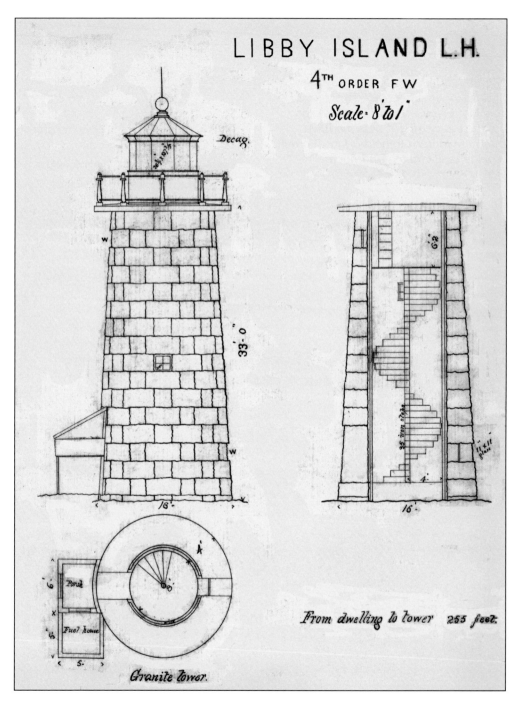

LIBBY ISLAND L.H.
4TH ORDER FW
Scale: 8' to 1"

Decag.

33'-0"

16'-

6'2

35 iron steps

11'x11' glass

4'

16'-

From dwelling to tower 255 feet.

Pond

Fuel house

Granite Tower.

PART I. Early Lighthouse Construction and Administration

The second tower at Libby Island was far sturdier than the one it replaced, and survives to this day. The lighthouse originally had 10 lamps with reflectors. This drawing (facing page) and United States Light-House Board photo (below) show the tower after it was modified with a new lantern to hold a fourth-order Fresnel lens. (Drawing and photo courtesy of U.S. Coast Guard)

I regret exceedingly the occasion for addressing you at this time, which is no less than to inform you of the complete demolition of the Lighthouse erected last year on Libby's Island. Cap. McKellar is here and will give you the particulars. He says that at eleven o'clock p.m. of the 8th inst. it fell down with a dreadful crash to the ground; the weather was fine and no difficulty was previously apprehended. The post had burst out a part of the wall during the winter, but by the attention of the Keeper it had been nearly reduced to its place. Whether this misfortune is charged to the unfaithfulness of the workmen, I know not. I tho't so far as I was capable of judging that the work was well done, and I am inclined now to believe, if the same work had been done at an earlier season, it would have remained firm.[59]

Keeper John McKellar elaborated in another letter:

The day previous to its falling it shew no signs of falling more than it had done for some time. The damage the Lanthorn & apparatus annexed to it has sustained, will cost about one tenth of the original cost to repair it, exclusive of the glass which is all broken. Three of my tin butts and four barrels of summer oil were crushed beneath the ruins.[60]

Collector Ilsley speculated on possible explanations for the building's collapse:

. . . The building was erected late in the Autumn and the mortar remained damp untill the frost came; during the winter a crevice was discovered in the column and continued increasing for some time. The Keeper, aware of danger, obtained assistance and placed braces against the work which prevented an increase of the aperture, and, he believed that would keep the Column in perfect safety for receiving repairs in the early part of the season; and which we were about commencing when the column fell. Whether the misfortune arose from the unfaithfulness of the workmen or from the frost penetrating the work before the mortar had cemented, I am not able to say; probably it was partially from both.[61]

Ilsley estimated that the cost of rebuilding the tower would be $1,000, and he urged that "the work should be commenced as early as practicable, in order that the mortar may have time to dry and cement before the frost comes on."[62] One of the potential contractors, Jairus Thayer of Portland, reported

I have examined the ruins of the Light House on Libby Island and find the column completely demolished, and that it will be necessary to rebuild it from the foundation; the Dome Lantern, Lamps, reflectors & apparatus much injured by falling, the glass all broken and soapstone deck much injured.

The whole may be repaired and put in complete order for sixteen hundred dollars. I will contract to do it for this sum, and believe it cannot be done for anything less.[63]

An advertisement soliciting proposals was issued, and Thayer was underbid by Noah Humphrey, who was given the contract for $1,449.[64]

Choosing contractors

The early lighthouses in Maine were plagued with problems: Many had been poorly constructed. Communicating with and supplying isolated locations was challenging at best. Keepers' lives were difficult (as evidenced by the many requests for increased salaries). And mariners complained about the quality of the lights.

According to a law written in 1809, all lighthouses were to be built by contract. After a request for proposals had been advertised, the lowest bid was selected unless the bidder was found to have previously deceived the government. This system discouraged expert architects and builders from bidding and often resulted in the use of inferior materials and methods of construction. If the local collector could not inspect the work, he appointed an "overseer" to monitor the progress of the job. The overseer was paid up to three dollars a day; the contractor would not be paid until the overseer certified that the job had been "faithfully done." The 1809 law also required the Lighthouse Establishment to advertise for proposals for obtaining oil and supplies.[65]

PART I. Early Lighthouse Construction and Administration

EARLY KEEPERS EARNED LESS THAN $1 A DAY

The most common type of communication from keepers during this early period was a request for higher compensation. One of the earliest requests was in the form of a petition dated August 10, 1812:

> The subscribers, citizens of Portland, hereby certify that for several years past they have known Barzillai Delano to be a careful keeper of the Light at the entrance of Portland Harbor, and that he has discharged his trust faithfully; and are of opinion that his present salary of two hundred and twenty-five Dollars is inadequate to the services performed by him, and that three hundred Dollars per year would be no more than a just compensation for the keeper of that light, and would be but a bare subsistence for a small family.[66]

The petition had 22 signatures, including that of the collector, Isaac Ilsley. On October 10, 1812, Secretary Gallatin responded "that the President[67] has decided that the Salary of the Keeper of the Portland Head Light House should be increased to three hundred dollars per annum."[68]

Salaries were based on a number of factors—the amount of work involved (i.e., the number of lamps to be maintained); the presence of a fog signal, etc.; the location of the lighthouse (i.e., an onshore station vs. an offshore station); and other advantages or disadvantages of the situation.

The correspondence makes clear that the Fifth Auditor in Washington and the superintendent in Portland had very limited knowledge of construction methods. An auditor is by definition someone who audits accounts, not a building contractor. The early contracts to build lighthouses contained minimal instructions—generally little more than a sketch of the desired structure and a page of specifications. Congressional appropriations for lighthouses were not generous; costs were to be kept at a minimum. Winslow Lewis, a contractor for many of the early lighthouses, criticized this frugality in an 1843 letter to the Secretary of the Treasury:

> I have been the Contractor for building about 80 of our lighthouses. From 1817 to 1837 there was on our extended coast & lake waters a rapid increase of light houses. Petitions came to Congress from every quarter, the consequence was the appropriations were extremely limited. In most instances from 4,000 to $6,000. In four instances 1,500, 1,600, 1,800 & $2,000 . . . . The land was to be purchased, light & dwelling house built & the lighting apparatus to be paid for. . . . This Sir, accounts for so many of your 2nd class

In 1831 Stephen Pleasonton described the condition of Petit Manan Lighthouse as

very bad indeed—built of worse materials than [Mount] Desert Light —the lanthern in good order as regarded the lamps & reflectors, but otherwise positively dirty—dwelling House much out of repair & leaking badly—the man has gone off, being tired of his state of independence. His wife had charge of the whole concern. This light I discover was built in 1817 by Frederick & William Pope, under Mr. Dearborn's superintendence. You will cause the necessary repairs to be made here, before the season be too far advanced; and if the keeper has actually left the establishment to his wife, you will report the fact and another appointment will be recommended.[69]

The 1817 tower was finally replaced with the tower shown here. Note the original tower without its lantern pictured on the right. (Ca. 1859 photo courtesy of U.S. Coast Guard)

PART I. Early Lighthouse Construction and Administration

of lighthouses not being built with more expensive & permanent materials. . . . a Light house built with hammered Granite dispensing with all wood, would be more durable than one built of brick or rubble stone with wood interior.[70]

Collector John Chandler, the Superintendent of Lighthouses in Maine, was at least in the field and could observe problems as they arose. In a letter to Stephen Pleasonton, dated November 28, 1829, he complained that

. . . one great defect in building all the Light Houses [towers] which have been erected in this state for many years past, is, in building them too large at the bottom, as they must come to about ten feet at the top, the water rests so long on them that it will find its way through the wall . . .. Some of them have been laid up with little mortar in laying the stone and pointed; and those which have had a sufficient quantity of mortar to lay the stone in, it is done so late in the season that the mortar freezes before it dries, and entirely destroys all the adhesive quality of the mortar, . . . I hope hereafter that no stone work of the kind will be done in this cold climate later than the middle of July, or August at the latest. The Light Houses which were built a year or two since on Cape Elizabeth never did dry. They were built so late in the season that the mortar froze, and whenever rain came, it ran amongst the stone and kept it continually wet.

. . . The truth is that the Light Houses already built give strong evidence of the necessity of having a man to superintend the building of the Light Houses, etc., who is a thorough workman, and a man of strict integrity; but such a man cannot be got for the sum which has been given . . . , and it is difficult for the superintendent of Light Houses to decide after the work is done, pointed and whitewashed, whether it ought to be accepted or not. This can only be known as the work progresses from day to day. There is also a difficulty in knowing from the keepers of the Lights, what repairs are necessary from time to time . . .. Some of them, probably from motives of economy, do not state all that ought to be done, and being neglected frequently require heavy repairs; others think more must be done than is really necessary.

It is very important that they should be kept well painted, pointed and whitewashed. The iron rusts very fast, if not kept painted. I am not sure but what it would be economy to select a good judge of what would be necessary to be done, and send the Cutter with him to inspect the whole of the Light Houses in the State early in the Spring, and report what is necessary to be done to each establishment.[71]

Pleasonton's response is not available. Two years later, on September 6, 1831, he wrote Chandler what Chandler must have already known:

. . . several of the Light Houses within your district have been so badly built and are now so much decayed, that if they are not speedily repaired, there will be great danger of their falling into ruins. For instance, it is represented that the one at Mount Desert Rock which was built & lit up only a year ago "is in a state of rapid decay, the materials all bad and work badly done, the mortar in particular is made with salt water and Sand mixed, no lime whatever. The dwelling house, too, leaks much and smokes badly."[72]

Pleasonton's 1831 report continued:

Moose Peak Light: This light was built by Jeremiah Berry in 1826 & the remarks made concerning it are—'worse & worse —'twill soon fall—mortar all sand—small stones all falling out—ran my arm in a foot—Lanthern in tolerable order— House very bad indeed.' The repairs which you may find necessary here you will cause to be made also. The remedy for bad mortar, as in this case, seems to be a coat of roman cement inside & out.

Libby Island Light: Is stated to be 'in a dilapidated state—will last a few short months unless something is done soon— the lanthern in tolerable order altho' not very clean . . ..'

As you may have other Light Houses in your District concerning which I have no particular information, . . . you could visit all the Light Houses this autumn in one of the Revenue Cutters and report their actual condition to me. In their standing instructions this duty is required of the Superintendants, once a year . . .[73]

A few weeks later, on September 28, 1831, Pleasonton replied to Chandler's explanation of the defects inherent in construction in Maine's climate.

The fact that you state that the mortar of many of the Light Houses on the Islands, however good originally, is destroyed by the frosts before it can become dry, in consequence of the prevalance of fogs & a damp atmosphere thro' the summer & fall months, seems to exonerate Messrs Berry and Small from blame in regard to the Light House at Mount Desert Rock. It would be improper therefore to prosecute or otherwise punish them for what they could not prevent. In the spring, as early as the absence of frost will permit, the several Light Houses in which the mortar has been injured, ought to be coated over with Roman Cement which it is presumed will become sufficiently hard before winter to resist the weather effectually. It will be expensive in the first instance, but it will be economical in the end.

Hereafter measures must be taken too, to build the Light Houses which may be authorized, early in the spring, and a superintendant in whom you have full confidence appointed to see that the mortar is properly made & the work substantially done.[74]

In further correspondence, Chandler suggested to Pleasonton that rather than coating the entire lighthouse with Roman cement, the mortar in the joints might be replaced "about an inch deep." Someone had told him that a coat of Roman cement over the entire surface would be washed off by storms before it had time to harden,

and whenever the water should get under any part of it, late in the fall or winter it may freese and heave off . . . . I will, however, follow your instructions if not otherwise directed. In either case, the expense will be considerable. If you can give me any information as to the best quality of Roman cement and the manner of preparing and using it, I shall be obliged to you. I am not sure but what there is a great difference in the quality, and it may be that our stone masons do not understand the best mode of preparing and using it, as it is very little in use here. I have taken much pains to seek out a good person to do the repairs on the Light Houses the coming season. There is no one whom I should think so well of employing as Col. Seward Merrill, who built the Boon Island Light. He is one of our best workmen; is very honest and faithful—no man more so. He proposes to find all the rigging to sling the stages on which to work, and board himself for three dollars per day, which is as low, I presume, as such a man can be got with the rigging, which will be necessary for the work. Shall I be authorized to employ him? There will be wanting a small vessel and some persons to sail her and it will be best to employ one other mason who can be got for less wages, and one common hand, so as to get the repairs through in good season, and employ the vessel as little time as possible; that number of hands will be necessary to hoist and manage the stagings. Shall I be authorized to employ the vessel and hands mentioned to make the repairs?[75]

The letters on the subject went back and forth, indicating that Pleasonton and Chandler were picking up ideas wherever they could find them. Pleasonton responded:

When I wrote to you on the 28 Sept. last I was under an impression that an entire coat of Roman cement over the Towers of the defective Light houses would be more efficacious than pointing the crevices between each layer of stones. If experienced workmen, whom you may have it in your power to consult, should be of opinion that pointing with Roman cement would be better than the other mode, I have no objection to your adopting that mode.

Instead of employing persons by the day to execute the work . . . you had better advertise for proposals and give it to the lowest bidder by Contract. The Keeper of each Light house to be repaired should be instructed particularly to oversee the work and cause it to be faithfully done.

I have no knowledge of where you will obtain the best Roman cement. Mr. Winslow Lewis, at Boston, who has used

PART I. Early Lighthouse Construction and Administration

a good deal of it, could probably inform you.[76]

On March 1, 1832, Collector Chandler wrote to Pleasonton:

I have this moment received your letter of the 25th ultimo in which you say that instead of employing men by the day, (as I proposed) to repair the Light Houses, it is your opinion that I had better advertise for proposals and give it to the lowest bidder, which I shall do of course; but I really fear that it will get into hands who will know little of the business and produce much trouble, and that the experiment in the use of the Roman Cement will not have a fair trial, nor the work be well done . . .[77]

Following Pleasonton's instructions, on March 9, 1832, Chandler advertised for proposals

. . . for repairing the Light Houses and Dwelling Houses connected with them

The repairs to the tower at Baker Island contracted for in 1832 did not last indefinitely. The tower was rebuilt in 1855 and shown here ca. 1859. (National Archives photo # 26-LG-1-19)

This granite tower at Mount Desert Rock replaced the earlier deteriorated tower in 1847. (Ca. 1859 photo courtesy of U.S. Coast Guard)

at the following places in the State of Maine, to wit—Wood Island; Pond Island; Monhegan; Owl's Head; Mantinicus Rock; Baker's Island; Petit Menan; Moose Peake; and Libby Island. The Contractor to take the lime mortar out [of] the joints of the outside walls of the buildings, three fourths of an inch deep, and deeper if the security of the walls render it necessary, and supply its place with the best of Roman Cement, properly prepared in such a way, as to make the walls perfectly water tight and strong . . ..[78]

In 1835, Chandler repeated the observation he made in 1829:

. . . Instead of having the base of the Tower from sixteen to twenty feet diameter, and ten feet at the Deck, when not more than twenty or twenty five feet high as is the case with many of them, I would have as little difference between the diameter of the Tower at the base and at the Deck, as can be, and have it stand strong. I suppose the object of building so large at the base was to have room for the Oil Butts, etc. but the Oil can very conveniently be kept in the Cellar. Where

Part I. Early Lighthouse Construction and Administration

the base is so large, when the storm beats against it, and the water lays so long upon it, it is impossible to have it tight. Whereas, if the wall is nearly perpendicular, it runs off immediately instead of running through the wall.[79]

The quality of many of the lighthouses built under Stephen Pleasonton left much to be desired. He took as much pride in saving money for the Treasury as in providing adequate aids to navigation. In 1843 Pleasonton wrote

. . . I do not hesitate to say that no similar establishment in the world now presents better lights, or is conducted with any thing like the economy. Being in possession of an official statement laid before Parliament in 1842, of the expenses of the British Lighthouses for 1840, I find the average was 3,602 dollars, whilst ours averaged 1,313 dollars only. This includes every expense of maintenance.[82]

Pleasonton's thriftiness included recycling used building materials and components. The lanterns being replaced at West Quoddy Head and Franklin Island were to be used at the lighthouses planned for Marshall Point and Browns Head. The latter lights were considered to be "harbor lights only. For such twenty feet will be sufficiently high and you will adopt that height with the proper proportions."[83] Pleasonton remarked, "This appears to be the best

way of disposing of the old lantherns, as they would bring a very inconsiderable sum if offered for sale, if indeed they would sell at all."[84]

In 1838, Congress was asked to authorize a number of new lighthouses, but some of the members were aware of

The lighthouse at Owls Head at the entrance to Rockland Harbor on West Penobscot Bay was completed in 1825.[80] The tower was most likely rebuilt or restored after that date—there is evidence that it was in a deteriorated condition soon after completion. On October 8, 1831, Captain Derby of the Revenue Cutter Morris *reported that the tower was*

. . . the most miserable one on the whole coast, & I am fearful it will not stand till spring. It has been patched

construction problems. A board of navy commissioners was appointed to appraise the current lighthouse system and the need for or suitability of the proposed sites. The inspecting officers found that the quality of the nation's lighthouses ranged from very good to

up since Sept. & is now apparently in good order, but it settles, and the stones drop out. The mortar is nothing but sand; you can see it on the ground. The Keeper says that the house is all hollow (I mean among the building stones), the mortar being decayed has run out & appears like Dust. . . . The interior of the Dwelling House was in neat order, & the Keeper & his wife to all appearance excellent people.[81]

(National Archives photo # 26-LG-4-60A)

very bad. The number of poorly constructed towers led many of the inspectors to conclude that future construction should be supervised by a qualified engineer.[85] In 1847, after more complaints, Congress went so far as to assign the construction of six new lighthouses to the Army's Bureau of Topographical Engineers.

Twin lights

Two sets of twin towers were built in Maine, the first constructed on Matinicus Rock in 1827 and the second set on Cape Elizabeth in 1828. Before distinguishing characteristics for lights were developed, twin lights were built in places where stations were located close enough together that one might be confused with another. At least 10 sets of twin lights were established in the United States.

On January 17, 1827, Collector Isaac Ilsley wrote to Pleasonton:

> I would beg leave to observe that the buildings on Mantinicus Rock should be so constructed that the Light may be distinguished from other Light Houses near the same, and for this purpose it is found necessary to have two Towers with Lanterns and Lights in each. The expense of two Stone Towers, built separate from the Keeper's House, would considerably exceed the appropriation made by Congress for erecting the buildings. Regarding these considerations, and also

that lofty Towers are not necessary on Mantinicus Rock, I deemed it advisable to advertise proposals for building the Keepers House of Stone, forty feet long and the walls two feet thick; on each end of the house to build an Octagon Tower, the posts of which to rest on the beams of the house, and to extend six feet above the ridge of the house. This method of erecting the building will be less expensive than any other, and, I believe, will answer the purposes for which they are designed. I would further observe that the Rock is a difficult place to build on and that to erect the buildings, even in the manner above named, they will cost five hundred Dollars more than the appropriation.[86]

Jeremiah Berry constructed the twin lighthouse for $3,700, and Winslow Lewis fitted up the two lanterns with patent lamps and reflectors for $800. John Alden Shaw, the first keeper, lit the lights for the first time on July 15, 1827.[87]

Cape Elizabeth Light Station marked Casco Bay and the approach to Portland Harbor from the south. The first aid to navigation on Cape Elizabeth was a windmill. It decayed and was demolished, and a beacon was erected around 1811. When a lighted aid was considered for Cape Elizabeth in the spring of 1827, Collector Ilsley reported that

> . . . I have, in company with six respectable Ship Masters and owners, visited Cape Elizabeth; and after a full

examination of the situation, the Gentlemen were of the opinion that Lights on two separate Towers should be placed on the Cape; the reasons in favor of two lights are that they may be distinguished from other Lights near the same, and that by the two lights a dangerous ledge lying about two and a half miles southeasterly from the Cape, may be avoided by the vessels passing coastwise, or bound into, or out of this port, by the Cape.[88]

Eight bids were received for constructing the towers on Cape Elizabeth; the lowest, $5,220, was from Jairus Thayer, who also outbid Winslow Lewis for fitting up the towers for $828. An extra 12 acres of land was purchased in order to access a spring for water.[89] The two rubblestone towers stood 300 yards apart, 144 feet above sea level. "Vessels coming from sea and bound into Portland Harbour, by giving these two lights a birth of 4 miles and run to the northward and eastward until Portland Light bears N.W., then stand directly for it, will clear all ledges."[90]

As the decades slid by and more and more lighthouses were constructed, the need for a feature that would distinguish one lighthouse from another during daylight hours became more urgent. The daymark could be a distinctive coloring or pattern, shape, or configuration of buildings. At the Cape Elizabeth station, the 1865 *Annual Report* noted, "in order still further to identify

Two separate towers designed by Alexander Parris were constructed on Matinicus Rock in 1857 and the building with the two towers was modified so that the roof line extended over the old towers. (Ca. 1859 photo courtesy of U.S. Coast Guard)

the two lights at Cape Elizabeth as day marks, four broad horizontal red stripes have been painted on the easterly tower, and on the westerly tower one vertical stripe."

Requests for higher salary

In 1830, Esaias Preble, keeper of the Mount Desert Rock Light Station, complained that his salary was inadequate for he was, "obliged from the great distance the rock is situated from the main land, to employ one, if not two men, to keep the Light in constant operation."[91] Preble asked for a second increase a year later, but on November 25, 1831, Pleasonton wrote to the Secretary of the Treasury:

> I consider it inexpedient to increase the salary in this case. In reference to other situations on the coast of Maine, it is already high. The Keeper at Martinicus Rock is subjected to nearly, if not quite, as many privations and inconveniences, and his salary is only four hundred and fifty dollars. In fact there is no salary higher than this for keeping a single Lighthouse in the United States.
>
> If we increase the salary of Mr. Preble, we must increase many others, and the average of four hundred dollars will not admit of it.[92]

In 1831, in response to a petition from the keeper at Dice Head Lighthouse for an increase in salary, Collector Chandler elaborated his position:

> . . . If it is believed that the Salary of all the Keepers are too low, then the one at Dice's Head is too low of course; but that Light is on the main land near a very respectable village, altho it is over rather rough ground to get to it. But I should think all those on Islands better entitled to an increase of salary than the one at Dices Head; and there are some of those on Islands that are not very well paid— particularly Mount Desert Rock, Martinicus Rock, Moose Peake and Petit Menan. I cannot therefore recommend the raising the salary at Dices Head, unless all are, on the coast of Maine, (with two or three exceptions) raised.[93]

On December 11, 1834, Pleasonton wrote to F. O. J. Smith:

> I have the honor to receive your letter of the 9th instant, recommending an increase of fifty dollars per annum to the Salary of the Keeper of Franklin Light house in Maine.
>
> Preparatory to fixing & regulating the Salaries of the respective Keepers of Light houses in 1829, I caused a report to be made to me by an intelligent and highly respectable man who had visited all of them, as to the advantages and disadvantages of each. With this report before us, with such additional lights as we could obtain, the Secretary of the Treasury and myself fixed the Salary of each Keeper with all the care and impartiality we could bestow upon the subject. On that oc-

> casion, I perceive, the salary of the Keeper of Franklin Island was raised from 300 to 350 dollars which corresponds with those of most of the other Keepers within the State of Maine. It is perhaps impossible to do precise and equal justice between the several Keepers, but I am of opinion that the Salaries as now fixed approximate as nearly to it as is practicable. As some evidence of this fact I send you enclosed a sketch [below] of the situation of several of the Keepers on the coast of Maine, with the Salary allowed to each from which you will perceive that the Salary of the Franklin Island Keeper bears a fair relation to that of others in his neighborhood and that if his Salary be increased it will afford a just claim to others for an increase. . . . I regret that I cannot find any good reason for recommending an increase of the salary of the Franklin Island Keeper.

The 'sketch':

> Petit Manan Light House is situated on the small Island of Petit Manan, 6 miles from the Main land, has a safe landing for a boat, land sufficient to keep a cow and a small garden. No other advantages. Salary of Keeper $350.00.
>
> Martinicus Rock Lights situated on a small barren Rock, near the Mouth of Penobscot Bay, 14 miles from the Main Land, accessible only in very moderate weather, not one foot of soil on the rock, and there are two lights to attend. Salary $450.00.

The first keeper at Cape Elizabeth, Elisha Jordan, was appointed on October 22, 1828. He received $450 per annum to tend both lights, a slightly higher salary than other mainland keepers.[89] At some point the rate was increased to $500. Keeper William Jordan, however, did not feel this to be an adequate sum. On August 6, 1852, he wrote Stephen Pleasonton:

I took charge as keeper of the Cape Elizabeth two Lights in the month of July, 1849, and have continued so to keep the Light, as I believe to the satisfaction of the Government, and to all navigators, as I have heard no complaints whatever; I have been faithful and economical, as the Superintendent of Lights will say. I feel confident that there is not a Light House Keeper any where to be found who has tried harder to save oil than I have—as my monthly and yearly statements will show.

I have two Lights to attend and a Fog Bell. The Lights are three hundred and twenty-five yards apart and the Fog Bell from dwelling House is about 110 feet distance. I have to hire a boy during the summer season, and a man during the winter months, and, if I did not do so, could not faithfully keep things in order. The location of the Lights is on a Cape, exposed to easterly storms and nothing to break them off, so that it is exceedingly hard work, especially in winter, to get from one Light House to another, in the night to trim lights twice—as the track in the snow, if made, fills up as fast as made, and each tower is fifty feet to ascend. In view of the above considerations, I would respectfully ask you to allow me One Hundred Dollars more per year, which would make my Salary $600 per year.[90]

Apparently his request was not granted. In 1853, Jordan was no longer keeper at Cape Elizabeth. Instead, Nathan Davis was listed as keeper with the same $500 salary; however, an assistant had been added to the station, at an annual salary of $200.[91] A few years later, a second assistant was added. Two more keepers were added to the station after a steam fog signal was installed in 1869. (Ca. 1859 photo courtesy of U.S. Coast Guard)

Maine Lighthouses: Documentation of Their Past

Hendricks Head Lighthouse was constructed on an island near the Sheepscot River mouth to guide mariners into the river and into Wiscasset Harbor, a prosperous shipbuilding center. The plan called for a combined dwelling and tower, not unlike that designed for Mount Desert Rock. John Upham lit the lamps for the first time on December 1, 1829.[100] On May 10, 1831, Collector Chandler reported that "the Keeper of the Light at Hendrick's Head writes me that he is in want of a boat; that establishment being on an Island. He also wants a well. He says he has to bring his water a quarter of a mile, except when it is wet."[101] In 1835, the keeper at Hendricks Head applied for a boathouse and slip. His request was denied because the "boat house and slip appear to be chiefly wanted with the view of launching the

PART I. Early Lighthouse Construction and Administration

boat more readily to aid vessels in case of distress" and this purpose was not one to which the Lighthouse Establishment could devote its expenditures.[102] The lighthouse is shown at left ca.1859. The old one-story rubblestone dwelling with a lantern on the roof was replaced with a new brick tower with a separate two-story wooden keeper's dwelling in 1875. (Courtesy of U.S. Coast Guard)

The original tower on Pemaquid Point (below) on the west side of the entrance to Muscongus Bay was erected in 1827 by Jeremiah Berry for $2,800. Winslow Lewis fitted up the lamps for $500.[97] Isaac Dunham was appointed keeper and the tower was lit on October 29, 1827.[98] By 1834 the tower was found to be "so decayed as to render it advisable . . . [to] be substituted by [a] new tower."[99] (Courtesy of U.S. Coast Guard)

Burnt Island Light situated in Booth Bay, 4 miles from the village of Townsend, and one mile from the mainland. No wood on the Island and only sand for a small garden. Salary $350.00.

Franklin Island Light situated near the entrance of St. George's River, 4 miles from the main-land, a small Island of Rocky Woodland, about one acre cultivated. Some fish are caught here in the Season for them. Salary $350.00.[103]

Pleasonton further explained his reasoning to Secretary of the Treasury Levi Woodbury on March 21, 1836:

I have the honor to return herewith the letter of the Hon. F. Ruggles with a letter from the Keeper of Pond Island Lighthouse enclosed, soliciting an increase of salary, and to state that when the salaries of the Keepers generally were revised by the Secretary of the Treasury and myself, in the year 1828, an increase of salary claimed by the then Keeper (Joseph Rogers) of this Lighthouse was duly considered and it was determined on comparing his case with that of others in his neighbourhood, not to increase the salary. With the view to do justice to the several Keepers, Mr. Winslow Lewis, who had frequently visited all the Lighthouses was applied to for a report of the condition of all the Lighthouses, upon which report some of the Keepers were increased, but the great majority of them received no increase whatever.

In regard to Pond Island and Seguin Island Lights, he reports as follows:

"Pond Island Light, situated on a small Island at the entrance of Kennebec River—no wood or land for cultivation, but the keeper has some advantage in entertaining the company that resort there in the Summer."

"Seguin Island Light—Situated six miles from the main land. The Lighthouse, with the Dwelling house is located three hundred feet above the level of the sea. The ascent of the road from the landing is an angle of forty five degrees up which all the supplies have to be conveyed. The Island contains about fifty acres of rocky land—no wood, and but very little land fit for cultivation, but produces sufficient grass to support several cows and a few sheep."

On considering the situation of these Keepers, it was thought the last mentioned was entitled to fifty dollars a year more than the former, and he was allowed that increase. I am still of opinion that this is a proper distinction.

If we raise the Pond Island Keeper, it will be necessary to raise those of half a dozen other Islands on the coast of Maine, all of whom receive the same salary with him.[104]

The subject came up again later that same year. Pleasonton replied to the Secretary of the Treasury on October 13, 1836, regarding John Simpson, keeper of the Petit Manan Lighthouse, soliciting an increase of salary:

The present high price of living has induced several Keepers to apply for additional compensation, and if this course should continue another year, it may be necessary to apply to Congress to increase the salaries generally, as the present average limit will not allow of an increase. The limit allowed by law is 400 dollars . . . .

I would respectfully recommend that all applications for increased pay be postponed until it shall become necessary to act upon all.[105]

Many keepers applied for and did receive additional compensation for ringing a fog bell. On August 7, 1837, Captain John Salter, keeper of the lighthouse at Seguin Island, was instructed that a bell had been placed at his station in a suitable building and was ready to be used during foggy weather.[106] Captain Salter received an additional $100 in salary until the machinery for ringing the bell was approved and attached.[107] That same year the keeper at Cape Elizabeth received an additional $50 to ring that station's fog bell.[108]

Problems with illumination at Browns Head Lighthouse

Six bids were received to build the lighthouse at Browns Head; the lowest—$1,800—was from Jeremiah Berry of Thomaston.[109] On July 27, 1832 Collector Chandler informed Pleasonton that

> The Light House at Brown's Head at the Western entrance of Fox Island Thorough Fare is now finished, except the fitting up, which will be done in a short time . . ..
>
> I found it necessary to procure the trees about the buildings to be pulled and cleared away to prevent the buildings being destroyed by fire. This I had done before the buildings were erected. . . . It will I suppose be necessary to lay out, say fifty dollars to make a road to the water, so that whatever may be brought by water for the use of the establishment may be got to the buildings . . ..[110]

On August 23, 1832, Collector Chandler reported that the lighthouse at Browns Head is "now completed, fitted up and ready for lighting—the oil is also there, and there being no keepers appointed, I am obliged to hire persons to take care of them . . .."[111]

Nine months later Collector Chandler reported that the lamps and reflectors were faulty. Pleasonton replied as follows:

> All the Lamps and reflectors in the Lighthouse at Brown's Head which were placed in it only last fall, are reported in your returns at the beginning of the year to be bad. In the contract you entered into for fitting up the Lighthouse, I find the contractor was bound to put 6 oz. of pure silver on each reflector. It is manifest that this could not have been done by him or the reflectors could not have been reported bad in a few months afterwards.
>
> As we are bound to deliver the Lamps and apparatus of all the Lighthouses to the new Contractors for supplying oil etc. in good order, it will be proper for you to call upon the Contractor for fitting up this Light to put the Lamps and every thing appertaining to them, in good order, as called for by his Contract. If he refuses to do so, it will be your duty to order suit against him, to enable you to sustain which, I will return to you the original Contract . . ..[112]

According to Collector Chandler the problem was caused by the lack of a vent hole:

> With respect to the fitting up of Brown's Head Light House, I am aware that the return of the Keeper reported the Lamps and Reflectors bad. And it is true that when the lamps were put in, they did badly, owing to the workman leaving no vent hole, through mistake, and the Keeper being new did not perhaps know what the difficulty was, at first, although he will, I think, make a very good Keeper . . .. After finding there was a difficulty with the lamps, the Contractor took his workman with him to Brown's Head, and made the alterations necessary, and I am informed that the Light has done very well since, and I have had no complaint from the Keeper. With respect to the reflectors, three of them were eighteen inch Reflectors taken from White Head Light, and had been but about two years in use, and were good. At the hole, where the tube goes through, they were a little tarnished by the fire of the lamp, as they will be very soon, but were three inches larger, over and above where they were tarnished, than the fourteen-inch ones, required by Contract. The others were furnished by Winslow Lewis, which he had made for the purpose, and the Contractor was furnished with a Certificate of the workman, who plated them for Mr. Lewis, that he had put six ounces of pure silver on each. . . .[113]

A replacement tower was completed and lit with a fifth-order lens in 1857.

The tower at Browns Head ca. 1859. (Courtesy of U.S. Coast Guard)

PART I. Early Lighthouse Construction and Administration

Endnotes

[1]Some of the introductory material in Parts I and III is based on J. Candace and Mary Louise Clifford, *Nineteenth-Century Lights: Historic Images of American Lighthouses* (Alexandria, Virginia: Cypress Communications, 2000).

[2]The first presidential administration included only an Attorney General and Secretaries of War, Navy, Treasury, and State. The Interior Department was not created until 1850.

[3]During the War of 1812, Pleasonton, then a young clerk in the State Department, distinguished himself by packing up the Declaration of Independence, the Constitution, international treaties, and the correspondence of George Washington and carting them to Leesburg, Virginia, where he locked them in an empty house and gave the key to the local sheriff. From Anthony S. Pitch, *The Burning of Washington*, reprinted on the White House Historical Association website at <www.whitehousehistory.org/08/subs/08_b04.html>.

[4]Arnold Burges Johnson, *Modern Light-House Service* (Washington, D.C.: Government Printing Office, 1890), p. 14. Francis Ross Holland in *Great American Lighthouses* (Washington, D.C.: The Preservation Press, 1989) claims there were 331 lighthouses and 42 lightships in 1852.

[5]The 1854 *Light List* indicates 38 lights in Maine, three of which were built after 1852.

[6]Francis Ross Holland, Jr., *America's Lighthouses: An Illustrated History* (New York: Dover Publications, Inc., 1972), p. 27.

[7]*A Biographical Directory of the U.S. Customs Service, 1771- 1989* (Washington, D.C.: U.S. Customs Service, Department of the Treasury, 1985).

[8]Letter from Boston customs office to Stephen Pleasonton, Fifth Auditor of the Treasury, March 25, 1820 (National Archives, Record Group 26, Entry 17J (NC-31): "Correspondence Relating to the Appointment of Lighthouse Keepers, 1801-52"). Hereafter abbreviated as NA, RG 26, E. All NA footnotes refer to the National Archives in Washington, D.C., unless otherwise noted.

[9]Collector Isaac Ilsley to Pleasonton, June 7, 1820 (NA, RG 26, E 17C (NC-31): "Letters Received from Superintendents of Lights, 1803-52").

[10]*A Biographical Directory of the U.S. Customs Service, 1771- 1989.*

[11]Winslow Lewis had been a ship captain whose career was interrupted by the Embargo of 1807. With a wife and six children to support, he turned to lighthouse improvements as a way to make a living. For a detailed account of Lewis's career, see Richard W. Updike, "Winslow Lewis and Lighthouses," in *The American Neptune*, January 1968, p. 32.

[12]Ilsley to Pleasonton, November 20, 1822 (NA, RG 26, E 17C).

[13]Johnson, p. 25.

[14]Captain Derby of Revenue Cutter *Morris*, "Remarks on Light Houses," August 16, 1831 (NA, RG 26, E 6 (NC-31): "Annual Reports, 1820-53").

[15]Holland, *America's Lighthouses*, p.14.

[16]Congress passed a law authorizing the Treasury to buy Winslow Lewis's patent and to contract with him "for fitting up and keeping in repair, any or all of the lighthouses in the United states or the territories thereof." The contract was to last not less than seven years, during which time Lewis would be solely responsible for keeping all the lighthouses in repair. (United States, *Statutes at Large*, II, 691) The appropriation for this purpose was $60,000. (Updike, p. 36).

[17]Collector John Chandler to Pleasonton, August 28, 1835 (NA, RG 26, E 17D (NC-31): "Superintendent of Lighthouses Replies to Circulars, 1830-38").

[18]Keeper Barzillai Delano to Collector Henry Dearborn, Superintendent of Lighthouses in Boston, June 1, 1809 (NA, RG 26, Regional Branch at Waltham, Massachusetts).

[19]Pleasonton to Superintendent of Lights in New York, August 18, 1843 (NA, RG 26, E 35 (NC-31): "Lighthouse Letters, Series P, 1833-64").

[20]Ibid.

[21]"Report of I.W.P. Lewis, Civil Engineer, made by order of Hon. W. Forward, Secretary of the Treasury, on the condition of light-houses, beacons, buoys, and navigation, upon the coasts of Maine, New Hampshire, and Massachusetts, in 1842," in U.S. Light-House Establishment, *Public Documents and Extracts from Reports and Papers Relating to Light- Houses, Light-Vessels, and Illumination Apparatus, and to Beacons, Buoys, and Fog Signals, 1789-1871* (Washington, D.C.: Government Printing Office, 1871), hereafter referred to as *Lighthouse Papers*, p. 356.

[22]Secretary of the Treasury Alexander Hamilton to Collector Benjamin Lincoln, Superintendent of Lighthouses in Boston, January 17, 1791 (NA, RG 26, Waltham).

[23]Commissioner of the Revenue Tench Coxe to Lincoln, July 19, 1797 (NA, RG 26, Waltham).

[24]Delano to Dearborn, June 1, 1809 (NA, RG 26, Waltham).

[25]Lewis to Secretary of the Treasury Albert Gallatin, November 14, 1812 (NA, RG 26, E 17J).

[26]Gallatin to Henry A.S. Dearborn, November 24, 1812 (NA, RG 26, Waltham).

[27]Ilsley to unknown, September 19, 1816 (NA, RG 26, Waltham).

[28]Ilsley to Pleasonton, August 21, 1821 (NA, RG 26, E 17C).

[29]Coxe to Lincoln, June 3, 1794 (NA, RG 26, Waltham).

[30]Keeper John Polerecsky to unknown, November 11, 1796 (NA, RG 26, Waltham).

[31]Coxe to Lincoln, June 3, 1794 (NA, RG 26, Waltham).

[32]Ibid.

[33]Coxe to Lincoln, August 31, 1795 (NA, RG 26, Waltham).

[34]Coxe to Thomas Blount and Benjamin Williams of North Carolina, September 29, 1795 (NA, RG 26, E 18 (NC-31): "Letters Sent Regarding the Light-House Service, 1792-1852").

[35]Coxe to Lincoln, August 31, 1795 (NA, RG 26, Waltham).

[36]Coxe to Dearborn, June 11, 1795 (NA, RG 26, E 18).

[37]Daniel Carey or Corey was appointed to inspect the construction of the lighthouse. Wolcott to the Commissioner of the Revenue, July 23, 1796 (NA, RG 26, E 17G (NC-31): "Miscellaneous Letters received (Numerical), 1801-52").

[38]Dearborn to Coxe, October 12, 1796 (NA, RG 26, E 17A (NC-31): "Letters received by the Treasury Department, 1785-1812").

[39]Coxe to Lincoln, March 16, 1796 (NA, RG 26, Waltham).

[40]Coxe to Lincoln, January 27, 1797 (NA, RG 26, Waltham).

[41]Dearborn to Coxe, August 30, 1797 (NA, RG 26, E 18).

[42]Dearborn to Coxe, August 30, 1797 (NA, RG 26, Waltham).

[43]Samuel Wheeler of Philadelphia contracted to make the lantern for New Point Comfort Lighthouse in Virginia in 1804.

[44]Petition, March 1798 (NA, RG 26, Waltham).

[45]Commissioner William Miller to Secretary of the Treasury, August 30, 1803 (NA, RG 26, E 18).

[46]Benjamin Beal and Duncan M. Thaxter to Lincoln, August 13, 1803 (NA, RG 26, E 17A); Miller to Lincoln, September 13, 1803 (NA, RG 26, E 18);

Gallatin to Lincoln, June 1, 1804 (NA, RG 26, Waltham).

[47]Contract by Lincoln, December 31, 1806 (RG 26, E 45 (NC-31): "Miscellaneous Material Received by the Fifth Auditor, 1812-52," December 31, 1806); Gallatin to Lincoln, January 28, 1807 (NA, RG 26, Waltham).

[48]Gallatin to Lincoln, August 27, 1806; Gallatin to Lincoln, February 23, 1808; Gallatin to Lincoln, May 25, 1807 (NA, RG 26, Waltham).

[49]"Schedule & Inventory of the Light House at West Quoddy with all appendages and articles thereto appertaining, the property of the United States, as Surrendered by Thomas Dexter, late Keeper to Peter Godfrey, present Keeper Confirmable to Instructions Received from the Superintendent of Light Houses in Massachusetts" (NA, RG 26, Waltham).

[50]L. Trescott, Custom House, Passamaquoddy, to Dearborn, April 8, 1815 (NA, RG 26, E 17C).

[51]Pleasonton to Chandler, December 9, 1830 (NA, RG 26, E 18); Chandler to Pleasonton, September 22, 1831 (NA, RG 26, E 17C).

[52]Chandler to Pleasonton, May 10, 1831 (NA, RG 26, E 17C).

[53]Chandler to Pleasonton, September 22, 1831 (NA, RG 26, E 17C).

[54]Chandler to Pleasonton, May 10, 1831 (NA, RG 26, E 17C).

[55]Pleasonton to Chandler, September 6, 1831 (NA, RG 26, E 18).

[56]Chandler to Pleasonton, September 22, 1831 (NA, RG 26, E 17C).

[57]Chandler to Pleasonton, August 25, 1835 (NA, RG 26, E 17D (NC-31): "Superintendent of Lighthouses Replies to Circulars, 1830-38").

[58]Ilsley to Pleasonton, July 5, 1822 (NA, RG 26, E 17C); Pleasonton to Ilsley, August 14, 1822 (NA, RG 26, E 18); Pleasonton to Ilsley, June 26, 1822 (NA, RG 26, E 18).

[59]Ilsley to Pleasonton, October 31, 1822 (NA, RG 26, E 17C).

[60]G. A. Morse, Custom House, Machias, to Ilsley, April 10, 1823 (NA, RG 26, E 17C).

[61]John McKellar, Libby Island keeper, to Ilsley, April 10, 1823 (NA, RG 26, E 17C).

[62]Ilsley to Pleasonton, April 20, 1823 (NA, RG 26, E 17C).

[63]Ibid.

[64]Jairus Thayer to unknown, Portland, June 25, 1823 (NA, RG 26, E 17C).

[65]Pleasonton to Ilsley, July 2, 1823 (NA, RG 26, E 18); Ilsley to Pleasanton, October 22, 1823 and November 13, 1823 (NA, RG 26, E 17C).

[66]Petition, August 10, 1812 (NA, RG 26, E 17C).

[67]James Madison.

[68]Gallatin to Dearborn, October 10, 1812 (NA, RG 26, Waltham).

[69]Pleasonton to Secretary of the Treasury, April 24, 1849, explaining how the construction of lighthouses is contracted and overseen (NA, RG 26, E 35).

[70]Lewis to Secretary of the Treasury, April 27, 1843 (NA, RG 26, E 35).

[71]Chandler to Pleasonton, November 18, 1829 (NA, RG 26, E 17C).

[72]Pleasonton to Chandler, September 6, 1831 (NA, RG 26, E 18).

[73]Ibid.

[74]Pleasonton to Chandler, September 28, 1831 (NA, RG 26, E 17H (NC-31): "Draft Copies of Letters Sent, 1813-52").

[75]Chandler to Pleasonton, February 17, 1832 (NA, RG 26, E 18).

[76]Pleasonton to Chandler, February 25, 1832 (NA, RG 26, E 17H).

[77]Chandler to Pleasonton, March 1, 1832 (NA, RG 26, E 17C).

[78]Newspaper clipping attached to letter from Chandler to Pleasonton, March 23, 1832 (NA, RG 26, E 17C).

[79]Chandler to Pleasonton, August 28, 1835 (NA, RG 26, E 17D).

[80]Ilsley to Pleasonton, July 20, 1825 (NA, RG 26, E 17C).

[81]Report by Captain Derby, October 8, 1831 (NA, RG 26, E 6).

[82]Pleasonton to Walter Forward, Secretary of the Treasury, February 15, 1843 (NA, RG 26, E 35).

[83]Pleasonton to Chandler, October 17, 1831 (NA, RG 26, E 18).

[84]Ibid.

[85]Holland, *America's Lighthouses*, pp. 28-29.

[86]Ilsley to Pleasonton, January 17, 1827 (NA, RG 26, E 17C).

[87]Ibid.

[88]Ilsley to Pleasonton, April 6, 1827 (NA, RG 26, E 17C).

[89]Ilsley to Pleasonton, June 16, 1828 (NA, RG 26, E 17C).

[90]Revenue Cutter Captain Howard, "description of part of the Light Houses on the Coast of Maine, with their bearings and distance from known Head Lands—height above the level of the sea—Latitude,

Longitude, etc.," reported by Chandler to Pleasonton, December 10, 1830 (NA, RG 26, E 17D).

[91]Pleasonton to Secretary of the Treasury, October 14, 1830 (NA, RG 26, E 18).

[92]Pleasonton to Secretary of the Treasury, November 25, 1831 (NA, RG 26, E 18).

[93]Chandler to Pleasonton, November 24, 1831 (NA, RG 26, E 17C).

[94]Ilsley to Pleasonton, September 20, 1828 (NA, RG 26, E 17C).

[95]Keeper William Jordan to Pleasonton, August 6, 1852 (NA, RG 26, E 17C).

[96]NA, RG 26, E 98 (NC-31): "List of Light-House Keepers and Other Employees 1845-1912" (National Archives Microfilm Publication M1373)

[97]Pleasonton to Ilsley, January 23, 1827 (NA, RG 26, E 18).

[98]Ilsley to Pleasonton, November 19, 1827 (NA, RG 26, E 17C).

[99]Pleasonton to Chandler, July 8, 1834 (NA, RG 26, E 18).

[100]Pleasonton to Chandler, August 10, 1829 (NA, RG 26, E 18); Chandler to Pleasonton, January 26, 1839 (NA, RG 26, E 17C).

[101]Chandler to Pleasonton, May 10, 1831 (NA, RG 26, E 17C).

[102]Pleasonton to Chandler, August 26, 1835 (NA, RG 26, E 18).

[103]Pleasonton to F.O.J. Smith, December 11, 1834 (NA, RG 26, E 18).

[104]Pleasonton to Secretary of the Treasury Levi Woodbury, March 21, 1836 (NA, RG 26, E 18).

[105]Pleasonton to Woodbury, October 13, 1836 (NA, RG 26, E 18).

[106]John Anderson to Captain Salter, August 7, 1837 (NA, RG 26, E 17K (NC-31): "Letters Received from the Secretary of the Treasury, 1830-52").

[107]Woodbury to Pleasonton, September 5,1837 (NA, RG 26, E 17K).

[108]Woodbury to Pleasonton, May 18, 1837 (NA, RG 26, E 17K).

[109]Chandler to Pleasonton, December 22, 1831 (NA, RG 26, E 17C).

[110]Chandler to Pleasonton, July 27, 1832 (NA, RG 26, E 17C).

[111]Chandler to Pleasonton, August 23, 1832 (NA, RG 26, E17C).

[112]Pleasonton to Chandler, May 22, 1833 (NA, RG 26, E 18).

[113]Chandler to Pleasonton, May 30, 1833 (NA, RG 26, E 17C).

PART I. Early Lighthouse Construction and Administration

PART II. Offshore Stations
The Challenges to Builders and Keepers

Captains of sailing ships were grateful for the lights that guided them into harbors, but the scattered shoals, rock ledges, and islands *offshore* were their greatest fear—particularly during the frequent fog that made them invisible. These dangers could be marked with lighthouses and other aids to navigation only when Congress made funds available. As the years went by, the majority of Maine's lighthouses and fog signals were placed on offshore rocks or islands.

Four of these treacherous spots— Mount Desert Rock, Matinicus Rock, Saddleback Ledge, and Boon Island— were described in an 1843 report by I. W. P. Lewis, nephew of Winslow Lewis (and one of his harshest critics), who worked as a civil engineer for the U.S. Lighthouse Establishment:

> These four places are lone rocks, standing several miles from shore. There is nothing but the naked barren rock & the lighthouses for the eye to rest upon. In storms the sea breaks furiously over the buildings & the keepers & their families are in danger of being swept away. Nothing can well be imagined more desolate & uncomfortable than such situation. All supplies of stores & fuel are necessarily obtained from the mainland during the summer season as these rocks are inaccessible during the fall & winter.[1]

Keepers on these islands found daily life far more trying than their colleagues onshore. Few offshore stations had towns, making it necessary to row or sail some distance to acquire supplies or medical assistance. Storms or bad weather could rule out trips to the mainland for days or weeks at a time. Landing on the islands, especially on rocky outcroppings, was often difficult, and occasionally a keeper drowned while trying to beach a boat in breaking waves. Structures, gardens, and supplies could be smashed by gale winds or washed away in high seas. Offshore stations were also the last to receive modern conveniences such as electricity, indoor plumbing, and telephones. Living in isolation, successful offshore keepers developed strong inner resources.

Boon Island Lighthouse and its keepers

Boon Island was a barren pile of rock six-and-one-half miles off York Beach. The first aid to navigation there was an unlighted wooden monument completed in 1799 and destroyed in an 1804 storm. A stone beacon was erected there in 1805, and in 1811 the Superintendent of Lighthouses in Massachusetts, Henry Dearborn, contracted with Thomas Heath and Noah Porter to construct a lighthouse for $2,377 and a stone dwelling house for $150.[2]

In March 1812, Isaac Ilsley, Customs Collector at Portland, reported that he had found a willing keeper:

> A person by the name of Thomas Hanna, of this place, will contract to keep Boon Island Light, one year for 300 dollars, provided 100 dollars is advanced him for the purpose of purchasing

Few men initially wanted to serve on desolate Boon Island. The first candidate declined the position. The first appointment, David Oliver, left without notice, bound for Europe as mate on a ship. Collector Dearborn wrote Secretary of the Treasury Albert Gallatin:

Boon Island is so peculiarly situated that it has been difficult to get any one who would consent to accept the appointment as keeper for the compensation allowed. All the fresh water, wood and necessaries for a family must be carried on to the Island, and it is far removed from the coast. In violent storms the sea makes a break almost entirely over the barren rock.

If a larger sum can be given, the person who faithfully tends the Light will earn his reward.[3]

(Ca. 1859 photo courtesy of U.S. Coast Guard)

PART II. Offshore Stations: The Challenges to Builders and Keepers

provisions, etc. to carry with him, for which he says he will give security.

Mr. Hanna appears to be an active, capable man, and from what I have seen of him, believe he will do well. He has a wife and two sons who will go with him, one son about 12 and the other 14 years of age. . . . [4]

Keeper Hanna soon found that $300 a year did not cover his expenses. On January 29, 1813, the Collector for the District of York reported to Dearborn that Hanna "shall be compelled to leave the Island in the spring unless he can have 450 Dolls. [dollars] per annum. He says that no person will furnish him with firewood for less than 7 Dolls. per cord in the fall of the year. They now ask him 8 Dolls. to deliver it on the Island and that it requires a considerable quantity of wood, more than he expected, . . ." Keeper Hanna needed the wood not only to burn in his stove for warmth but also to melt ice for water.[5]

All increases or reductions in pay required the approval of the Secretary of the Treasury. In pleading Hanna's case, Collector Dearborn wrote Secretary of the Treasury Albert Gallatin:

From the known unpleasant situation of the Keeper of Boon Island Light; its distance from the coast; the difficulty of going to or coming off from the Island; the trouble & expense which he must necessarily be subject to for the procurement of the necessaries of life, make it equitable that his compensation should be made adequate to the services rendered. It is certainly the most disagreeable residence in this Commonwealth for a Light House Keeper.

I . . . hope the sallary of Mr. Hannah will be increased, as his conduct has been perfectly satisfactory. The Cutter, I have sent there twice since the Lantern was Lighted & the Officers reported to me that there was not a Light House on the Coast Kept in more perfect order.[6]

Keeper Hanna wrote directly to Collector Dearborn on March 15, 1813:

It will be one year on the first day of April next since I have lived on this desolate Island and discharged my duty faithfully in taking care of this Light House. My contract with the Government (made with Mr. Ilsley, Collector at Portland) was for the sum of three hundred Dollars and [I was] to be provided with all necessaries for myself and family. I have fulfilled my part of the contract but the Government have not theirs. It has not provided me in any manner with any article for my support. My portion of the $300 I have received but cannot exist here with[out] that provision for me.

I now must state that unless the Government provide for me and my family as agreed, I shall, on the first day of April leave this Place. If the sum of $150 be added to the salary ($300) I shall be satisfied and will provide for myself.[7]

Gallatin authorized a $100 salary increase on March 24, 1813.[8] Three years later, in May 1816, Keeper Hanna resigned and was replaced by Eliphalet Grover.[9] On March 12, 1818, Jeremiah Bradbury of York, Maine, wrote to Collector of the Customs H. A. S. Dearborn:

Grover the Keeper of Boon Island Light was in yesterday and desired me to inform you that on the 4th Feby. last during the violent S.E. gale the sea washed over the whole Island, compelling him & his family to take refuge in the Lighthouse. The dwelling house, he says, sustained some damage by the washing out of the lime and many small stones from the walls of the house. The platform leading from the house to the light house was torn up. The slip still remains, but was considerably loosened & several of the rollers carried away. He thinks if the slip should not be secured very soon a Northeast storm may rip it up and carry it away.[10]

Apparently the keeper's salary had become attractive enough to prompt some competition. Keeper Grover's son wrote Collector Dearborn on behalf of his father on November 11, 1818:

I have just been informed that by the report of two or three people that they have got in the portsmouth print that I am dead, but I am yet alive and hope to live to see those people brought to justice for making the report; one of the three is the man that has sent you his recommendation. I think he is layzy idle fellow, a brick layer by trade, and he has seen me in Portsmouth with a little money and because he had none, he has raised this report about me thinking to get my Birth [berth] which is not so pleasant as he thinks it is . . . But I hope that government is not a going to remove me to gratefy one man unless I have done something worthy of being removed. There is many people that would like well to have my pay but few would like the birth. I have always endeavored to due my duty and to give you & the contractor Mr. Lewis satisfaction for every thing that I am entrusted with that belongs to govern-ment and have taken as much pains to keep a good light as any man in the world could, and what the cause of my Being envied so much is I cannot tell. I wish you would have the goodness to converse with Mr. Lewis and see wether he finds any fault with me or not and I beg of you Mr. Dearborn, as soon as you receive this to send me back by the next mail an answer to inform me wether I am to be removed or not . . . I am not alone; my son is as capable of tending the lights as I am, and I don't think but what he is as well acquainted with the island and ways of tending the lights as any man in the states. . . . There is five of us all told heare on the island and if one should die, I think the other four could tend the lights. Mr Dearborn sir send me a letter and my boat shall wait on shore for it.[11]

In 1825, Winslow Lewis petitioned for a higher salary for several Maine lighthouse keepers, including Keeper Grover on Boon Island. In making his case to the Fifth Auditor, Stephen Pleasonton, he stated that

The situation of Boon Island Light is different from any other in the United States, on a small barren rock over the whole of which the sea breaks in heaving gales, situated 12 miles from any land, no fresh water, every thing to be brought from the main, it is only in very moderate weather that a boat can land on the island. Months often elapse in the winter without the keeper having any intercourse with the main land. Thus situated, there would be no surety of the light with only one man on the island. Should anything happen to him consequently the keeper always has to keep some one with him. The salary that has been allowed for the keeper of this light has never been propor-tionate to that of other light houses, considering its peculiar situation. It is a light of the first importance and the present incumbent is a valuable man in whom confidence can be placed that his duty will be strictly attended to.[12]

In 1831 Colonel Seward Merrill was contracted to build a new tower on Boon Island for $2,900.[13] On September 22, 1831, Collector John Chandler reported to Pleasonton that the new tower was lit up on July 21, 1831.[14] Eliphalet Grover was still listed as keeper in 1837 at an annual salary of $600, the maximum rate paid to a lighthouse keeper during that period. Other Maine lighthouse keepers receiving that amount included Esaias Preble at Mount Desert Rock and Samuel E. Haskell at Whaleback Ledge. Most mainland keepers received $300 per annum.[15]

On January 26, 1839, near the end of his tenure on Boon Island, Grover reported a heavy southeast gale:

. . . at 10 P.M. the sea was up around the buildings; Sunday morning between the hours of 9 and 11 the sea broke upon the buildings, and the family then retreated to the Light House as a place of safety. The sea broke into the porch . . . and unhung the doors and forced the door of the dwelling house and entered the lower rooms; it also entered the Light House and done considerable damage, washing shells and sea-weed into the rooms. It washed away the plat-form which was built for the purpose of getting from one building to another. . . . at 3 P.M. the tide being down, some of the family ventured out and beheld an astonishing spectacle. Fragments of wood were scattered over the Island, and large rocks which had laid quiet for more than 20 years, were torn from their places. The sea continued rough for three days, but the wind coming from the North West it gradually subsided.[16]

Grover left the station that same year after serving 23 years there. A petition was submitted for a John Kennard of South Berwick to take his place. "Mr Kennard is a gentleman of good moral character, temperate, industrious, and persevering in his business, and is, and always has been a firm supporter of the Democratic cause in our country." A few months later, Kennard also petitioned for the keeper position at Whaleback Light, but received neither appointment.[17]

In 1854, the station received its first paid assistant, who earned $300 per annum while the head keeper continued to earn $600. A second assistant keeper was appointed soon thereafter. Family members often served in the assistant keeper positions. The island lacked an additional keeper's dwelling to house an unrelated assistant.

The tower was again rebuilt in 1854, requiring two congressional appropriations. According to the 1853 *Annual Report* the additional appropriation was needed because the District Engineer ascertained that "the materials of the present tower and building are unfit for use in the construction of the new building" and that the old tower was needed as an aid while the new tower was being constructed.

The keeper with the longest tenure at Boon Island was William C. Williams. He reported as second assistant keeper on August 5, 1885, and became first assistant keeper on November 5, 1886. He was promoted to full keeper on November 21, 1888. He started at an annual salary of $450, received $20 more as first assistant, and was given an additional increase of $10 in 1888. As head keeper he earned $760 and never received a single raise during the 23 years he served in that position. Williams retired in 1911, having spent 26 years on the station. For eight of those years, 1897 to 1905, Charles S. Williams is listed as first assistant keeper, having been promoted from second assistant.[18]

Boon Island Lighthouse Keeper William C. Williams appears to be on the far right. (Courtesy of Maine Maritime Museum, Bath, Maine)

Soon after the beginning of Williams's career at Boon Island Light, the station was described in the 1887 *Annual Report*:

This tower is of ashlar masonry, 25 feet in diameter at the base, 12 feet in diameter at the top, and 118 feet high to the base of the lantern. The tower was strained and kept leaking by its vibration. The fourteen windows in the tower, with iron frames and sash, did not exclude water, and could not be opened for ventilation; and the floor was so low that the water flowed on to it from the entrance of the covered way, keeping the entire interior of the tower in a damp and unsightly condition. The vibration was checked by six sets of iron ties, with struts, attached to the top of the lantern and anchored to the masonry 40 feet below the watch-room deck; the windows were torn out and replaced by double windows, with wooden frames and sash, which readily open for ventilation; the floor was raised 18 inches with concrete, and the tower, which was found in anchoring the iron ties in much greater need of it than was anticipated, was thoroughly repointed. The stone dwelling designed for two keepers is occupied by three, two of whom have families. It is old and its interior is in bad condition, needing thorough renovation. The island is a bare rock; communication with the coast is infrequent in winter, and the keepers have had to store their vegetables and provisions in the halls adjoining their bed-rooms. For the proper preservation of such supplies a house 12 feet by 20 feet in plan was built, sheathed, covered with paper, clapboarded, rough plastered, and back plastered.

The crowded living conditions on Boon Island continued, as indicated in the 1891 *Annual Report*:

There are at this station one keeper and two assistants, and but two sets of quarters in one double dwelling. The second assistant keeper has to board either with the family of the keeper or with that of the first assistant keeper. This forced arrangement is unsatisfactory to all, and is quite unfavorable to the retention of a second assistant of the needed qualifications. The station is isolated and exposed, the tower is tall, and this second-order light is an important one. A third dwelling which is urgently needed, it is estimated can be built for $3,400. It is therefore recommended that

Keepers, family members, and visitors at Boon Island during William C. Williams's tenure as principal keeper. (Courtesy of Maine Maritime Museum, Bath, Maine)

PART II. Offshore Stations: The Challenges to Builders and Keepers

an appropriation of this amount be made therefor.

The need for the third dwelling was repeated in subsequent annual reports, until finally $4,000 was appropriated in 1904 for a dwelling completed in 1905. Maintaining harmony among several unrelated keepers must have been difficult in such close quarters on a small island. Disputes did arise. On June 29, 1893, the Engineer Secretary queried the First District Inspector over a letter from Charles W. Torrey, first assistant keeper at Boon Island, "charging the Keeper of that station with neglect of duty, in not properly keeping an account of oil expended at the station, and a waste of the Government property in throwing surplus oil away in order to make his account of expenditures tally."[19] As far as is known, no charges were levied against Keeper Williams; Assistant Keeper Torrey was dismissed on September 1, 1893.

Many years after he retired, Keeper Williams was interviewed by Robert Thayer Sterling (who served as keeper at Maine lighthouses from 1913-46) about his life on Boon Island. He stated that

> There were days when I first went on station that I could not get away from the idea that I was locked up in a cell. . . . All we had was a little stone house and a rubblestone tower. When rough weather

came we didn't know as it would make much difference as to whether we went into the tower or not . . . The seas would clean the ledge right off sometimes. . . . When the terrible seas would make up and a storm was in the offing, I was always thinking over just what I would do in order to save my life should the whole station be swept away . . . I believe it is these things which gradually wear on the mind and finally upset the brain.[20]

Keeper Williams noted a number of shipwrecks off Boon Island. He reported a particularly memorable one that occurred on a frigid morning in early December 1892, when the schooner *Goldhunter* struck on Boon Island Ledge,

The boathouse at Boon Island Light Station. (Courtesy of Maine Maritime Museum, Bath, Maine)

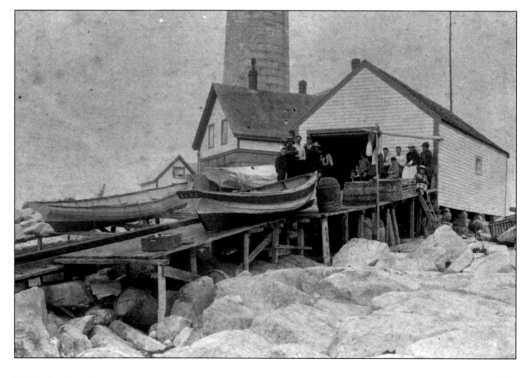

about three miles from the light station. The crew succeeded in getting to their yawl boat and after a six-hour row reached the light station at 1:30 in the morning.

> We were aroused by the barking of the dog. . . . We got out our lanterns and climbed down over the icy rocks and made out the little boat just outside the breakers. The castaways were instructed to follow the lights [of our lanterns] around the rocks . . . [and we] watched their chance to run in on the top of a sea. The three keepers covered with flying spray, grasped the boat rails and the dog at the same time took the painter line in his teeth and ran up the rocks. The little craft was hauled beyond the reach of the next sea. . . .
>
> The crew was frozen to the thwarts and almost helpless. The keepers and their wives had a desperate task for the next few hours to resuscitate the almost lifeless men.[21]

During heavy storms, Keeper Williams noted that

> . . . we would remain up in the lantern, for if anything happened to the light it would take some time to climb 133 feet. . . . There was no lounging place at the top of the tower, only an old soap box or camp stool for a seat. As you set there just watching your light, all the enjoyment you got was hearing the wind making a cotton-mill din around the lantern. With such a noise and being so many feet up from the ground, the seas battering the rocks down below is utterly drowned out. . . .[22]

By the 1930s, some modern improvements had reached Boon Island, but the keepers still faced challenges on this barren rock outcrop. On August 20, 1932, a letter from a Boon Island keeper was published in the *Rockland Courier-Gazette*:

> A fine evening on Boon Island. A shower has just passed, leaving the air clear and refreshing, stars shining brightly. If it is fine, the station boat will go in to York Harbor tomorrow after mail and supplies, also to take mail in. We sometimes wonder if people on the mainland really understand what it is to live out here. We tell of the pleasant things, and indeed we do enjoy our lighthouse life, but there are things not so pleasant—such as waiting a week, or even two or three weeks for letters from our loved ones. Also when one of our number is sick and it is too rough to get off or on the island, the keeper has to be doctor, and really has quite a leaning that way. He calls up a doctor by telephone, but if the telephone is out of order, as it often is, he has to rely on his own knowledge and the remedies on hand in the medicine chest supplied by the government.
>
> One has to have a varied knowledge of things to be a lightkeeper. As one keeper here recently said, "I thought all one had to know how to do out here was to clean, paint, and polish brass, but I have found out that one has to be doctor, painter, steeplejack, glazier, boatman, gasoline engineer, electrician, stonecutter and even a cook when the women folks leave us in the fall."[23]

Another letter published in the *Gazette* on October 22, 1932, reported,

> The first week in September we had a very rough spell with high winds . . . . The men lost nearly all their lobster pots . . . .
>
> The engines that generate the electricity for the light decided to lay down on the job a few days ago. The keepers worked day and night to fix them and get them going, but no use. They need new parts, which must be sent. In the meantime the old vapor light is being used.[24]

The last keepers at Boon Island Light were removed by helicopter after the Blizzard of 1978. When the storm hit, two Coast Guard keepers were on duty. The two men stayed in the tower as boulders washed over the island, damaging the generator building, fuel tanks, and helicopter pad, as well as destroying the boathouse and boat launch.[25] The station was automated soon thereafter. (Historic American Building Survey/Historic American Engineering Record (HABS/HAER) copy of U.S. Coast Guard photo ca. 1950)

Problems at Moose Peak Light Station

Jeremiah Berry completed the lighthouse on Moose Peak on Eastern Bay's Mistake Island in September 1826, and "a respectable shipmate," Alexander Milleken, was appointed keeper.[26]

On January 28, 1829, Ilsley responded to Congressman Jeremiah O'Brien's inquiry regarding a pay raise for keeper Milleken:

Your letter of the 23rd inst. in relation to the application of A. Milleken, Keeper of Moose Peak Light, for an increase of salary, is received.

Moose Peak Light is on a small barren Island, called Mistake, at a considerable distance from the main land and from any other inhabited place, the inconveniences of obtaining supplies are considerable, and the lonely gloomy situation make it very unpleasant for the Keeper and his family. Taking into consideration the peculiar disadvantage of the station and the privations to which the Keeper is subjected, it would seem that a salary of 400 Dollars would be no more than a fair average compensation with other Keepers.[27]

Keeper Milleken got his increase.[28]

The Moose Peak tower very early showed signs of poor construction. In 1831 Revenue Cutter Service Captain Derby reported that the mortar consisted of sand with small stones falling out of it; he was able to run his arm a foot into the wall.[29] Pleasonton recommended that the tower be coated with Roman cement inside and out.

According to the Collector, "The distance from dwelling-house to Light House at Moose Peak is too far for the Keeper to walk in the night-time in a violent rain or snow-storm, and dangerous especially in crossing the bridge of about one hundred feet in length."[30] A covered walkway is shown in this photo of Moose Peak Light Station ca. 1859. (National Archives photo # 26-LG-3-73)

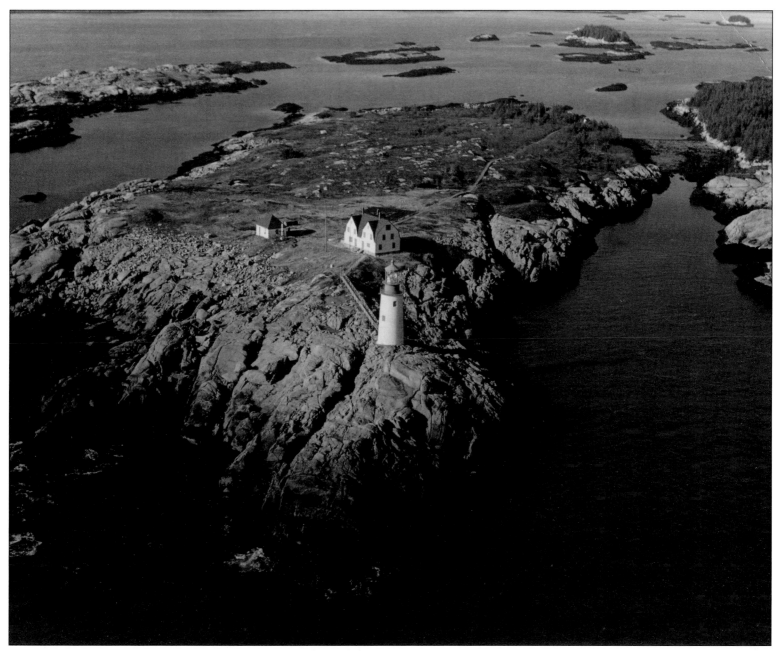

Moose Peak Light Station ca. 1950 . (Courtesy of U.S. Coast Guard)

Maine Lighthouses: Documentation of Their Past

By 1850, the tower had again deteriorated. In 1851 Collector Luther Jewett wrote:

> There is a rent or fisure from the base of the deck, which has weakened the Tower so much that last year the Keeper informed me that it had settled or inclined so much to the westward, that he had, with the assistance of another person, to be in the lantern all night, for ten nights in succession as the weights to the clock-work laid so hard against the box or well which contained them, that there was not power sufficient to revolve the Chandelier.
>
> Besides, the Tower is wrongly located, the Keeper being obliged to pass a long bridge to get to the Light; and this bridge is not always passable, obliging the Keeper in almost every heavy storm to creep on his hands and knees over the rocks. . . . it appears to me that it is not economical to put a new Lantern and new lighting apparatus on a Tower of this kind; and yet the Lantern is so old and rusty that it is difficult to keep the glass whole.
>
> If, however, you still adhere to the opinion that it is best not to re-build, but put on a new Lantern and new lighting apparatus, I will put the Tower in as good a situation and in as economical a manner as is possible.
>
> I would observe that there is a good granite ledge, very near the dwelling-house, so that, in case of re-building, the rock-material could be had very reasonable.[31]

Apparently Jewett's advice for replacing the tower was not heeded. Although a new lantern and optics were installed in the 1850s, a replacement tower was not completed until 1886.

Landing a boat at offshore stations was often tricky and dangerous. On May 11, 1920, Harry E. Freeman, Second Assistant Keeper of Moose Peak Light Station, reported a tragedy:

> While attempting to land at 12:30 p.m. the Keeper Henry C. Ray and Maurice R. Beal, 1st Assistant, were thrown from the dory by the sea. While I was rescuing Mr. Beal from the breakers, Mr. Ray had got back into the dory again and was either trying to help Mr. Beal or make a landing on the Rock. The seas turned the dory over and again threw Mr. Ray into the sea. But after getting Mr. Beal safely on the Rock, it was impossible to launch a boat from the slip and rescue Mr. Ray, the tide having carried him into the breaking seas on the point where he sank from sight . . . in view of his wife and myself. The dory belonging to the station equipment was lost.[32]

Competing claims on Baker Island

A lighthouse was established in 1828 on Baker Island, one of the five islands that make up the Cranberry Isles. Built to mark the mouth of Frenchman Bay, it was the first light in the vicinity of Mount Desert Island. Although the lighthouse was advertised in 1825, construction was delayed until a deed to the property could be obtained. Builders Humphrey & Thayer completed the lighthouse for $2,944 and Winslow Lewis fitted up the light for $450.[33] Although Pleasonton recommended to President John Quincy Adams the appointment of Samuel Moody as keeper (one of 17 candidates), Pleasonton's letter was returned with the notation "Let William Gilley be appointed—J. Q. Adams."[34]

Keeper Gilley had been the first resident of Baker Island. A fisherman, wood-cutter, and farmer, Gilley moved to the island in 1812. He and his wife had 12 children, nine of whom were born at the lighthouse.[35] Gilley served as keeper until 1849, when the Whig party came into power in Washington and he was replaced by a political appointee. Gilley moved to Great Duck Island, but his sons continued to live on Baker Island and squabbled with subsequent keepers over who owned the property. On March 13, 1852, replacement keeper

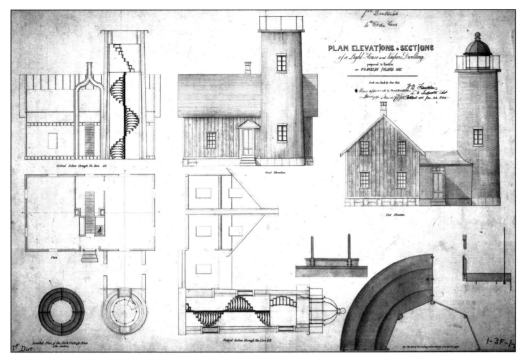

The 1853 Annual Report *indicated that the Baker Island and Franklin Island lighthouses "are entirely worthless, the lanterns are worn out, and the keepers' dwellings are so old and leaky that they are unhealthy. I recommend that both be rebuilt and fitted up with Fresnel lens lights of the fourth or fifth order." The towers were rebuilt in 1855. (Architectural drawing for Franklin Island from National Archives, RG 26; photo of Baker Island courtesy of U.S. Coast Guard)*

Maine Lighthouses: Documentation of Their Past

John Rich complained to Stephen Pleasonton:

> I would respectfully call your attention to my situation as Keeper of the Light on Bakers Island, Hancock County, State of Maine. First I took possession of Bakers Island Light by Instructions from Mr. Jewett as Superintendent of Lights for the State of Maine. I called on the former Keeper & reported the facts & gave him 6 or 7 weeks time to vacate the premises to me and at the expiration of that time he did give up the possession of the Light House Dwelling House and what he considered the government property but said the Island belonged to him excepting three acres.
>
> Secondly, Mr. Gilley left the Island in charge of his sons Joseph & Elisha. Soon after I took possession of the Light House these Mr. Gilleys commenced to abuse & insult me at every opportunity. . . . I then informed Esq. Jewett & he said that I should enjoy some privileges there & he, Mr. Jewett, notified the Mr. Gilleys that they must leave the Island, but here the matter rested and they since continued to live on the Island and enjoyed all the privileges as they did when Old Mr. Gilley lived on the Island . . . I have lived on the Island since the removal of Mr. Gilley and have received no benefits of the Island whatever . . . and even this last winter have had to winter my Cow off the Island. I was even forbid[den] picking up drift wood . . . [36]

Many letters went back and forth between the collector and Pleasonton regarding the Gilleys' claim to the island. When it was finally determined that their claim could not be supported and that the Gilleys were "squatters on public lands," a federal marshal was engaged to deliver a letter telling them to quit the Island.[37] Apparently the Gilleys convinced the marshal that they were reasonable and wanted to compromise. This agreement proved ineffective and an increasingly exasperated Keeper Rich fired off another letter:

> . . . I can stand the Base insults and insinerations no longer. I cannot leave the Island for any emergency for one hour at a time without my family being subject to insults of the most indecent & vilest kind. The Locke on the door of the Light House was destroyed by forcing nails into the Key hole between the hours of Lighting and 10 o'clock at night. The door & stove was covered with the vilest filth, so much that in going into the Light House I carried it on my shoes into it & many other things that is not decent for any common man to mention and as such it seems as insufferable to bear any longer and as regards the privileges of the Island the Gilleys promised me last spring if I would consent for them to stay there this season, they would agree that I should have hay enough to Keep one Cow for which they have allowed me barely one half ton which is hardly 1/4 part of the hay that is necessary to Keep a Cow & further more while getting that they called me a thief repeatedly.[38]

John Rich departed his post in 1853. After years of legal battles the ownership disputes were settled in court, with the government having jurisdiction over the area containing the light station with a right of way for access, and the Gilleys retaining the remainder of the island.

Problems with contractors on Mount Desert Rock

Planning for the construction of a lighthouse on Mount Desert Rock, south of Mount Desert Island, began in 1829 and was fraught with politics. Collector John Chandler indicated that the light was intended to mark where the rock was,

> . . . and not for a direction to any other point. It is therefore unnecessary to have a very high Light, and it can not only be cheaper built, but it will be better that the dwelling house and Light House should be connected so that the keeper should not be obliged to go out of the building in the night, for I understand the Sea at times breaks over the greater part of the Rock, and the spray quite over.

[Gamaliel] Smith, the lowest bidder for building at Mount Desert Rock, is himself a stone mason and a man of understanding (although it seems to me his bid is no evidence of it). He says he will find surety for the faithful performance of the contract, if his bid is accepted. I am sure he will lose money by it, but he must judge for himself. If his proposals are not accepted (his bid being the lowest), I have no doubt he will make much noise about it, and try to make people believe that it is because he is not friendly to the administration that his bid is rejected, and that you are paying for the Light Houses much more to the friends of the administration than they were offered to be built for. I am not sure that the bid is not made with that view, for he is a noisy politician. I think it best to let him take it if he will find surety. It may be, when he finds he can have the contract, he will not take it. It may be well, therefore, to provide for such a contingency in your instructions.[39]

Gamaliel E. Smith was given the contract and construction begun. When colder weather arrived in October, Smith applied for an extension. Collector Chandler's confidence in Smith's abilities, however, had dwindled even further.

The erection of the buildings must necessarily be postponed, as they cannot now be completed this season, and I very much doubt whether they will ever be done by him in the manner they ought to be. He appears to understand nothing of the work and has scarcely begun it. I have kept a man there to superintend the work until the third instant, when he left the work. Smith had been gone weeks, and left only two men, and they could do nothing of use, and the Superintendent left in consequence.

Indeed, from all Smith's movements, I am satisfied that there is little prospect of his fulfilling his contract in years, and that the work would never be well done. . . . Under the circumstances, I do not think it proper for me to extend the time, but will obey such instructions as I may receive from time to time from the Department.

Perhaps I ought to state that Smith's proposals were so much lower than it is possible the work could be done for, and knowing the character of the man, I doubted his intention of ever closing the contract, when he put in his proposal. I did suppose that he expected that the Government would doubt his fulfilling the contract and not accept his proposals, and then he could blaze it abroad that his proposals were rejected because he was opposed to the Administration, and that twice or three times the sum was given to a friend of the Administration for erecting the buildings, more than his offer.

. . . I think it best for the Government, and for him too, that he should have nothing further to do with the erection of the buildings. And I hope that, in all future Contracts it will be provided that the Light Houses and Dwelling Houses shall be finished by the fifteenth of July, and that advertisements for proposals will be seasonally issued for that purpose.

Owing to buildings of this description not having been completed until late in the fall, . . . several of the Light Houses are nearly falling down, and will incur a great annual expense to keep them standing.[40]

A month later, Collector Chandler wrote,

With respect to the Light House to be built on Mount Desert Rock, since writing you on the 19th of October last, Capt. Drinkwater of the Revenue Cutter, has returned from the rock. He informs me that Smith the Contractor was laying up the Walls of the House without any mortar, and where he had got the walls high enough in spots, was putting on the beams, although the cellar was not entirely excavated, nor the whole of the cellar wall laid up. The Contractor seems to pay no regard to the Contract in doing the work, and as I before stated to you, I do not believe it will be done by him so as to answer any purpose.[41]

Smith forfeited his contract and it went to the next lowest bidder, Joseph Berry, for $2,770. Berry had just completed the Hendricks Head Lighthouse, using similar specifications. Collector Chandler emphasized the importance of appointing a superintendent of construction—"a man who is a judge of work and one who cannot be cheated in it, and nerve enough to resist the Contractor's course

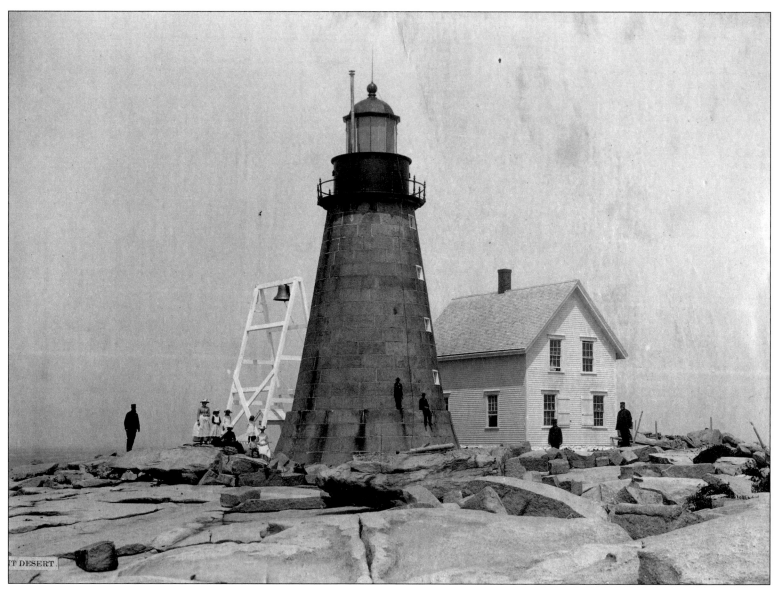

"Mount Desert Rock is 20 miles south of the 'Mountain Desert,' destitute of all herbage except a few Beets, Carrots, Potatoes, etc, which the Keeper with more industry than I presumed he had, has raised."[42] (USLHB photo of the 1847 replacement tower at Mount Desert Rock courtesy of U.S. Coast Guard)

if he is disposed to sham the work or do it in an improper manner."[43]

The tower on Mount Desert Rock was completed in July of 1830 and Esaias Preble appointed keeper.[44] The fixed light, 56 ½ feet above sea level, was first lit on August 25, 1830.[45]

A year later, in his "Remarks on Light Houses," Captain Derby of Revenue Cutter *Morris* recorded the following:

. . . found the lighthouse [on Mount Desert Rock] in a state of rapid decay. It must have been badly built; the material is all bad. The mortar in particular is made with salt water sand & mixed with salt water. If you analyze it, you can see no Lime whatever. The Lantern & its apparatus in good order, & at a distance of 20 miles, it was plain to be seen. The dwelling House in bad order; leaks much and smoaks badly.

Unless something is done, the Lighthouse will be down. I should advise to point it with good Mortar & board it over slightly, painting the covering white, 4 coats. In addition all the Lights want an attendant, one who can weekly look at them. Give him two hundred Dollars, or if the Government cannot afford to pay, make the Capts. of the Cutter attend to them, dividing the Lights from Boon Island to Quoddy Head. A Collector never sees the Lights.[46]

A few weeks later Pleasonton wrote Collector Chandler:

I have received information from a source entitled to respect that several of the Light Houses within your district have been so badly built and are now so much decayed that if they are not speedily repaired there will be great danger of their falling into ruins. For instance, it is represented that the one at Mount Desert Rock which was built & lit up only a year ago "is in a state of rapid decay . . ." This Light House I perceive was built by Joseph Berry and the work superintended by a person appointed by you of the name of Isaac F. Small. Neither of these persons should ever be employed by the government hereafter, and indeed Berry should be required to do this work over again, or at any rate rough cast it with roman cement without charge. If he will do neither you must cause it to be put in a state of repair and bring suit against him for a breach of his contract and practising a fraud upon the Govt.[47]

In response, Collector Chandler defended Berry's reputation as a builder:

[Capt. Derby] is undoubtedly mistaken as to the manner in which that Light House was built. He says he does not judge altogether from what he saw, but was informed by some person where he had been that it was built without lime. This report no doubt grew out of the fact that, when it was partially built by Gamaliel E. Smith, the walls of the House were put up without any mortar whatever, of which I gave you notice, and you directed me to give the contract to the next highest bidder, which was Joseph Berry. Mr. Berry is a very honest, faithful man, as much so as any man I know, and so is Mr. Small. I should have full confidence in either of them. But that the mortar has now become inadhesive, I have no doubt, for I find that however good the mortar used on those islands, where they are almost continually enveloped in the fog, and where there is such a body of stone and mortar, it never gets dry the first year. Winter comes, it freezes and destroys all the adhesive qualities of the best lime mortar ever made in two years; and, on taking out a stone, the mortar will crumble like sand; and indeed I thought at first on my coming here, that all the Light Houses were built as your informant thinks the one of Mount Desert was built, without lime. If you will turn to my letter of the 18th of November 1829, you will find that I have there stated the difficulties attending this subject. The Light Houses which I have built this year are all pointed with Roman Cement, and I hope this may prove usefull. But all the Light Houses in Maine will require constant or annual repairs to a great extent. They all leak in our most violent and driving storms, and almost every Dwelling House on the Islands smokes badly. I have been trying to remedy the one at Seguin for a year without success. Mr. Joseph Berry has been employed repairing the Light Houses for some time past, and will have the whole done in a short time, if not now finished. I employed him because I had

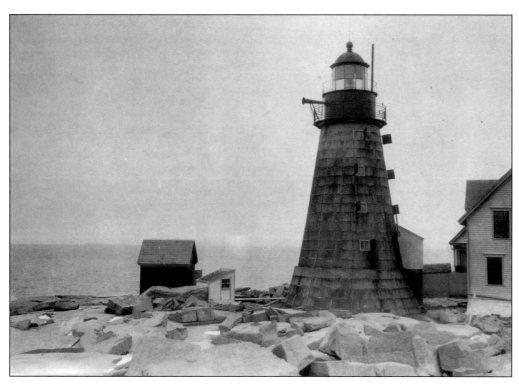

The 1847 tower on Mount Desert Rock was designed by Alexander Parris, a professional architect and engineer who specialized in granite construction. In 1875 the conical tower was described as being three floors with a watchroom and lantern above and a cellar and cistern underneath. A separate dwelling housed the keeper.[48] (1931 photo by R. C. Smith courtesy of U.S. Coast Guard)

confidence in him; but as you say he should be no more employed, I will hereafter govern myself accordingly, although I think it unfortunate, and, if after his statement of facts, you so direct, I will prosecute him according to your suggestion. You state that the remedy for bad mortar seems to be a coat of Roman Cement, inside and out. It is late in the season to put it on them this autumn, and they will soon all have been repaired for this season, but I will have it done next spring if you so direct. The expense will be very considerable.[49]

Pleasonton accepted Chandler's explanation and Berry was exonerated.[50]

Joseph Berry, a Georgetown stone mason, went on to rebuild the tower at Pemaquid Point in 1835. In certifying Berry's work, keeper Isaac Dunham indicated, "Captain Berry has completed the Light House in a good workmanlike manner and according to the Contract in every way—and I will venture to say, a better tower and lantern never was built in the State."[51] Modified in 1856 to support a Fresnel lens, the Pemaquid light tower is still standing.

In November 1831, Keeper Preble at Mount Desert Rock requested funds for building a woodhouse. The collector supported his request,

for it would be very difficult for him [Preble] to keep his wood in order to burn unless it is under cover, and it costs too much to get wood to the establishment to have it injured or lost; indeed it would seem that all those establishments should have some place to put their wood under cover. A number of them have at their own expense erected them, and several have applied to have pay for them; but I thought it not proper to give them any encouragement until I knew your views on the subject. Will you authorize me to pay Mr. Preble any thing for the above purpose or not?[52]

Pleasonton's response was negative:

If a Wood House is allowed Mr. Preble, I am apprehensive that all the other Keepers would claim the same advantage, of which many of them would not stand in as much need; and it is my desire to place them all as nearly on a footing as is possible. If you think his case is a peculiar one and can reconcile the other Keepers to the exception made in his favor, you may allow the Wood House, but if there be danger that the other keepers will claim the same indulgence, and will be dissatisfied if not yielded to them, then it must be denied to Mr. Preble.[53]

Bringing supplies to an offshore station such as Mount Desert Rock was a never ending problem for the keeper and for the government as well. Collector Chandler justified leaving an extra oil butt at Mount Desert Rock in a letter to Pleasonton, dated September 5, 1832:

> . . . The usual number of Oil Butts or Cannisters were furnished for Mount Desert Rock by the Contractor for fitting it up for lighting; but it was early discovered that a Boat could not land Oil for months together at some seasons of the year, and for fear the Contractors would be unable at some times to land Oil in season to keep the light burning, I thought it necessary to furnish an additional Butt, that a greater quantity might be kept on hand than is required at Light Houses generally, because if the Light should become extinguished for the want of oil, it would be a thousand times more dangerous than if a Light had never been there.[54]

All keepers were required to keep reports of oil consumption so that the collector could ensure that enough oil was supplied to each station. Stormy weather often interrupted the filing of those reports from offshore stations. On February 2, 1833, Chandler wrote,

> I have this day received a letter from Esaias Preble, Keeper of Mount Desert Rock Light House, in which he says he shall not have winter oil enough to carry him through the cold weather; had only sixty-two gallons to commence the year with. Not knowing that a new Contract is entered into, I thought proper to state the facts to you, and wait your directions in the case. Several of the Keepers state that it is necessary to have ladles to dip the oil out of the Butts, when it is so cold it will not run. Shall they be furnished to them?
>
> It was not until this morning that I have been able to get the whole of the special returns required from the Keepers, although I have three times sent the Cutter for the purpose of getting some of them, but it was impossible to land at Mount Desert Rock and Mantinicus Rock. Will forward the statement required as soon as possible.[55]

In addition to ladles, the government contractors supplied the keepers with lamps, tube cleaners, wicks, scissors, funnels, measures, and other articles for heating the oil.

Locating a light on Saddleback Ledge

When the Board of Navy Commissioners was trying to determine the need for a lighthouse on Saddleback Ledge, they requested the assistance of Joseph Smith, captain of the Revenue Cutter *Morris*.

Captain Smith mentioned that there were many advocates for placing the light on the west head of Isle au Haut, but he considered the surrounding sunken ledges a potential danger to vessels. His remarks concluded,

> There is no light between Matinicus & Bakers Island, a distance of about forty miles. In viewing the coast about the Isle au Haut & the Islands in the Penobscot bay, the necessity of a light-house in that vicinity, as a guide to vessels through the eastern channel is very apparent, the navigation is of importance sufficient to warrant the erection & support of it & Saddleback ledge is decidedly the best location.[56]

The navy commissioners followed Smith's advice.

In his 1842 report to the Secretary of the Treasury on the condition of lighthouses in Maine, New Hampshire, and Massachusetts, I. W. P. Lewis described the light station on Saddleback Ledge as it stood a few years after its completion.

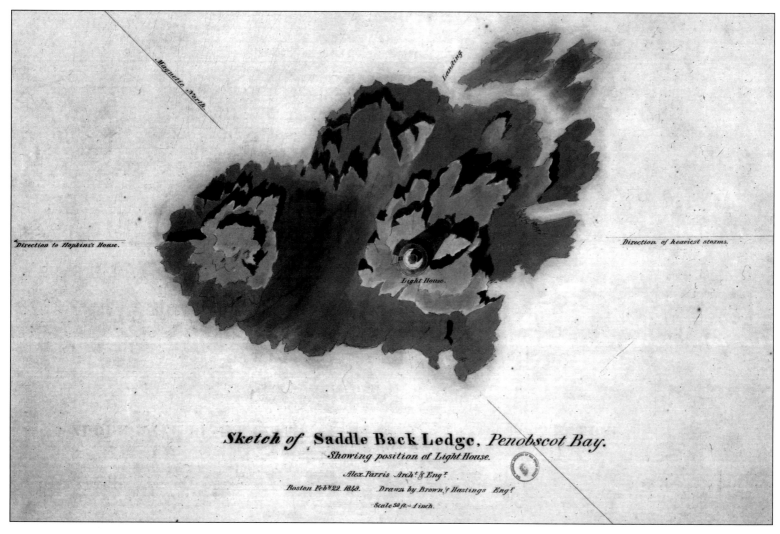

Sketch of Saddle Back Ledge, Penobscot Bay.
Showing position of Light House.
Alex. Parris Arch.t & Eng.r
Boston Feb.y 22 1848. Drawn by Brown & Hastings Eng.r
Scale 50 ft. = 1 inch.

Captain Joseph Smith of the Revenue Cutter Morris *recommended a light on Saddleback Ledge:*

In selecting proper sites for Light Houses, I have had two objects principally in view, viz, a bold shore & conspicuousness of location. Saddleback ledge, the place named in the appropriation, has there two advantages. It is near the centre of Isle au Hautt bay, has seven fathoms of water within thirty yards & twenty five fathoms within sixty yards of it in every direction. A vessel may therefore run directly for, & so near to it on any course, that the distance may be accurately judged so as to shape a course from it with confidence.[57]

(Drawing found in National Archives, RG 26)

PART II. Offshore Stations: The Challenges to Builders and Keepers

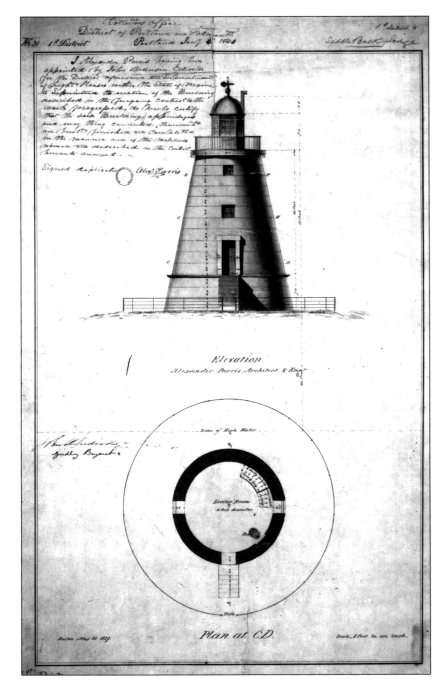

The granite tower on Saddleback Ledge on the east side of the entrance to Isle au Haut Bay was constructed in 1839. The tower was designed by Alexander Parris, who in January 1840 noted in the upper lefthand corner of one of the drawings:

> I Alexander Parris having been appointed by John Anderson Collector for the District . . . and Superintendent of Light Houses within the State of Maine to Superintend the erection of the Building ascribed in the foregoing contract as the work progressed, do hereby certify that the said Buildings, appendages, and every thing connected therewith are built, finished and completed in the manner and of the materials named and described in the contract. . . .

(Drawings found in National Archives, RG 26)

Maine Lighthouses: Documentation of Their Past

. . . [It is] simply a conical tower of hammered granite, the base being sunk below the surface of the rock, and resting upon a level plane, quarried out for the purpose. The stones of each course are equal to the thickness of the wall, and the joints, being very close, are filled with hydraulic cement of pure quality. The sea breaks quite over the lantern in a southeast gale. The tower contains four apartments for the use of the keeper, but no convenience for collecting fresh water, nor any means for securing the boat— both important omissions.

However, the cost of the work was but $15,000, and it is the most economical and durable structure that came under observation during the survey, and, what is worthy of special remark, the only one erected in New England by an "*architect and engineer*."[58]

Other early offshore stations

Pumpkin Island

Reporting on the light on Pumpkin Island in East Penobscot Bay in 1874, District Engineer J. C. Duane observed,

> . . . this light, together with several others on this part of the coast, are not only useless, but actually the cause of disasters . . . they frequently [draw] vessels into passages obstructed by ice, and as a remedy I would respectfully recommend that the Inspector be authorized to cause such lights to be extinguished when in his judgement it may be necessary.[59]

Apparently the Light-House Board heeded his advice. A year later, an inspection report described Pumpkin Island as:

> . . . about 1½ acres. None cultivated. One acre in grass, ½ acre rocky with small spruce trees at S.W. end. Station kept in fair order. Is of little service as the waters hereabouts are landlocked, and the light can be serviceable only about three miles at the farthest. The *Lewiston* Steamer, which runs during summer months, is about the only vessel using it. It is discontinued when the ice makes.[60]

(Ca. 1859 photo courtesy of U.S. Coast Guard)

Pond Island

The light station on Pond Island at the west side entrance to the Kennebec River was established in 1821. In 1823 the keeper petitioned for a well or cistern at his station:

I am the keeper of the Light House on Pond Island at the entrance of Kennebec River and live on the same Island. I suffer great inconvenience on account of having no means to obtain fresh water but by transporting it from the mainland. It is usual I am told to have a well or Cistern on the Islands where Light Houses are placed. The object of this letter is to request you to make application at the proper department to have this inconvenience remedied. I have applied a number of times to the superintendent, who observes he has no orders on the subject. A well or a Cistern to hold rain water would be of material consequence to any person who may keep the Light and live on the Island.[61]

Pleasonton directed that a cistern be built if good water could not be procured by digging a well.[62] (1885 photo courtesy of U.S. Coast Guard)

Whaleback Ledge

The lighthouse on Whaleback or Whale's Back Ledge sits in Maine waters off Portsmouth, New Hampshire. The first tower, completed in 1829, was so poorly constructed that it had to be cased over with wood in 1831, "to prevent the keeper from being drowned out by the sea washing through all the crevices."[63]

Various fixes were applied to the tower over the years, but "no human art can, however, make a firm structure of it. When there is a heavy swell rolling in, the base of the tower is struck with such force as to shake the whole edifice in the most alarming manner. The keeper asserted that the vibration was so great as to move the chairs and tables about the floor."[64] By 1869,

. . . the iron clamps which were intended to secure the stones of the foundation pier are all broken, and the stones on the upper side are cracked and started out. By putting an iron band of six inches by two around the upper course of stone of the pier an attempt has been made to put the station in a condition to last through the coming winter, but there can be no reliance upon this expedient for any length of time, and there is no doubt but the station should be rebuilt as soon as possible . . ..[65]

Congress appropriated $70,000 for a new tower to be constructed on Whaleback Ledge in the manner of other "wave-swept" masonry towers.

. . . The position is one of the most difficult to work upon on the coast, as the rock is covered by the waves except at low water and is exposed to the full force of the Atlantic. The new structure will be a masonry tower, solid to a height of 20 feet above low-water mark, and the blocks of granite which will form a facing for the interior mass of concrete will be tied together by dovetail joints, as is usual in similar sea structures. The diameter of the tower at the base will be 27 feet, and height of the focal plane above the sea will be 68 feet.[66]

Work on the foundation was begun in 1870. The tower was completed in 1872 and lit in May of that year. First District Inspector Thomas Selfridge wrote, "It is very desirable on the occupation of a new light that an intelligent Keeper should be appointed" and suggested that rations be furnished to this station as an incentive.[67]

The fog bell was located on the old tower 39 feet from the new one.[68] Until it was torn down around 1880, the old tower also served as a boathouse.[69]

After a gale on January 26, 1839, the keeper at Whaleback Ledge reported:

. . . such was the effect of the sea, that the assistants of the keeper could not hear each [other] speak when in the lantern, on account of the noise produced by the shaking of the apparatus in the lantern, when the sea struck the foundation of the light house, and he [the keeper] describes the shocks as that of sudden and heavy blows and a passing off with a shaking and quivering motion.

A large rock adjoining the lower tier of the foundation stone, and into which the foot of the iron ladder was inserted, was carried away, ripping up the ladder with it.

The reader may form some idea of the unenviable situation of the keeper . . . during the late storm from the fact that the building is situated on a ledge of sunken rocks, visible only at low water and about a mile distant from any human habitation.[70]

(Ca. 1859 photo courtesy of U.S. Coast Guard)

PART II. Offshore Stations: The Challenges to Builders and Keepers

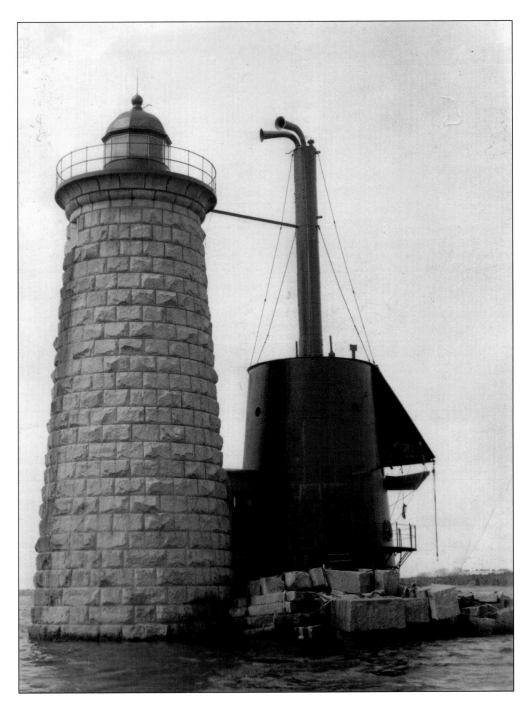

Whaleback Ledge light tower and fog signal in 1939. (Courtesy of U.S. Coast Guard)

Maine Lighthouses: Documentation of Their Past

Endnotes

[1] I. W. P. Lewis, survey on various keeper salaries in New England, February 6, 1843 (NA, RG 26, E 35).

[2] Gallatin to Dearborn, July 30, 1811 (NA, RG 26, Waltham).

[3] Dearborn to Gallatin, March 18, 1812 (NA, RG 26, E 17C).

[4] Ilsley to Dearborn, March 16, 1812 (NA, RG 26, E 17C).

[5] Collector for the District of York, Maine, to Dearborn, January 29, 1813 (NA, RG 26, E 17C).

[6] Dearborn to Gallatin, February 23, 1813 (NA, RG 26, E 17C).

[7] Hanna to Dearborn, March 15, 1813 (NA, RG 26, Waltham).

[8] Gallatin to Dearborn, March 24, 1813 (NA, RG 26, Waltham).

[9] Smith to Dearborn, May 9, 1816 (NA, RG 26, Waltham).

[10] Jeremiah Bradbury to H. A. S. Dearborn, March 12, 1820 (NA, RG 26, E 17C).

[11] Grover to Dearborn, November 18, 1818 (NA, RG 26, Waltham).

[12] Lewis to Pleasonton, December 14, 1825 (NA, RG 26, E 17E (NC-31): "Letters Received from Winslow Lewis, 1811-44").

[13] Chandler to Pleasonton, April 7, 1831 (NA, RG 26, E 17C).

[14] Chandler to Pleasonton, September 22, 1831 (NA, RG 26, E 17C).

[15] Official Register of Federal Employees, 1837.

[16] Grover's January 31, 1839, letter was reprinted in The Portsmouth Journal of Literature and Politics, February 9, 1839.

[17] Petitions dated February 14, 1839, and July 4, 1839 (NA, RG 26, E 17G).

[18] NA, RG 26, E 98.

[19] Engineer Secretary Captain F. A. Mahan, to First District Inspector, June 29, 1893 (NA, RG 26, E 23 (NC-31): "Letters Sent to District Inspectors and Engineers, 1852-1910").

[20] Robert Thayer Sterling, Lighthouses of the Maine Coast and the Men Who Kept Them (Brattleboro, Vermont: Stephen Daye Press, 1935), p. 54.

[21] Ibid., pp. 56 -57.

[22] Ibid., p. 60.

[23] Reprinted with permission from the Courier-Gazette, Rockland, Maine.

[24] Ibid.

[25] "Lighthouse Badly Damaged By Winter Gale," Down East Magazine (May 1978).

[26] Ilsley to Pleasonton, July 6, 1826, and September 28, 1826 (NA, RG 26, E17C).

[27] Ilsley to Congressman Jeremiah O'Brien, January 28, 1829 (NA, RG 26, E 17C).

[28] Pleasonton to O'Brien, February 19, 1829 (NA, RG 26, E 18).

[29] Pleasonton to Chandler, September 6, 1831 (NA, RG 26, E 17H).

[30] Jewett to Pleasonton, October 1, 1851 (NA, RG 26, E 17C).

[31] Collector Luther Jewett to Pleasonton, April 12, 1851 (NA, RG 26, E 17C).

[32] Letter to Superintendent of Lighthouses, Portland, Maine, found in 1920s keeper's journal for Moose Peak Light Station (NA, RG 26, E 80 (NC-31): "Lighthouse Station Logs, 1897-1941").

[33] Ilsley to Pleasonton, February 16, 1828 (NA, RG 26, E 16 (NC-31): "Miscellaneous Records, 1816-1929, 1918-36").

[34] Pleasonton to President John Quincy Adams, June 3, 1828 (NA, RG 26, E 16).

[35] The Keeper's Log, spring 1997, and "Lighthouses Guide Sailors Around Mount Desert Island," The Bar Harbor Times, August 12, 1982.

[36] John Rich to Pleasonton, March 13, 1852 (NA, RG 26, E 16).

[37] William Paine of the U.S. Marshal's Office, Portland, Maine, to Jewett, April 26 and May 5, 1852 (NA, RG 26, E 16).

[38] Rich to Pleasonton, August 9, 1852 (NA, RG 26, E 16).

[39] Chandler to Pleasonton, June 16, 1829 (NA, RG 26, E 17C).

[40] Chandler to Pleasonton, October 19, 1829 (NA, RG 26, E 17C).

[41] Chandler to Pleasonton, November 18, 1829 (NA, RG 26, E 17C).

[42] Report dated August 16, 1831 (NA, RG 26, E 6).

[43] Chandler to Pleasonton, March 12, 1830 (NA, RG 26, E 17C).

[44] Pleasonton to Secretary of the Treasury, July 12, 1830 (NA, RG 26, E 18); and Pleasonton to Chandler, July 13, 1830 (NA, RG 26, E 18).

[45] Chandler to Pleasonton, January 27, 1831 (NA, RG 26, E 17C).

[46] Report dated August 16, 1831 (NA, RG 26, E 6).

[47] Pleasonton to Chandler, September 6, 1831 (NA, RG 26, E 17H).

[48] J. L. Davis, Capt., Member, USLHB, "Inspection Report of First Light-House District," August 1875 (NA, RG 26, E 9 (NC-31): "Reports Submitted to the Board by Committees, 1874-1900"). Hereafter referred to as 1875 inspection report.

[49] Chandler to Pleasonton, September 15, 1831 (NA, RG 26, E 17C).

[50] Pleasonton to Chandler, September 28, 1831 (NA, RG 26, E 18).

[51] Quoted in Bill Caldwell, Lighthouses of Maine (Camden, Maine: Down East Books, 1986), p. 108.

[52] Chandler to Pleasonton, November 20, 1831 (NA, RG 26, E 17C).

[53] Pleasonton to Chandler, November 24, 1831 (NA, RG 26, E 18).

[54] Chandler to Pleasonton, September 5, 1832 (NA, RG 26, E 17C).

[55] Chandler to Pleasonton, February 2, 1833 (NA, RG 26, E 17C).

[56] Captain Joseph Smith to Board of Navy Commissioners, May 29, 1837 (NA, RG 26, E 25 (NC-31): "Correspondence of the Naval Committee, 1837-38").

[57] Ibid.

[58] Lighthouse Papers, p. 357.

[59] J. C. Duane to Professor Joseph Henry, Chairman of the USLHB, February 5, 1874 (NA, RG 26, E 24 (NC-31): "Letters Received From District Engineers and Inspectors, ca.1853-1900" or Letterbook 337).

[60] 1875 inspection report (NA, RG 26, E 9).

[61] S. L. Rodgers to Honorable E. Herrick, April 20, 1823 (NA, RG 26, E 17C).

[62] Pleasonton to Ilsley, May 13, 1824 (NA, RG 26, E 18).

[63] 1842 report of I. W. P. Lewis, quoted in Lighthouse Papers, p. 304.

[64] Lighthouse Papers, p. 357.

[65] 1869 Annual Report.

[66] 1870 Annual Report.

[67] Selfridge to Henry, May 21, 1872 (NA, RG 26, E 24 or Letterbook 297).

[68] Duane to Henry, May 31, 1872 (NA, RG 26, E 24 or Letterbook 297).

[69] 1880 Annual Report.

[70] The Portsmouth Journal of Literature and Politics, February 9, 1839.

PART III: The U.S. Light-House Board (USLHB) Revamps the System

As mid-century approached, the increasingly noisy chorus of complaints that Winslow Lewis's system of lamps and reflectors was inadequate spurred action in Washington. In 1851, Congress appointed another board to scrutinize every aspect of the Lighthouse Establishment. The investigation uncovered myriad problems. Some towers were not tall enough to provide the necessary range for their lights. Also, their placement along the coast was erratic: they were bunched together in populated areas and too widely scattered in sparsely settled areas. Mariners testified that they could not see or distinguish the lights, placing blame on the now-obsolete lamps and reflectors.

A new approach to administration

By 1851, Stephen Pleasonton had administered lighthouses through nine presidencies.[1] The investigating committee recommended that he be replaced by a nine-member board and that the whole system be revamped under its direction. The U.S. Light-House Board (USLHB), established by Congress in 1852, would remain under the jurisdiction of the Secretary of the Treasury, but the Board was directed to

> . . . discharge all administrative duties relating to the construction, illumination, inspection, and superintendence of light-houses, light-vessels, beacons, buoys, sea-marks, and their appendages, and embracing the security of foundations of works already existing, procuring illuminating and other apparatus, supplies, and materials of all kinds for building and rebuilding when necessary, and keeping in good repair the light-houses, light-vessels, beacons, and buoys of the United States; and shall have the charge and custody of all the archives, books, documents, drawings, models, returns, apparatus, and other things appertaining to the Light-House Establishment.[2]

The Light-House Board was made up of two navy officers, two army officers, two civilians of "high scientific attainments," and an additional navy and army officer to serve as the Naval and Engineering Secretaries. The Secretary of the Treasury served as the ex officio president. In his absence, a chairman elected by the Board presided over the quarterly meetings. To expedite decision-making, the Board had six standing committees: finance, floating aids to navigation, lighting, experiments, location, and engineering. The day-to-day administrative duties were performed by the two secretaries.[3]

The Board redivided the country into 12 districts; the first district encompassed the coast of Maine and New Hampshire. Army and navy officers were appointed to serve as district engineers and inspectors.

NUMBERS OF AIDS IN THE FIRST DISTRICT UNDER THE USLHB

The annual reports prepared and published by the Light-House Board tracked its activities and summarized the extensive paperwork produced by the agency. The 1864 *Annual Report* indicated that Maine and New Hampshire had 44 lighthouses. The 1868 *Annual Report* provided a more detailed breakdown:

Light-houses and lighted beacons	46
Light-vessels	None
Beacons unlighted	41
Buoys actually in position	303
Spare buoys to supply losses	234
Tenders (steam)	1
Tenders (sailing)	None

In 1872, a category for "fog-signals operated by steam or hot-air engines" was added to the list, with eight reported in the first district. By 1892, the first district contained

> ...57 light-stations with 59 lights, 2 beacon lights, and 1 independent fog signal. Of these stations 28 are provided with fog signals. Seventeen of these signals are bells struck by machinery, 8 of them are operated by steam, and 3 of them are worked by hot-air engines. The independent fog signal of Manana Island is run by hot air. There are in position 104 day or unlighted beacons, 11 whistling buoys, 16 bell buoys, and 606 other buoys.[4]

The number of lighthouses and lighted beacons in Maine under the Light-House Board peaked at 80 in 1905 and 1906. In 1907, three years before the U.S. Light-House Board was dissolved and its duties taken over by the U.S. Bureau of Lighthouses, the following statistics were given for the first district:

Light-houses and beacon lights	78
Light-vessel in position	1
Day, or unlighted, beacons	133
Fog-signals operated by steam or oil engines	17
Fog-signals operated by machinery	31
Gas-lighted buoys in position	2
Whistling buoys in position	23
Bell buoys in position	31
Other buoys in position	822
Steamers, *Lilac* and *Geranium*, buoy tenders for supply and inspection	2
Steamer *Myrtle*, for construction and repair in the First and Second districts	1[5]

Lighthouse construction under the Light-House Board

The Light-House Board developed a practical system for building lighthouses. Extensive and detailed architectural drawings were prepared, leaving nothing to the discretion of the builders. "Plans of light-houses of different classes, with modifications adapted to different localities, would promote economy by the frequent repetition of the same pieces, which in stone-work, brick-work, iron-casting, carpenter's work, glazier's work, and the like, is productive always of a decided economy."[7] The Board's Engineer Secretary scrutinized all plans, drawings, specifications, and estimates of the cost of any construction or new illuminating apparatus. The old contract system of hiring the lowest bidder to construct a lighthouse was discarded. "A knowledge of the qualities of stone, cements, mortars, and other materials used in their construction, is not to be acquired in a day, and belongs only as a general rule, to a competent engineer, architect, or builder."[8] The Board tapped personnel from the U.S. Army Bureau of Topographical Engineers to design and construct many of the lighthouses.

Standard plan of a second-order lighthouse. (Drawing in National Archives, RG 26)

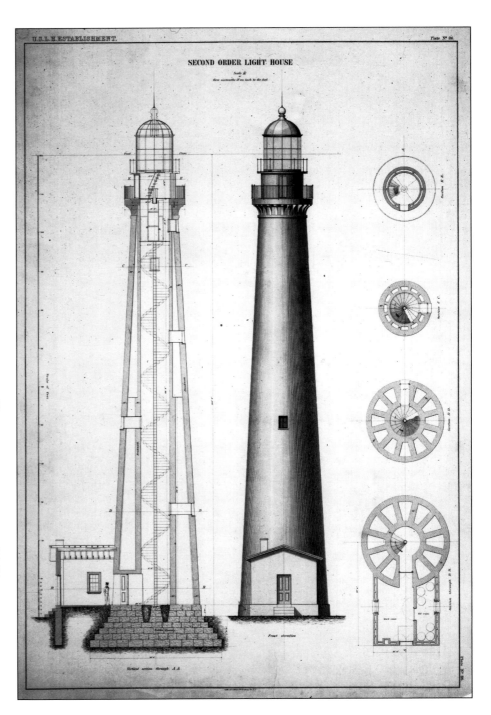

The lighthouse at Prospect Harbor was established in 1850 and discontinued in 1859 when the Light-House Board decided that since "the harbor is not used as a harbor of refuge, and the village near which it is situated has only a small coasting trade. . . . the light is not of sufficient service to the general or local interests of navigation to justify its maintenance . . ."[6] In 1870 the Board reversed its decision and the light was re-exhibited. In 1891 a separate tower replaced this attached one. (Courtesy of U.S. Coast Guard)

PART III: The U.S. Light-House Board (USLHB) Revamps the System

The Board also put into place a regular system of inspection of the lighthouses by district inspectors. "Frequent visitation and minute examinations by competent inspectors would insure vigilance, economy, and order on the part of the keepers. The inspectors should be men thoroughly acquainted with all the details of lighthouse management and superintendency, with the manner of adjusting the lamps and reflectors, and of keeping them in order."[9]

The Light-House Board also addressed problems caused by leaky lanterns and poorly ventilated towers. Lack of storage space for oil and other supplies was noted, as was the frequent necessity for repointing the towers and checking for disconnected lightning rods. Other problems needing attention included the lack of comforts in the keepers' dwellings; inadequate and hasty repairs at the lighthouses; and ineffective notices of changes in the lights.[10]

No new construction occurred during the 1860s. The district inspector and engineer having been recalled for more urgent war duties, the first district was compelled to rely upon "civil assistance." The 1870s, however, saw a number of cast-iron towers erected (discussed in the next section), as well as traditional wooden or brick lighthouses established at Avery Rock, Burnt Coat

Maine lighthouses rebuilt during the first decade of Light-House Board supervision included Baker Island, Bear Island, Boon Island, Browns Head, Fort Point, Franklin Island, Goat Island, Matinicus Rock, Petit Manan, Pond Island, Seguin Island, and West Quoddy Head. In that same decade, new stations were established at Bass Harbor Head, Blue Hill Bay, Deer Island Thorofare, Heron Neck, Narraguagus Island, Portland Breakwater, Pumpkin Island, Tenants Harbor, and Winter Harbor. With a few exceptions, the Light-House Board preferred brick in the construction of new or replacement masonry towers.[11] Tenants Harbor Light Station in 1892. (Courtesy of U.S. Coast Guard)

Harbor, Egg Rock, Halfway Rock, and Hendricks Head. Towers were also rebuilt at Grindle Point, Indian Island, Little River Island, and Nash Island. With the exception of Ram Island Light Station, very little major construction took place in the first district during the 1880s, but the 1890s brought the construction of lighthouses on Great Duck Island and Two Bush Island as well as the new Kennebec River lights and four spark-plug towers discussed in Part IV. The last traditional lighthouse built in Maine was the station at Whitlocks Mill on the south bank of the St. Croix River, lit in early 1910.

Cast-iron construction

The first cast-iron-plate lighthouses were constructed in the early 1840s. James Rodgers completed a cast-iron tower for the Spanish government in Cuba before any cast-iron towers were constructed in this country. Rodgers cited the tower's advantages: durability and strength, the fact that the tower could be moved, roominess inside for the keeper, and resistance to fire.[12] Because cast iron was lightweight (compared to brick and stone), inexpensive, strong, and watertight, and because it deteriorated slowly, cast-iron towers soon proliferated. Most cast-iron towers were lined with brick for additional stability and insulation.

The twin towers at Cape Elizabeth were rebuilt of cast iron in 1874, as were towers at Portland Breakwater (1875), Little River Island (1876), and Cape Neddick (1879). In addition, all four spark-plug towers were constructed of cast iron, as were their foundation tubes.

The use of cast iron for the new towers at Cape Elizabeth was in part due to a shortage of bricks caused by the rebuilding of Boston after the Great Fire of 1872. Another factor influencing the decision may have been cost. Engineer Duane estimated a brick tower would cost $18,948, whereas an iron tower (with a brick lining) would cost $16,548.[13]

The original dwelling at Narraguagus Island Light Station was wrapped around the tower. In 1875 a new detached dwelling was erected and the old dwelling torn down, leaving the tower to stand by itself. This photo was taken after a new lantern was placed on the tower in 1877. (Courtesy of U.S. Coast Guard)

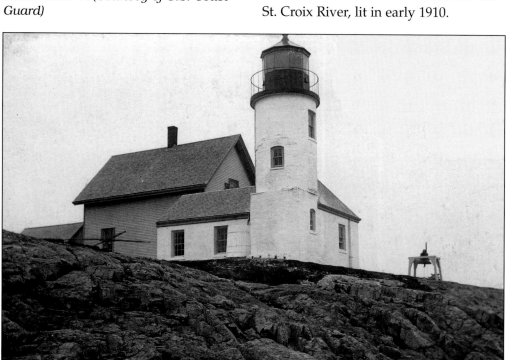

PART III: The U.S. Light-House Board (USLHB) Revamps the System

DEL. T. E. PEACOCK · 1962

BRUNSWICK H.A.B.S. FIELD OFFICE
MAINE
MID-COAST SURVEY II
UNDER DIRECTION OF UNITED STATES DEPARTMENT OF THE INTERIOR
NATIONAL PARK SERVICE, BRANCH OF PLANS AND DESIGN

PORTLAND POINT

PORTLAND BREAKWATER LIGHTHOUSE
NAME OF STRUCTURE
PORTLAND SOUTH PORTLAND CUMBERLAND COUNTY MAINE

SURVEY NO. Me 112

HISTORIC AMERICAN BUILDINGS SURVEY
SHEET 5 OF 5 SHEETS

THIRD LEVEL

¼" PLATE GLASS

CAPITAL MISSING

6'-7"

SECOND LEVEL

6'-7⅛"

FIRST LEVEL

CAST CONCRETE BASE

½" = 1'-0"

GRANITE

APPROXIMATE HIGHWATER MARK

SOUTHEAST ELEVATION
SCALE ½" = 1'-0"

The 1875 cast-iron tower built on the Portland Breakwater did not use the standard design for cast-iron lighthouses. Rather than featuring a plain cylindrical tube, it was decorated with classical columns. The 1875 tower replaced a wooden tower built in 1855. (Historic American Building Survey/Historic American Engineering Record (HABS/HAER) drawing)

Maine Lighthouses: Documentation of Their Past

67

The plans for the lighthouse on the Portland Breakwater did not include a dwelling. Instead, the keeper lived in a house on shore and walked out the 1,900-foot breakwater to reach the lighthouse—not a pleasant journey in severe weather. In 1889, the inspector stated

> . . . that the accommodations at this station are entirely inadequate for the Keeper, and the proper, clean, and orderly care of the station, and recommend that a wooden structure to contain two rooms so situated as to be protected against the worst seas, be attached to the tower. . . . this would leave the watch-room free, and

provide better recommendations [accommodations] for the Keeper, as during the winter he ought to remain at the light, day and night; and that the roofs would also provide fresh water for the Keeper, which now has to be brought a distance of three-quarters of a mile.[14]

A keeper's dwelling was attached to the tower that same year. The dwelling was removed in 1934 when the light was electrified and the keeper at nearby Spring Point Ledge assumed responsibility for tending the lights at both stations. (Photo courtesy of Ken Black, Shore Village Museum, Rockland, Maine)

Although the Board of Navy Commissioners investigated the need for a lighthouse upon the "York Nubble" as far back as 1837, no formal request for an appropriation was submitted to Congress until 1874. Having been petitioned for a light by the president of the Portland Steam Packet Company and others, the Board asked the first district inspector to prepare a report evaluating its importance. The inspector's report along with the other paperwork was then submitted to the Board's Committee on Lighting which responded,

> The Committee on Lighting to which were referred by the Board at its meeting on the 10th of August, the papers relating to the necessity for a light house at Cape Neddick (York Nubble), Maine, have had the same under consideration, and beg leave to report that, in the opinion of the Committee, a light of the 4th order should be established at York Nubble, and therefore, recommend that Congress be asked for an appropriation for the same.[15]

The request for a $15,000 appropriation was repeated in 1875 and granted in 1876. Construction was postponed until 1879 because of delays in acquiring title to the site. (1949 photo (facing page) courtesy of U.S. Coast Guard)

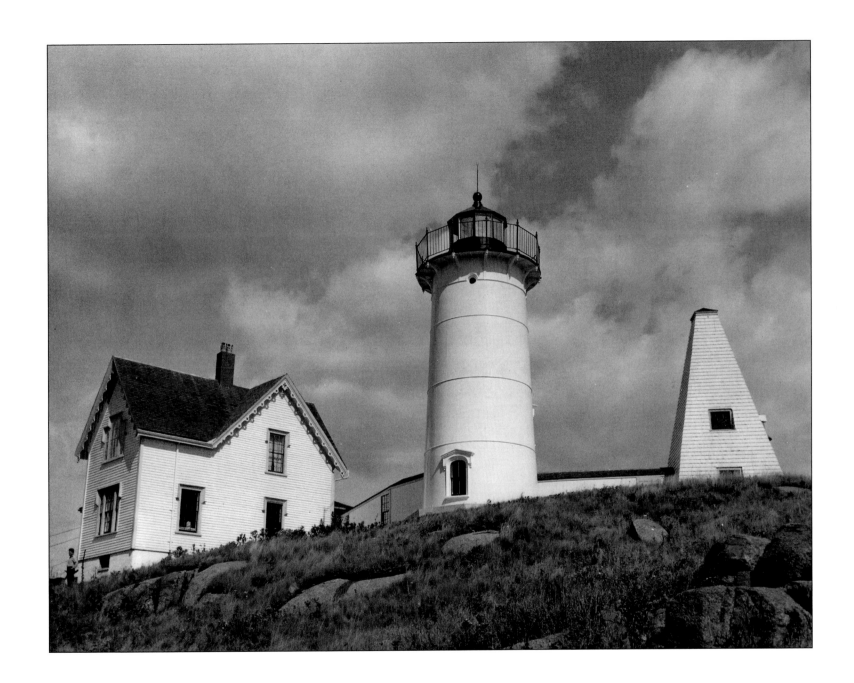

Maine Lighthouses: Documentation of Their Past

Iron (cast, wrought, or rolled) was also used for lighthouse components such as stairs, galleries, railings, doors, shutters, and door and window frames, and for joists, flooring, partitions, etc.[16] Shown here is the stairway in the tower at Dice Head. (HABS/HAER photo by Richard Cheek, 1990)

PART III: The U.S. Light-House Board (USLHB) Revamps the System

Details of cast-iron steps for the Petit Manan Lighthouse. (National Archives drawing, RG 26)

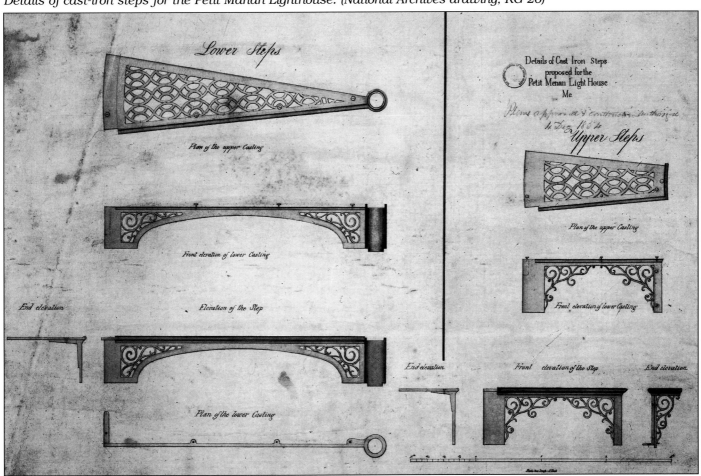

Four spark plugs

The need for light towers in deep water with no rock bottom to provide a foundation led to the introduction of the caisson or "spark plug" lighthouse. The caisson foundation was a pre-assembled cast-iron cylinder, fitted with either a temporary watertight bottom or a permanent wooden crib. The cylinder was towed to the location and sunk by controlled flooding of the interior. Rip-rap was put around the outside to add stability and prevent bottom scour. Next the cylinder was pumped out and filled with stone and concrete. A cellar was generally put inside the caisson to provide for a water cistern and storage. A keepers' quarters of several stories and integral lantern formed the tower built above the water level.

The light on Goose Rocks was first exhibited on the night of December 31, 1890, as reported by Principal Keeper Ira D. Trundy in his logbook. The next day, Leo Gillis reported for duty as Trundy's assistant.[17] Families were not posted to this station, so the keepers rotated ashore for visits or to spend the Sabbath. Until a motorboat was provided in 1938, the keepers relied on government-issued dories that were easier than a rowboat to haul up on the rocks at the station, but more difficult to maneuver. (Courtesy of U.S. Coast Guard)

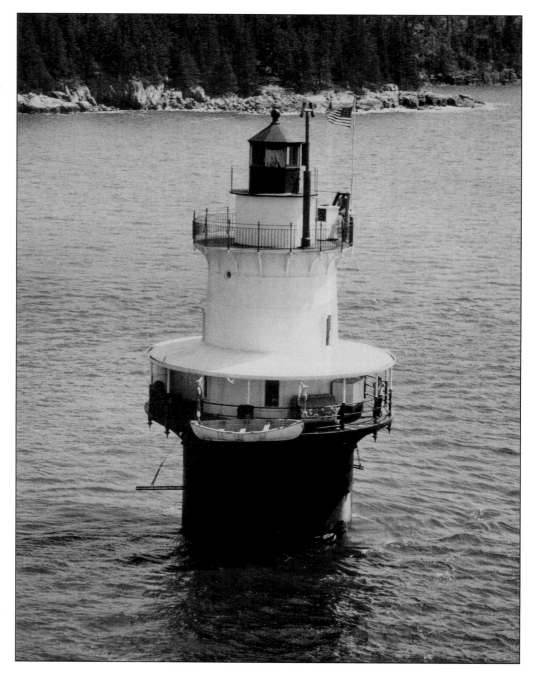

PART III: The U.S. Light-House Board (USLHB) Revamps the System

Four caisson-type lighthouses were built in Maine:

Crabtree Ledge. When asked to report on the "necessity, advisability, and practicability of establishing a lighthouse on Crabtree Ledge, Frenchmans Bay," Inspector Oliver A. Batcheller responded positively:

> Travel over this route has of late assumed larger proportions, and is constantly increasing. In winter there are three lines of steamers running with more or less regularity, and in summer the various steamers plying in these waters make from fifteen to twenty trips (many of them at night) daily.
>
> From the character of the traffic—mostly passenger in connection with the Maine Central R.R.—and from the absence of sufficient hotel accommodations at Mount Desert Ferry, these steamers, carrying large numbers of people are obliged to run regularly, and at high speed, in order to maintain the popularity of the route.
>
> Crabtree Ledge lies directly in their route, and is a serious danger to navigation.[18]

The $25,000 Congress appropriated in 1886 was found to be insufficient for constructing the tower on Crabtree Ledge, so an additional $13,000 was appropriated in 1888. According to the 1890 *Annual Report*:

> The light-house recently constructed consists of a cylindrical iron caisson, 25 feet in diameter and 32 feet in height, founded upon a rock 15 feet below mean sea-level. It is filled with concrete and surmounted by an iron tower, 37 feet high from base to focal plane, and was finished December 31, 1889.[19]

The fifth-order lens was lit on January 15, 1890. The lighthouse was discontinued in 1934, and sold at public auction. It later collapsed in a storm.

Goose Rocks. The lighthouse on Goose Rocks was completed in the last decade of the nineteenth century to mark the east entrance to the Fox Island Thorofare between Vinalhaven and North Haven Island. The 1888 *Annual Report* claimed that "this thoroughfare is one of the most important passages on the coast of Maine for large fleets of coasting and fishing vessels." A $35,000 appropriation was obtained and construction began in 1890. The metal work was contracted to a firm in Boston; Portland cement was delivered to Widow's Island about a quarter of a mile from the site where a temporary storehouse and quarters were constructed. "The casting of the tower and the breaking of the stones" took place at Crotch Island, "about 8 miles from the station."[20]

Lubec Channel. The light at Lubec Channel was lit the same night as that at Goose Rocks—New Year's Eve, 1890. The bell fog signal was put into operation on February 1, 1891. Fred W. Morong was the first keeper, Loring W. Myers his assistant. On October 1, 1895, Myers took over as principal keeper when Morong was transferred to Libby Island Light. Herbert Robinson became assistant keeper.

On May 21, 1899, keeper Myers noted that "the assistant keeper had to go home to stay with his son through sickness and death of his son. The principal keeper had to take his wife on as the assistant—could not get a man to take his place at the time."[21] When Robinson was transferred to Libby Island on February 15, 1902, Myers noted how long Robinson had served at Lubec Channel and what a good assistant he had been. Almon Mitchell replaced Robinson and served until November 10, 1909, when he left to take charge of Petit Manan Light Station. Wilson Joy arrived from Ram Island Ledge to replace Mitchell. Keeper Myers trained several more assistants before retiring on October 1, 1923, after 33 years of service.[22]

Spring Point Ledge. The lighthouse on Spring Point Ledge, on the westerly side of the main channel into Portland Harbor, was the final spark plug lighthouse built in Maine. Two steamers and seven steamship companies petitioned the Light-House Board stating that they carried more than a

After the War Department dredged a channel between Lubec and Campobello Island, a light was needed at the entrance of "Lubec Narrows." The station consisted of a

cylindrical iron caisson, 33 feet in diameter and 48 feet high, cast in eight sections of thirty-two plates each, expanding, in the upper section, to 37 feet 9 inches in diameter, to be sunk 6 feet into the site (11 feet below extreme low and 36 feet below extreme high water), filled with concrete, and surmounted by an iron tower, 37 feet in height from base to focal plane.[23]

(Courtesy of U.S. Coast Guard)

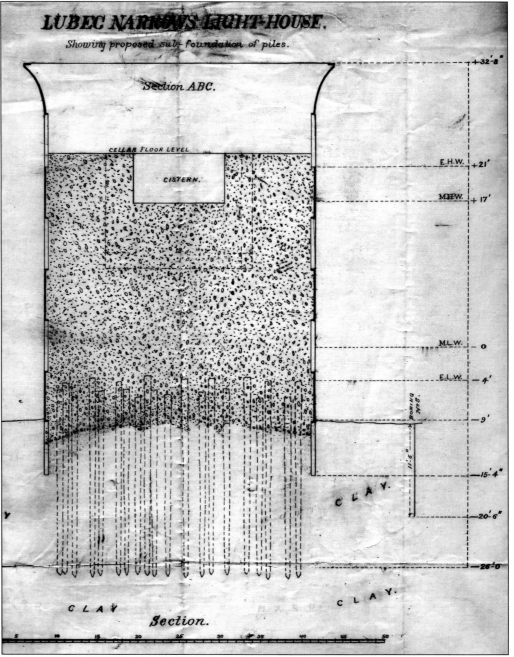

half million passengers past the ledge annually. The breakdown appeared in the 1891 *Annual Report*:

Casco Bay Company	317,285
Portland Steam Packet Company	75,482
International Steamship Company	40,325
Maine Steamship Company	4,495
Harpswell Steamboat Company	6,000
Portland and Boothbay Steamboat Company	3,000
Steamer *Greenwood*	36,000
Steamer *S. E. Spring*	35,000
Allan Steamship Line	775
Total	518,362

The Light-House Board repeatedly requested $45,000 from Congress to build a lighthouse on Spring Point Ledge. Funds were authorized in 1895. In May 1896 the Board accepted the $27,490 construction bid of Thomas Dwyer of New York, New York.[24] Despite work stoppages caused by bad weather and arguments over the quality of the cement used, the tower was completed in March 1897. A *Notice to Mariners* announced that a fifth-order light showing a flash every five seconds would be established on or about May 24, 1897. William A. Lane, transferred from his position as mate of the tender *Myrtle*, became the first keeper.[25]

Keeper Lane's new circular home consisted of four floors, watch room, and lantern room. The first level provided a cellar for coal and equipment storage. The next level served as a kitchen and the third level

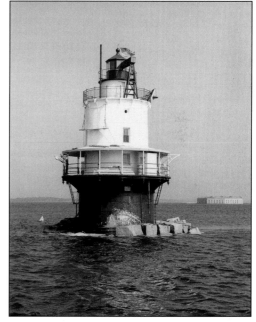

Spring Point Ledge Lighthouse in 1949 (two years before a granite breakwater connecting the lighthouse to the shore was completed), and in 1989. (1949 photo (above) courtesy of U.S. Coast Guard; 1989 photo (left) by Richard Cheek courtesy of HABS/HAER)

Maine Lighthouses: Documentation of Their Past

was Lane's office and quarters. The assistant keeper occupied the fourth level below the watch room. A fog bell hung outside the watch room with its striking machinery located inside; the weights had to be wound up from their position in a central column inside the tower.[26]

Lighting the Kennebec River

Before 1898 the navigational aids along the Kennebec River were maintained by private companies whose vessels traveled to the important harbor at Bath and other upriver communities. The 1892 *Annual Report* indicated that

There were 3,137 arrivals of vessels in this river during the year, not counting the steamers which ply daily. The steamers *Kennebec*, 1,652 tons, and *Sagadahoc*, 1,413 tons, made ninety-six round trips each from Gardiner to Boston. Other passenger steamers ply on the river from Bath to Augusta, Boothbay, and Popham Beach, and intermediate places. The number of passengers carried was 232,150. Seventeen tugs were engaged on the river in towing. Thirty-nine vessels of 32,063 gross tons were built on the river, valued at $50 per gross ton, or, say, $1,603,150. The vessels arriving will average 450 tons. Some 24 feet draft can be carried to Thwings Point, 6 miles above Bath, 16 feet draft from Thwings Point to Gardiner, and 8 feet from Gardiner to Augusta. The Kennebec River is kept open by the

towboats during the winter from Bath to the sea. Above Bath the buoys are taken up about November 20, and the river is likely to freeze at any time after this date. The ice usually goes out early in April. The river not only has the sea fogs, which extend to Bath, but its own river fog or mist, which is dense and at times low

down. On dark nights it is sometimes impossible to tell where the water ends and the shore begins. The Light-House Establishment maintains no lights or fog signals in the Kennebec, but the Kennebec Steamboat Company and the towboat companies have united for many years in maintaining lanterns hung on the

The Doubling Point Range Lights (above), marking the channel from Ram Island to Fiddlers Reach, consisted of two frame towers, dwelling, and barn—shown here in 1975. The Perkins Island Light Station (facing page) *was established in 1898. A boathouse and boatslip were completed in 1901 and a bell tower with a 1,000-pound bell established in 1902.[27] (Courtesy of U.S. Coast Guard)*

Maine Lighthouses: Documentation of Their Past   77

buoys at turning points or other difficult places. The above facts establish, in the Board's opinion, the necessity for and advisability of increasing the aids to navigation in the Kennebec River . . ..

The needed appropriation of $17,000 was not made until 1895. The four-station system, completed in 1898, consisted of Squirrel Point, Perkins Island, Doubling Point, and Doubling Point Range. They were no sooner built than the local Congressman made his interests known:

There will probably soon be appointed Keepers for the new Light Houses recently established on the Kennebec River, in my Congressional District. If the positions are to be filled by promotions, I trust the promotions will be made of Assistants in my Congressional district, as far as possible. I notice that a large proportion of appointments by promotion in recent years have been from lighthouses outside my district, & there has been complaint frequently made to me that there seemed to be small chance for promotions of assistants within the district. I do not know how much grounds there may be for this complaint, but I have called your attention to the matter in order that all reason for it may be avoided. I shall expect that the three new places will be filled from my Congressional district.[28]

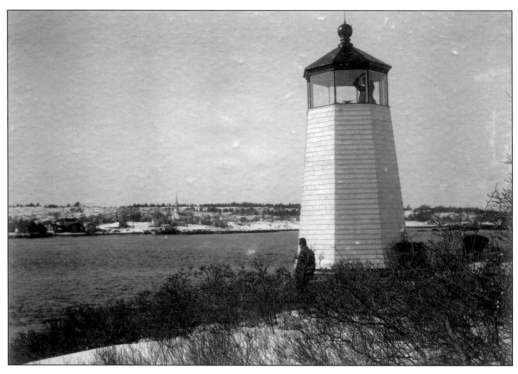

The tower at Squirrel Point Light Station (above) before the lens was installed. (Courtesy of U.S. Coast Guard)

Drawings (facing page) of the two towers that form the range at Doubling Point. The design for the front range was also used for the towers at Doubling Point, Perkins Island and Squirrel Point. (Courtesy of U.S. Coast Guard)

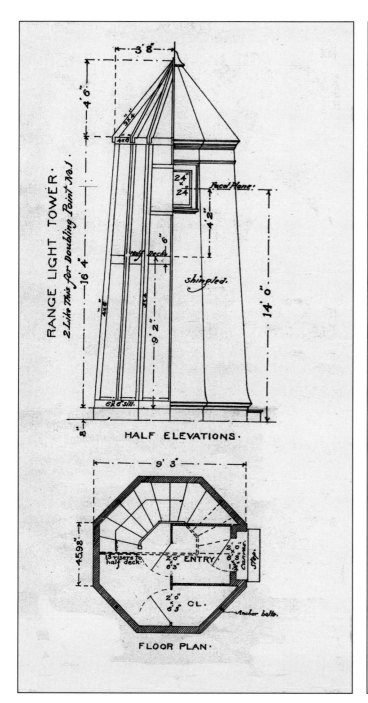

RANGE LIGHT TOWER.
2 Like This for Doubling Point No.1.

3'8"
4'6"
3'4"
4x6"
24x24
Focal Plane.
4'2"
16'4"
Half Deck.
6"
9'2"
4x6"
3'4"
Shingled.
14'0"
6x6 Sill.
8"

HALF ELEVATIONS.

9'3"
45.98"
13 risers to half deck.
2'0" 6'3"
2'0" 6'3" ENTRY
Canvas.
Step.
2'0" 6'3" CL.
Anchor bolts.

FLOOR PLAN.

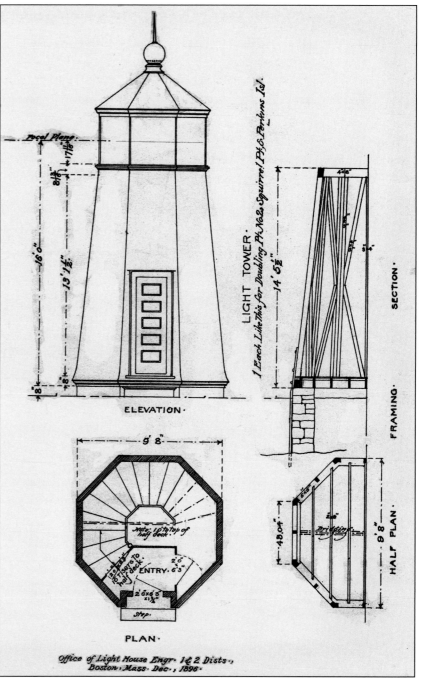

LIGHT TOWER.
1 Each Like This for Doubling Pt. No.2, Squirrel Pt. & Perkins Isl.

Focal Plane.
+1'7 1/8"
8'3"
16'0"
13'1/2"
8"
8"
4x6"

ELEVATION.

SECTION.

FRAMING.

9'8"
Note 10' to top of half deck.
12 RISERS TO half deck.
2'0" 6'3" ENTRY
2'0"x6'5" x1 1/2"
45.04"
Step.

PLAN.

9'8"
6x6"
2x6"
Bridging.

HALF PLAN.

Office of Light House Engr. 1 & 2 Dists.,
Boston, Mass. Dec., 1896.

Additional stations built or rebuilt under the USLHB

The station on Heron Neck on Green Island in East Penobscot Bay was lighted for the first time on February 6, 1854. It is shown here ca. 1859. The 1875 inspection report indicated that the one-and-a-half-story brick keeper's dwelling was leaking and "the wall paper was all wet . . . ."[29] In 1891 the dwelling was described as,

    . . . having 8-inch brick walls separated by 2-inch air space from a 4-inch brick lining and having interior 4-inch brick partitions. It is, however, understood to have been built by contract, and so little mortar was used that many of the joints do not appear to have been filled. In driving rainstorms they receive large quantities of water which keep the walls very damp and almost incessantly exudes moisture into the dwelling. The dampness of the dwelling is further increased by the character of the site, which is underlaid by a sloping ledge over which the water flows, saturating the soil surrounding the dwelling and keeping its cellar wet. From these causes the dwelling is unhealthy and it is unsuitable for occupancy in so severe a climate. It is claimed that on this account five deaths have occurred in it since its erection in 1853.[30]

In 1895 a new wooden keeper's dwelling was finally completed. (Ca. 1859 photo courtesy of U.S. Coast Guard)

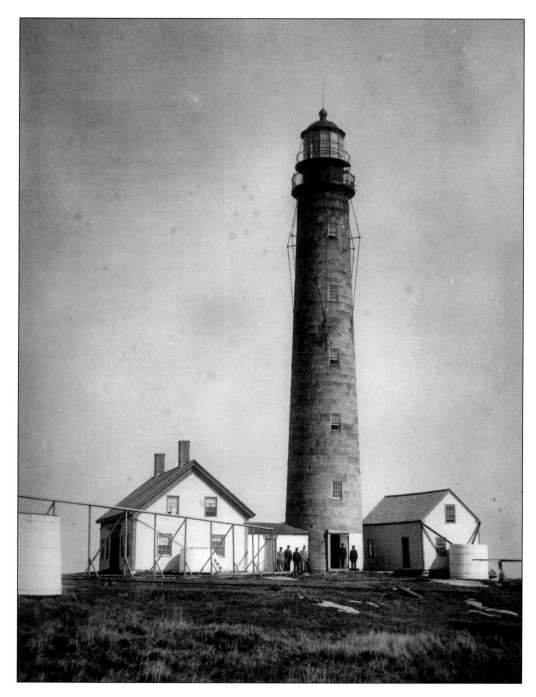

The lighthouse at Petit Manan was established in 1817, and the U.S. Light-House Board rebuilt it and fitted it with a second-order Fresnel lens in 1855. By 1881, the first district inspector complained that the tower was "very shaky" and "it vibrates so much during heavy weather that the plate glass of the lantern is cracked. In a recent gale three panes were thus broken."[31] In 1882, "a cast-iron capping was put on the top of the light-tower, the lantern braced and strengthened and reglazed where required, and the joints in the tower walls repointed."[32] Apparently this did not solve the problem as indicated in the 1888 Annual Report:

> This tower, of ashlar masonry, is 96 feet in height to the watch-room deck, 20 feet in diameter at the base, and 12 feet at the top. The entire horizontal joint, two courses below the deck, was loosened by vibration, which became alarming in high winds. In September last the watch-room and lantern were firmly secured to the tower with six sets of 1 1/8-inch iron tie-rods, passing each from an iron collar inclosing the lantern to an iron strut set in the masonry and thence to a bolt set in the granite 34 feet below the deck. Fortunately, the lantern was thus secured before the severe gale of December, 1887, which might otherwise have proved disastrous at this station.

(National Archives photo # 26-LG-4-26)

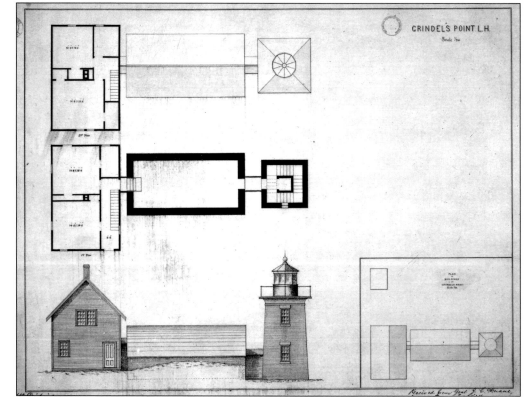

In 1875 on Grindle Point, a square brick tower with a separate one-and-a-half-story keeper's dwelling (top of facing page) replaced a one-and-a-half-story brick dwelling with a lantern on top (above). The walls of the old dwelling were taken down to near the surface of the ground and the roof lowered, converting it into a covered passageway between the tower and dwelling. The passageway was used for storing provisions, fuel, oil, and other supplies.[33] (Photos courtesy of U.S. Coast Guard; National Archives drawing, RG 26)

PART III: The U.S. Light-House Board (USLHB) Revamps the System

The station established as a guide to Blue Hill Bay in 1856 was originally called Eggemoggin. Upon the recommendation of the first district inspector, the Committee on Location changed the name to Blue Hill Bay in 1872.[34] The station (left) is shown here ca.1859. (National Archives photo # 26-LG-1-36)

The light station on Ram Island in Booth Bay Harbor was first lit on November 5, 1883. A footbridge on iron piles connected the tower to the shore. In reviewing the plans, the Committee on Engineering was "of opinion that it will be safe to omit the cover to the bridge leading to the tower until necessity shall show it is required; but in the meantime a storm vestibule should be added to the tower."[35] (Courtesy of U.S. Coast Guard)

PART III: The U.S. Light-House Board (USLHB) Revamps the System

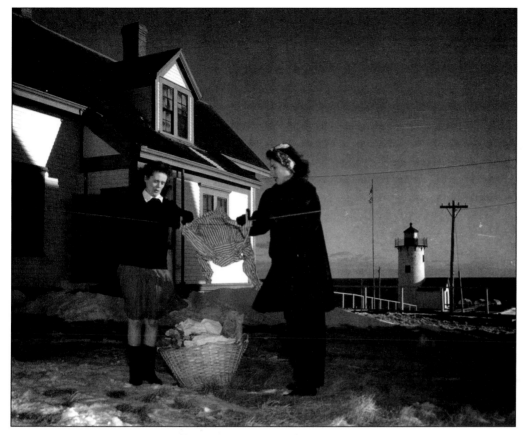

shed 130 by 30 feet in plan, with a storage cistern holding 5,350 gallons, and with coal bunkers of 60 tons' capacity; three dwellings of six rooms each, with outbuildings, a barn 20 feet by 30 feet in plan, a boat and store house at the landing measuring 30 feet by 40 feet, a double boat-slip 200 feet long, and an enginehouse with steam windlass.

The station included a duplicate steam fog-signal apparatus and a 1,200-pound fog bell to be rung by hand in emergency.

Some considered Great Duck Light the roughest station on the Maine coast because it was so exposed to wind and weather off the Atlantic. The island was the only light station having two boathouses and two slips, one on either side of the island, to be used according to which way the wind blew. Gasoline hoists hauled boats up the slips. One of the boathouses is shown below in 1950. (Courtesy of U.S. Coast Guard)

The 1885 Annual Report of the Light-House Board *indicated that a light and fog signal station at Great Duck Island*

would be of great aid to the commerce going to, from, or past this portion of the coast of Maine, to guide vessels caught in easterly gales and the usually accompanying snow storms, into Bass Harbor or Southwest Harbor. Both are frequently used by coasting vessels at all seasons as harbors of refuge. It is especially essential that a fog-signal should be established here, as the fog-signals nearest, on either side, are those at

Matinicus Rock and Petit Manan, which are 60 miles apart.

Strategically located between the primary light on Mount Desert Rock and the approach to Blue Hill Bay and Mount Desert Island, Great Duck Island Lighthouse was finished in December 1890.[36] The 1891 Annual Report *described the Great Duck Light Station as*

a brick tower 35 feet high to its focal plane, with a brick service room 8 feet by 10 feet in plan; a brick fog-signal house 32 feet square, with a service cistern holding 25,000 gallons; a rain-

In 1890, $25,000 was requested to build a fog signal station on The Cuckolds,

two rocky islets rising about 15 feet above high water in the westerly edge of the channel at the entrance to Booth Bay . . . much dreaded by mariners in thick weather and are a great peril to a large number of vessels, as it is estimated that from three to four thousand enter the bay for refuge in Booth Bay Harbor, which is well protected and is one of the most useful and important harbors of refuge on the coast of Maine.[37]

The appropriation was passed on March 3, 1891, and work began on The Cuckolds fog signal building in the Board's Portland workshop in January 1892. Later that year construction moved onsite.

. . . The structure consists of a semicircular granite pier 36 feet in diameter and 12 feet high, hollow in the center for fresh-water cisterns and storeroom. It is surmounted by a brick fog-signal house of a similar form, but of smaller diameter. A substantial double dwelling having a heavy, hard pine frame, well bolted to the ledge, is in the rear of the pier. A bulkhead of hard pine, 60 feet long, protects the dwelling and outbuildings. The boathouse and boat slip are on the west side of the rock, protected from the sea.

There were used in the construction of the station 105 yards of granite masonry, 430 casks cement, 60,000 bricks, 100 tons sand, 200 tons of broken stone and pebbles, 70,000 feet of lumber, inclusive of the false work, 3,400 pounds wrought-iron work, 5,900 pounds columns and railings,

4,000 pounds of beams, about 650 tons in all.

The material was bought under contract, and the greater part was carried to the station by the tender *Myrtle* in connection with other work in the vicinity. The work was done by hired labor, with the plant belonging to the Light-House Establishment and kept in this district. Work was commenced at the site April 22, 1892, and was finished November 16, 1892. The cost of the structures and machinery complete in place was $24,750.[38]

The signal consisted of duplicate first-order Daboll trumpets operated by compressed hot-air engines. In 1895, a 1,000-pound bell was installed for use while the keeper waited for the air pressure to build up to run the trumpet.[39] (National Archives photo # 26-LG-1-82B)

PART III: The U.S. Light-House Board (USLHB) Revamps the System

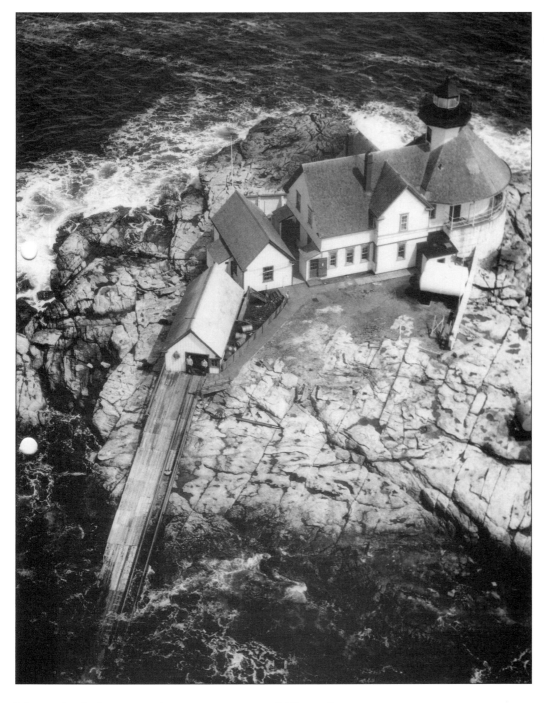

A light tower was placed on top of the fog signal building at The Cuckolds station in 1907. (Courtesy of U.S. Coast Guard)

Maine Lighthouses: Documentation of Their Past

On March 8, 1872, Engineer Secretary Major G. H. Elliott wrote to First District Engineer General J. C. Duane in Portland, Maine:

Please find herewith copy of petition to Congress signed by E. P. Walker and many others, and referred to this office, for a light on Two Bush Island, at the entrance to Penobscot Bay, ...

'To the Honorable Senate & House of Representative in Congress assembled.

The undersigned ship-masters, owners & citizens of Vinalhaven, Maine, respectfully represent to your Hon. Body the great need of a light in Two Bush Island so called. Said Island is situated on the western side, and at the entrance to Penobscot Bay and a light on this Island would be a

great benefit as a guide to vessels passing in and out of this Bay, where more than five thousand vessels annually pass by this Island . . .. The passage into Penobscot Bay by this Island is the only safe passage for vessels running into the ports of Rockland, Camden, Belfast, Searsport, Bucksport, Bangor and many smaller places. The mercantile community and inhabitants generally feel that

PART III: The U.S. Light-House Board (USLHB) Revamps the System

they would be very much benefitted and hope to realize what has long been a necessity in having a light placed on said Two Bush Island.'[40]

More petitions followed until in 1892 an appropriation was requested. A call for bids went out in 1896. The contract for Two Bush Island Light station called for a combined tower and dwelling for two keepers, of brick; a fog-signal tower with fuel room and work room, of brick; an oil house of brick; a boat house of wood; and a barn of wood.[41] W. H. Glover Co. of Rockport won the contract with a bid of $12,250.[42]

Two Bush Island Lighthouse was built the following year midway between Matinicus Rock and Whitehead Island Lights, marking the entrance to Two Bush Channel. Four miles from Spruce Head, Maine, and an additional seven miles from Rockland, the island had no harbor, and because it was surrounded by ledges, it was a very dangerous place to land a boat. (National Archives photo # 26-LG-4-70)

Evolving Technology

The Light-House Board constantly experimented with different types of technology. The Committee on Experiments was tasked with testing oils and other illuminating materials and accessories, and lighting apparatus; investigating the relative value of signals by sound or sight; checking the ventilation of lighthouses and light-vessels, and their protection from lightning; examining ways of preventing corrosion or decay of materials used in the lighthouse service; and doing experiments or observations to determine the value, or cost-effectiveness of other measures.[43]

Lamps and Lenses

Although the 1838 reports of the Board of Navy Commissioners investigating the Lighthouse Establishment noted structural flaws in many of the lighthouses, criticism of the quality of the light was the most common complaint. The superiority of the French lenses used in Europe was alluded to as early as 1829 in a letter from Nathaniel Niles to Secretary of the Treasury Samuel Ingham. Reporting on the administration of lighthouses on the French coast, Niles wrote of "improvements made in the construction & lighting the lanterns. The old method of using *reflectors* has been renounced & a series of glass prisms or *refractors* substituted which are so arranged as to throw all the light in a horizontal direction . . ."[44]

Although these lenses required a large initial investment, they were far more durable than lamps and reflectors and required only one lamp. Pleasonton did not test the Fresnel lens until 1841. Although he placed Fresnels at Navesink and two other lighthouses, he took no further steps to introduce them in this country. Frugal to the end, Pleasonton may have based his reluctance to adopt the superior lenses on Winslow Lewis's assessment that they would require far more manpower. Because Treasury had purchased Lewis's patent for his lamps, and he was contracted to install them, he had a vested interest in continuing their use. Even after visiting the "French Lenticular Lights" being tested at the twin Highland Lights at Navesink, New Jersey, Lewis maintained that his own lamps and reflectors were adequate and much simpler to operate:

The whole [Fresnel] apparatus taken together, exhibits a beautiful specimen of workmanship, but far more complicated than any opinion I had formed; more particularly the Lamp and its appendages, are extremely complicated,—many of its parts are of so delicate a texture, as to require constant attendance—so liable is the machinery of the Lamps to get out of order & being but one source of Light, that it requires two Keepers for each Light house, to stand watch & watch through the night, & one skilful machinist, with workshop & tools. . . . [45]

Blaming the shortcomings of the reflector system used previously at Navesink on the small panes of the lantern, Lewis concluded,

> That the Lenticular Lights are a brilliant affair & produce a strong light . . . but too complicated & liable to get out of order . . . As a Lantern fitted up with our large reflectors will produce a Light that can be seen from 30 to 35 miles, as far as any light can be useful to navigators—I doubt, if hereafter, it will be thought advisable to go to the expense of the French Lenticular.[46]

The new U.S. Light-House Board decided otherwise and decreed that Fresnel lenses be introduced in all American lighthouses. In Maine, the Board set a deadline of June 30, 1858, for replacing the old system of lamps and reflectors with lenses.[47] In most cases the installation of these lenses required a larger lantern, and many towers were modified or rebuilt to accommodate a new illuminating apparatus.

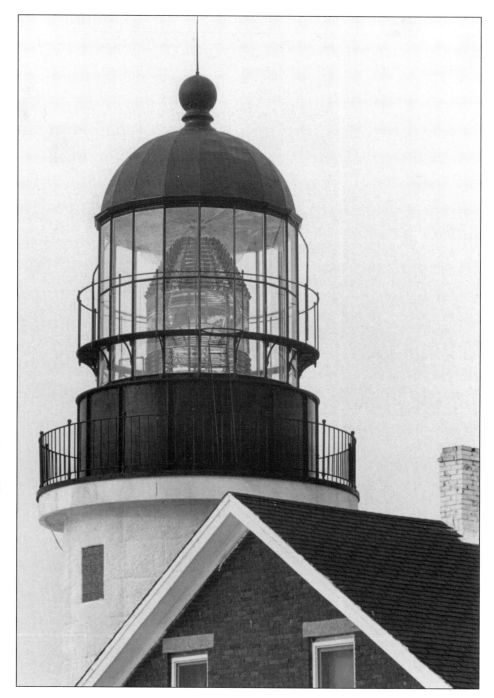

PART III: The U.S. Light-House Board (USLHB) Revamps the System

Fresnel lenses, named for their French inventor, Augustin Fresnel, have prisms at the top and bottom to refract light to the center of the lens, where it is intensified by powerful magnification through central bulleyes.[48] The lens at Seguin Island Light Station (facing page) is a first order. (Courtesy of U.S. Coast Guard)

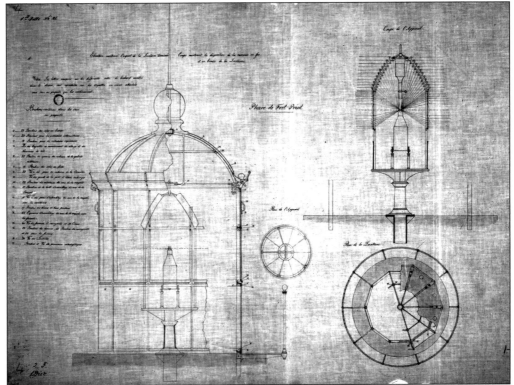

Fresnel lenses were classified into six orders: the strongest or first-order lenses were placed in primary lights on important headlands; second- and third-order lit secondary lights on less important points along the coast or on large bays or sounds. Fourth- to sixth-order lights, the smallest, were used to mark bays, sounds, or obstructions in rivers, or on piers or wharves. Included in the last classification were range, beacon, and pier lights.[49] Shown above is a French drawing of the lantern and lens for Fort Point and left, a photo of the fourth-order lens at Owls Head. (Drawing from National Archives, RG 26; HABS/ HAER photo by Richard Cheek, 1989)

Four orders of lanterns were based on uniform plans. First-, second-, and third-order lanterns were used for corresponding orders of lenses. The fourth-order lantern was used for fourth-, fifth-, and sixth-order lenses. Under the USLHB, lighthouse towers were designed to support a specific order of lens and lantern. (National Archives drawing, RG 26)

Because shore lights were difficult to distinguish from one another, some lenses were revolved by clockwork, with a few colored or multiple lights providing further distinction. Aids to navigation were also distinguished in the daytime by their daymark or "shape, arrangement, and color, according to the peculiarity of the respective localities, the kind of background, and the characteristic features of adjacent structures."[50] To preserve the overall appearance of a site, an old tower or building was modified or removed when a replacement was erected. The U.S. Light-House Board ruled that new buildings could not be erected, colors of buildings changed, nor trees cut down without its approval.

The improved lenses and lamps were more complex. Keepers were expected to have the basic mechanical skills to maintain and operate their equipment, with lampists and machinists called in only for major repairs.

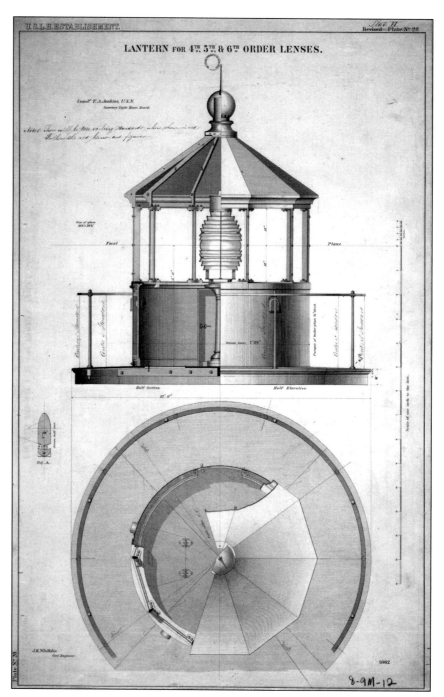

PART III: The U.S. Light-House Board (USLHB) Revamps the System

. . . Lampists are required to visit every light in their charge at least once a quarter, to accompany the Inspector during his tour of inspection, should he require their services, to visit and remain several days at those lights to which new keepers have been appointed, and make frequent inspections of the Steam fog-signal in their charge.[51]

Illuminants

In 1848, calculations for the amount of whale or sperm oil needed under a new contract indicated that the 256 American lights were lit by a total of 2,670 lamps, requiring 72,120 gallons of oil per year.[52] The single lamp in the Fresnel lens used less oil than the earlier reflector apparatus. The price of sperm oil, however, continued to rise with diminishing whale catches and an increase in the use of sperm oil as a lubricant. After unsuccessful experiments with colza or vegetable oil in the early 1860s, lard oil was found to produce an adequate light at a cost savings. A few decades later, when further economy was sought, mineral oil or kerosene replaced lard oil, and a new lamp was invented specifically for its use. By 1885, kerosene was the principal illuminant and was used in Incandescent Oil Vapor (IOV) lamps. Because kerosene was highly combustible, separate oil houses were built to house it. Gas was also tested as an illuminant, but was not widely adopted. In the late 1880s, the use of electricity as an illuminant was first tried in several aids to navigation, including the Sandy Hook East Beacon and the Statue of Liberty in New York Harbor.[53]

A variety of lamps were used under the Light-House Board. Many were imported from the same companies in France that manufactured the Fresnel lenses. Others were manufactured at the Lamp Shop in the General Lighthouse Depot on Staten Island, New York. In 1873, the following lamps were in service in Maine lighthouses (the choice of lamp depending on the order of the lens): Funck's Constant Level Lamp, Wagner Mechanical Lamp, Franklin's Constant Level Lamp, Lepaute's Escapement or Mechanical Lamp, and Lepaute's Moderator Lamp.[54]

AUG 15 1892

The oil house at West Quoddy Head, 1892. (Courtesy of U.S. Coast Guard)

USCG Lighthouse Keeper George Woodward cleaning the fourth-order lamp at Owls Head Light Station in 1946. (Courtesy of U.S. Coast Guard)

　　　　　　PART III: The U.S. Light-House Board (USLHB) Revamps the System

Fog Signals

The first fog signal used in the United States was a cannon installed at Boston Harbor Light Station in 1719. The Boston keeper answered a shot from a ship entering the harbor, giving the mariner a sense of the lighthouse's location. The most common early fog signal was a bell. Some fog bells were rung by hand, but Maine's frequent and lingering fog made mariners particularly insistent that light stations adopt mechanical fog bells. These were operated by a striking mechanism and weight that was raised by either a flywheel or clockwork. Many of these bells were located in a wooden pyramidal bell tower.

One of the earliest fog bells in Maine appears to have been placed at West Quoddy Head in 1820.[55] The machinery for ringing the bell had to be replaced several times, however, when mariners complained that the signal was faint. Collector Solomon Thayer, in Lubec, explained in a letter dated July 12, 1827:

> Some years since a fog bell was put up on West Quoddy Head in this Town & when rung by hand is found to be of the highest importance in guiding vessels into Passamaquoddy Bay. They cannot indeed find this way without it for half the time from the first of June to the last of September. The fog prevails when the wind is on shore & a bell to answer the

object must be powerful & rung by powerful machinery or it cannot be heard.

Two sets of machinery have been made for the West Quoddy Bell, neither of which answered the purpose by reason of this want of power. And the only way for the bell to be of any use is to ring it by hand & this is done whenever a signal gun is fired by vessels in the Bay of Fundy.

... Since the establishment of a line of Steam Boats from the British Provinces to Boston, fog-bells along the coast are

Bass Harbor Head Light Station in 1950. Note two fog bells—one hanging from the building at the right and one to the left of the tower. An earlier pyramidal bell tower sits behind the newer fog signal building. (Courtesy of U.S. Coast Guard)

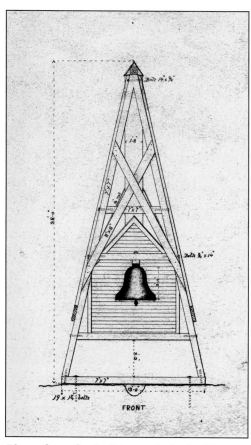

Plans for a fog bell tower to be built on Pemaquid Point. (Drawings courtesy of U.S. Coast Guard)

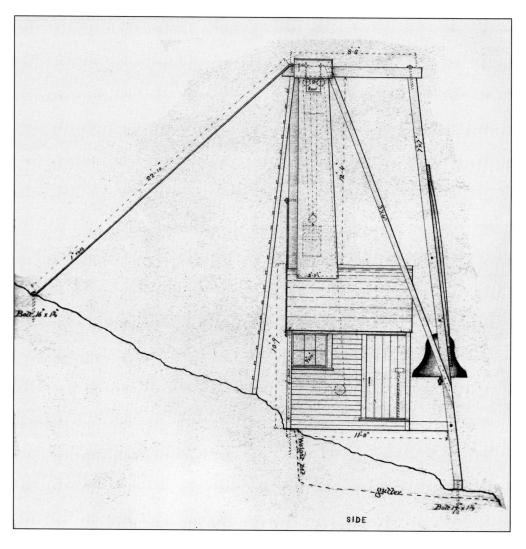

PART III: The U.S. Light-House Board (USLHB) Revamps the System

deemed an object of greater consequence. They are obliged to run during the foggy season & to them, at such times, light houses are of no sort of use. I have frequently heard the Masters of these vessels & Packet Masters say they had rather have fog-bells on the headlands in three or four places than all the lighthouses between this and Boston.

It is of the utmost consequence to the commercial interests of this part of the country that the Bell at West Quoddy be made to perform its office & I do hope you will take measures to procure the construction of such machinery as will fully effect the object.[56]

Mariners continued to have trouble hearing the fog bells. In 1850 Collector Luther Jewett commented, "They are not heard at distances at all satisfactory which in a measure is owing to the state of the atmosphere or weather, but mostly owing to the imperfectness of the machinery. In a heavy fog the sound of the bells is generally heard from one to two miles; whereas in a thin fog they are heard from two to five miles."[57]

The U.S. Light-House Board experimented with different types of steam-powered fog signals beginning in the late 1850s. In 1865 Joseph Henry, chairman of the Committee on Experiments, reported that there were four types of fog signals in use at U.S. lighthouses:

1. Bells rung by clock machinery

2. Whistles sounded by steam from a boiler

3. Whistles sounded by air condensed by the waves

4. Trumpets blown by an Erricson engine[58]

Of these, bells were still the most commonly used: "their efficacy depends upon the size of the bell and its position with regard to reflecting objects."[59] The steam whistle was found to be expensive and the wave-powered whistle limited in its application.

Celadon L. Daboll conducted experiments to improve the air trumpet and plans were made to install some of these devices in the summer of 1866.

The various fog-bells established for the guidance during thick weather of mariners along this rocky and dangerous coast, have rendered as useful service as their character would permit. The board, however, being impressed with the necessity of erecting some apparatus capable of producing more effective signals, applied for and obtained, at the last session of Congress, an appropriation for establishing at the outlying stations such improved apparatus as careful scientific research and experiment might indicate as best adapted to the purpose.[60]

By 1872, the stations at West Quoddy, Petit Manan, Matinicus, Whitehead, Seguin, and Cape Elizabeth all had 10-inch steam whistles. Monhegan had a six-inch steam whistle and Portland Head had a Daboll air trumpet.

According to various annual reports, a siren was introduced at Seguin in 1875 but was soon disassembled. A siren was in use at Cape Elizabeth in 1876 and was supplemented by a whistle in 1880. By 1880 all steam-operated fog signals had backups or substitutes. In 1882, many stations were provided with small hand bells "for the purpose of indicating to vessels their proximity during thick weather, sounded in answer to their signal."[61]

Because maintenance of the machinery required special skills, machinists were often hired as keepers at stations with first-class steam-operated fog signals. After the engine-driven fog signal was introduced at Cape Elizabeth, the Board issued the following directions for its operation:

There are now four keepers at Cape Elizabeth Light-Station. This number is deemed quite sufficient to take care both of the lights and the fog signal. If the Principal Keeper does not possess the skill required in the management of the fog-signal, he should be removed and a proper person nominated. One of the Assistants also, should be competent to manage any steam machinery.

The Keeper and each of his assistants should be given to understand, that he must take his turn of duty in attending to the fog signal as well as the light.[62]

The 10-inch steam whistle was operated in the fog signal building pictured at right in this 1892 photo of West Quoddy Head Light Station. (Courtesy of U.S. Coast Guard)

PART III: The U.S. Light-House Board (USLHB) Revamps the System

Acquiring enough fresh water to produce the needed steam became a problem in some locations. On September 19, 1881, USLHB Engineer Secretary Major F. W. Farquhar wrote that it had become necessary to discontinue the fog signal at Seguin because the water supply had run out. He recommended "arrangements of gutters, pipes, etc., as will ensure the catchment of all the rain-fall from the buildings of the station."[63] This still did not solve the problem, for in 1886 the Board authorized a 1000-pound bell to be rung by hand as a backup at Seguin.[64] In 1889, the First District Lighthouse Inspector was "authorized at his own suggestion to have the tanks at Seguin, Me., light-station filled with salt water by steam tugs at the expense of about $100, for the purpose of keeping the steam fog-signal in motion."[65] Saltwater, of course, gummed up the machinery. In 1895, $200 was authorized "for supplying the Seguin, Me., fog-signal with 12,700 gallons of fresh water . . . the water being necessary to keep the signal in operation and the case therefore being one of emergency."[66]

Before 1876 the fog signal at Petit Manan

> . . . was supplied with water from a well excavated in the rock, and as the greater part of the water in the well came from an adjacent swamp, it was impregnated

with decomposed vegetable matter, and proved very injurious to the boiler. In order to procure a supply of pure water, an old stone building, 34 by 20 feet, and an addition 16 by 14 feet, formerly used as a keeper's dwelling, were roofed over and fitted with gutters and water-conductors, and two wooden tanks, each 12 feet in diameter, were placed in the cellar. The two water-sheds, 50 by 30 feet each, erected last season, are located one at each end of this building, and are fitted with water conductors and gutters leading to the cisterns in the cellar of the old house. A one-story brick engine-house, 32 by 14 feet, has been erected; it contains the duplicate fog-signal and a large wooden tank which will hold four days' supply of water. The water-sheds are 150 feet distant and the water is conveyed through pipes.[67]

Even though the water capacity was doubled when a new boiler house was built at Petit Manan in 1887, periods of drought strained the system. In 1889, "the supply of fresh water became so nearly exhausted during the protracted period of dense fog, with little or no rain in the spring and early part of the present summer, that temporary means had to be provided for supplying the boilers with water from the sea."[68] Saltwater was used several times until a new brick cistern, measuring 15 by 28 feet, was built in 1890.[69]

In 1935, Assistant Superintendent Thomas Sampson described the station at Petit Manan:

> . . . station is located on easterly point of Petit Manan Island; double dwelling 30 ft. northwest of tower and single dwelling 135 feet west of tower, double dwelling has 6 rooms each and single dwelling 6 rooms to house keeper and two assistants; cisterns in each cellar, 2 in rainshed, and 1 in oil house; wooden tanks in dwellings; surface reservoir about 40 feet southwest of whistle house 26,504 gallons; 32,405 gallons used for signal and 7,555 gallons for domestic use.[70]

In 1885, the Light-House Board began publishing the number of hours steam- or hot-air engine fog signals were in operation each year. West Quoddy's 10-inch steam whistle tallied the most with 1,945 hours in operation. The whistle at Petit Manan came in second with 1,926 hours and the one at Seguin followed with 1,401 hours. In 1888 these statistics included the amount of coal each signal consumed.[71]

The number of fog signals operated by engines kept increasing. The 1907 *Annual Report* shows additional fog signals at Mount Desert, Egg Rock, Great Duck Island, Rockland Breakwater, Cuckolds, Cape Elizabeth (Portland) Lightship *No. 74*, Relief Lightship *No. 53*, and Halfway Rock.

Petit Manan Light Station in 1892. In 1888 the 10-inch steam whistles, in duplicate, were in operation 2,271 hours, consuming 153,482 pounds of coal. (Courtesy of U.S. Coast Guard)

PART III: The U.S. Light-House Board (USLHB) Revamps the System

Just like the lights, fog signals had individual characteristics to distinguish them from other signals. These characteristics were constantly adjusted to best serve the mariner. In 1895 the Committee on Lighting outlined the changes to signals in the first district based on recommendations by the inspector and engineer:

Blast/Silent Interval/Blast/Silent Interval [in seconds]

Station	Blast	Silent Interval	Blast	Silent Interval	
W. Quoddy Head	3	57	3	57	
Libby Islands	2	13	2	13	(no change)
Petit Manan	3	9	3	45	
Mount Desert Trumpet	3	17	3	17	
Great Duck Island	2	28	2	28	
Matinicus Rock	3	27	3	27	
Whitehead	3	9	3	45	
Manana Island Trumpet	2	13	2	13	
Cuckolds Trumpet	3	17	3	17	(no change)
Seguin	3	57	3	57	
Cape Elizabeth Siren and Whistle	3	9	3	45	
Portland Head Trumpet	2	13	2	13	
Whaleback Trumpet	3	17	3	17[72]	

A *Notice to Mariners* was published to alert mariners to these changes as well as revisions made to the annual *Light Lists*.

Manana Island Fog Signal Station

In 1853 Joseph Farwell, master of the steamer *Daniel Webster*, wrote:

> The island of Monhegan is the island that all of our vessels on this coast take their departure from on leaving the coast . . . and it is the only land that steamboats wish to make between Portland light and Whitehead light . . . before you change your course either from Portland or Whitehead. The Manana is a small island, taken . . . out of Monhegan Island on the westerly side, and makes the harbor of Monhegan. . . . A sailing vessel is obliged to run until she judges herself up, and then lay to until the fog clears up. Often a vessel or steamboat may be within a cable's length of this island in the fog, and not know whether they are very near or not, or whether they are inside or outside of the island. A bell, well arranged on Manana, would announce to a vessel the position of the island . . ..[73]

In 1855, a 2,500-pound bell was mounted on a wooden frame attached to the dwelling provided for the man appointed to attend it. The keeper struck the bell by hand until a striking mechanism was installed in 1856. In 1870 the bell was replaced with a six-inch Ericsson steam engine and ten-inch Daboll trumpet. Two years later, it was replaced with a whistle. In 1876, the fog signal at Manana Island became an independent station, separated administratively from the light station on adjacent Monhegan Island. The whistle was still not powerful enough, so the signal was again changed to a first-class Daboll trumpet in 1877. In 1899 the steam engines were changed to oil. In 1912 the trumpet gave way to a first-class air siren. The signal was changed to diaphone horns after 1933. [74]

In 1928, Keeper Ernest V. Talbet described the following duties at Manana:

> My work as a lightkeeper is to assist in the operation of a fog signal station. The station consists of an engine house with two crude oil engines with air compressors attached. Clock works for regulating the whistle blast, air tanks and air siren.
>
> I stand a regular watch of six hrs. alternating with the other keeper which make 12 hrs. of watch per man in the 24 hrs., 6 hrs. in the day time and 6 at night. The object of this watch is to note the approach of fog, snow, vapor, heavy rains or smoke and start the fog signal.
>
> I operate the engines and assist in keeping the engine cleaned, engine room cleaned and painted inside and out.

There are also two dwelling houses, two sheds, two oil houses, one barn, one donkey boiler house and one boat house and boat. I assist in keeping these buildings cleaned and painted inside and out, whitewash cellar walls and basement and doing such repair work as we are capable, also help keep grounds in order.

There is also a track with a car which will hold about a ton of coal. This track and car is used to transport coal, oil and lumber or any other heavy material from the wharf at the shore to the oil houses and dwellings.

I assist in loading and unloading the car, storing the coal 16 tons and kerosene oil from 200 to 400 gals., 100 brls. of crude oil for engines, lumber and paint and other material which is landed yearly. I operate the donkey boiler and hoister which is used to haul the car up the hill. The wood work of this track is covered yearly with a wood preservative and the rails painted with red lead on which I help.

I go for mail and household supplies to another island daily, weather permitting.

When the lighthouse machinist is on the station to overhaul the engines or make repairs, I assist him when called on to help handle heavy parts of the machinery, cut pipes or cut threads on the pipes or such work as I am capable of doing when it does not interfere with my regular station duties.

I give such assistance as I can to working parties at the station.

I give assistance or summon aid to vessels in distress and assist in saving life and property when it is practicable to do so.[75]

A first-class Daboll trumpet was installed at the Manana Fog Signal Station in 1877. (Courtesy of U.S. Coast Guard)

PART III: The U.S. Light-House Board (USLHB) Revamps the System

Lighthouse tenders: lifeblood of the system

While lighthouses depended on keepers to keep their lights shining, the entire system of aids to navigation relied on lighthouse tenders and their crews. In the first half of the nineteenth century contractors were relied upon to deliver oil and maintain a variety of buoys. Communication from the keepers was infrequent and often sparse, so it was difficult to ascertain the condition of the various stations and the efficiency of the keeper in his work. The administration in Washington encouraged the local custom collectors and revenue cutter captains to visit stations in their jurisdiction and complete inspection reports. This arrangement was not always efficient or satisfactory.

As the number of buoys increased, Stephen Pleasonton saw the advantages of government ownership of vessels specifically devoted to maintaining aids to navigation. Most of the vessels acquired for this work had been built for other purposes. It was not until the U.S. Light-House Board took over that vessels were designed specifically for tender work. Gradually, most lighthouse districts came to own at least one tender, some powered by sail, others by steam. The steam-powered tenders proved much more maneuverable in tending buoys than their sail-rigged counterparts, allowing more accurate placement.[76] They could also operate in most types of weather and wind conditions.

When the Light-House Board took over in 1852, there were two tenders servicing the first district—both sailing vessels. In 1859 the Board made the case for replacing these slower, less efficient vessels with a steam-propelled vessel:

> In the first district, comprising the rock-bound and dangerous coast of Maine, and part of the coast of New Hampshire, there are two tenders employed. These vessels are frequently delayed by fogs and head winds and strong adverse tides; and the duties of the district tax their energies to the utmost during the short time they are permitted to work. One propeller could easily perform all the labor now performed by these two sail vessels, and afford the inspector, besides, increased facilities of visit. The cost of her maintenance would not exceed that of the sail vessels.[77]

In addition to maintaining buoys, tenders supplied light stations with replacement parts, paint, oil, coal, wood and other fuel, and other provisions. Tenders transported the machinists and lampists who installed and repaired the lighting apparatus and fog signal. Keepers had to be delivered to their stations, along with their families, property, livestock, official mail, etc. Lighthouse inspectors traveled on tenders and had special accommodations on board. Tenders were also responsible for moving lightships on and off their stations.

By 1875, the first lighthouse district had a fleet of four vessels homeported at their depot in Portland: the steamers *Iris*, *Myrtle*, and *Mary*, and the schooner *Wave*. The steamers burned coal, *Iris* consuming 350 pounds of coal per hour, and *Myrtle* 700 pounds underway. *Iris* had been purchased from the U.S. Navy in 1865 and rebuilt in 1871. Taking on the duties of two sailing vessels in the first lighthouse district, *Iris* proved to be an efficient and economical replacement.

> So valuable have been the services of this steamer in replacing important buoys that instances have occurred in which buoys driven from their moorings by stress of weather, have been replaced by others within twenty-fours hours afterward. It would certainly require two, and perhaps three sailing vessels to perform the same efficient service. Previously to the employment of a steamer in this district it was not unusual to be compelled to wait days, and even weeks, for fair weather to replace buoys adrift from their positions off the harbor of Portland, although they were, of all in the district, the most conveniently reached.
>
> . . . Whenever assistance could be rendered to vessels in distress the *Iris* has not failed to do all that she could, and

has saved from wreck the steamer *Wm. Tibbetts*, and the ship *Fannie Fish*.[78]

Captain J. L. Davis, member of the Light-House Board, who inspected the district in 1875, felt the crew on *Iris* was inadequate. The crew consisted of

Captain Johnson, Mate Day, engineers Merrill and Smith, 6 men on deck: 2 firemen, cook, steward, and boy. The latter acts as berth deck cook. A 2nd Mate at $40 per month and one additional deck hand are greatly needed. The work is almost constant; the Captain looks out for the safety of the vessel in steering, etc., and the Mate in directing the work on board. In supplying Stations with coal, provisions, etc. and handling buoys, [they] have no relief. A 2d Mate or leading man can be made very useful. . . .

The *Iris* is kept actually employed the whole year except February, when she stops to repair boiler and engines, etc. During the year she takes care of 383 buoys, lands supplies, coal (650 tons), rations, lime, stone, etc., and makes quarterly inspections. She takes up in the rivers about 100 buoys in the fall and replaces them in the Spring—in St. Croix, Pembroke, Damariscotta, Penobscot, and Kennebec. This work occupies 2 months in the Spring and six weeks in the Autumn. A small Schooner properly fitted with derrick, etc. could be advantageously employed at this work at comparatively small expense. When not employed at buoys, she could be delivering coal, etc. to Stations. [79]

After 21 years in service, *Iris* was sold at auction in 1892, a year after the new tender *Lilac* was placed in service.[80] Built by the Globe Iron Works at Cleveland, Ohio, in 1892, *Lilac* was planned specifically for the first district lighthouse inspector. During her first year of service—1893—*Lilac* steamed 14,469 miles and consumed 841 tons of coal.[81]

Some of the early steam tenders retained the traditional sailing rig. Among these was USLHT Myrtle (below and facing page), built in 1872 to serve both the first and second lighthouse districts in "works of construction and repair."[82] In 1897, around the time these photos were taken, Myrtle steamed about 11,380 miles and consumed 770 tons of coal.[83] (National Archives photos # 26-LSH-30-3 and 26-LSH-30-4)

PART III: The U.S. Light-House Board (USLHB) Revamps the System

Maine Lighthouses: Documentation of Their Past

The deck logs for the tender *Lilac* reflect the daily routine of a tender after the turn of the twentieth century.[84]

December 2, 1910, Underway at 7:30 A.M. Changed Little River buoy, thense to Davis Straits and changed Gig Rock Bell buoy. Away at 11:40 A.M. proceeded west to Cape Elizabeth Light Vessel at 3:30 P.M. supplied her with fresh water. Away at 4:30 P.M. made fast to Custom House wharf Portland at 6:00 P.M.

December 3, Underway at 7:20 A.M. made fast to Buoy Depot Little Diamond Island. Landed 2 bell buoys, 1st class can. Coaled ship. Took on board 30 feet 1 1/4" chain 15 feet 1" chain and 2 bell buoys. Underway at 2:30 P.M. made fast to Custom House wharf Portland. Employed balance of day loading Light House supplies and cleaning ship.

December 4 [Sunday], At Custom House wharf, Portland. Only necessary ship duty done this day. Gave part of crew liberty.

December 5, At Custom House wharf, Portland. Captain Sterling reported at the Inspectors Office. Comdr J. D. McDonald U.S.N. came on board at 10:00 A.M. Underway steamed to and inspected the following stations: Halfway Rock, Seguin, Cuckolds, and Ram Island. Anchored in Boothbay Harbor for the night at 5:30 P.M.

December 6, Underway from Boothbay at 6:30 A.M. Steamed to and inspected the following stations: Manana, Monhegan, Tenant Harbor, and Goose Rock. An-

chored in Fox Island Thorofare at 4:30 P.M.

December 7, Commenced work at 7:00 A.M. rigging bell buoy. Underway at 7:30 A.M. changed Channel Rock Bell Buoy. Thense . . . inspected & delivered supplies at the following stations: Eagle Island, Isle au Haut, and Burnt Coat Harbor. Thense to NE Harbor and came to anchor for the night at 4:50 P.M.

December 8, Underway from NE Harbor at 6:30 A.M. Steamed to & inspected Crabtree Ledge Light and delivered one Royal Atlanta Range [stove]. Thence to Egg Rock Light and inspected the same. Away at 11:00 A.M., steamed to Gt. Duck Island, landed on NW end of the Island and made inspection of the station. Thence to Bass Harbor and came to anchor for the night at 3:30 P.M.

December 9, Underway from Bass Harbor at 6:30 A.M. Steamed to Mount Desert Rock to make inspection, could not make a landing on account of heavy surf. Thense to Bear Island wharf at 11:30 A.M. Took on board 12 tons of coal for ships use . . . Cast off at 3:30 P.M. steamed to Bass Harbor and came to anchor at 4:20 P.M.

December 10, Underway from Bass Harbor at 6:15 A.M. Steamed to Mount Desert Rock Light Station and inspected the same at 8:00 A.M. Also delivered supplies. Thence to Matinicus Rock Station at 1:00 P.M. Inspected the station and delivered 2 automatic clocks. Away

at 2:20 P.M. Inspected Heron Neck Light Station. Came to anchor in Hurricane Sound for the night at 4:50 P.M.

December 11, Underway from Hurricane Island at 6:00 A.M., proceeded west to Hendricks Head Light and inspected the same at 11:15 A.M. Thence to Kennebec River and inspected the following stations: Pond Island, Fort Popham, Perkins Island, Squirrel Point, Doubling Point. Anchored on Parker Flats Kennebec River for the night at 5:00 P.M.

December 12, Underway from Kennebec River at 6:15. Steamed to Cape Elizabeth to make inspection. Could not make landing on account of rough NE sea. Thence to Ram Island Ledge Light and inspected the same at 10:00 A.M. Thence to and inspected the Buoy Depot. Landed 2 Bell Buoys and one Stone sinker. Cast off at 11:20 A.M. Steamed to Portland made fast to Custom House wharf. Employed balance of the day cleaning ship.

December 13, At Custom House wharf, Portland. Only necessary ship duty done. Gave crew liberty as ordered by Inspector.

December 14, Underway from Custom House wharf at 7:15 A.M. Made fast to Buoy Depot. Coaled ship and worked 3 hours cleaning and painting buoys on wharf. Cast off at 4:15 P.M. Made fast to Custom House wharf Portland for the night at 4:40 P.M.

[Repeated work at Buoy depot on 15th, 16th, 17th, and 18th]

PART III: The U.S. Light-House Board (USLHB) Revamps the System

According to the 1907 Annual Report, lighthouse tender Lilac *"was employed in buoy work, inspections, carrying supplies to stations and coal and water to the light-vessel. She steamed about 12,798 miles and consumed some 1,162 tons of coal. She established 16 buoys, replaced 59 buoys, changed 114 buoys, painted 213 buoys, recovered 33 buoys, delivered 55 tons of coal to light-vessel No. 74 and 18 ½ tons to light-stations, delivered oil and general supplies to 39 light-stations and worked 219 hours at the light-house depot on buoys."* Lilac *worked with a variety of buoys—nun buoys, can buoys, spar buoys, iron buoys, gas and whistling buoys, as well as bell buoys. In addition to transferring and positioning the buoys, the crew was responsible for cleaning and painting the buoys at the depot. The tender also frequently assisted other vessels in distress. (National Archives photo # 26-LSH-27-1)*

December 19, At Buoy Depot. Coaled ship. Took onboard 3 tall type 2nd class buoys and 1 1st class iron spar, also 2 stone sinkers. Landed 2 wooden spar buoys. Underway at 4:00 P.M. made fast to Custom House wharf Portland at 4:30 P.M. Filled water bottoms with fresh water and took onboard ship stores. Received 10 tons coal for ships use.

December 20, Underway from Custom House wharf Portland at 7:00 A.M. Steamed to Cape Elizabeth Light Vessel and supplied with fresh water. Away at 11:00 A.M. proceeded east outside. Came to anchor in Seal Harbor at 5:00 P.M.

December 21, At anchor in Seal Harbor at 1:20 A.M. Capt. & mate from Schooner *Mary Curtis* came alongside and said their vessel was at anchor in a dangerous position close to the breakers under Two Bush Light and requested assistance. Underway at 2:35 A.M. steamed to Two Bush, hove up schooner's anchor and took her in tow. Came to anchor in Seal Harbor with the vessel at 5:30 A.M. Underway at 7:00 A.M. Steamed up the Bay to off Rockport. Sounded out Fourteen Foot patch. Shut down thick snow. Could not get angles to establish the buoy. Waited for weather to clear till 11:15 A.M. when we came to anchor in Rockport Harbor.

December 22, Underway from Rockport at 7:00 A.M. Steamed out in the Bay and established Tall type 2nd class nun buoy painted red & black horizontal stripes on Fourteen Foot Spot off Deadmans Point. Removed Deadmans

Point Buoy. Changed Spruce Head Buoy from Spar to tall type 2nd class can. Changed Squaw Pt. Buoy. Removed Sears Island Gas Buoy and replaced it with iron spar. Changed Brigadier Island Ledge Buoy. Anchored in Searsport Harbor at 4:00 P.M.

December 28, Underway from Custom House wharf at 7:00 A.M. made fast to buoy depot. Set gas buoy overboard for testing. Cast off at 9:20 A.M. Steamed to Portland, took on board lumber for Spring Pt. Ledge Light. Underway at 10:50 A.M. Delivered lumber at Spring Pt. Ledge. Thence to Buoy Depot at 12:00 noon. Took on board one combination gas & whistling buoy, 1 3rd class nun and 1 stone sinker. Cast off and made fast to Custom House wharf Portland at 4:30 P.M.

January 8, 1911, Underway from Port Clyde at 6:30 A.M. Steamed out by Marshalls Point Light, ran into thick vapor. Dropped anchor at 7:15 A.M. to wait for weather to clear. Underway at 9:45 A.M. Steamed to Marshalls Point Whistling Buoy and changed the color of the same from white & black perpendicular stripes to all black Number I. M. P. Away at 10:35 A.M. Steamed west. Towed U.S.L.S. crew boat from Thrubeup Island to Damariscove Island. Thense to Sheepscot River and replaced Bull Ledge buoy which had gone adrift. Left at 3:00 P.M. Steamed to Portland, landed liberty crew. Made fast to Buoy Depot at 8:30 P.M.

January 10, Underway at 7:00 A.M. Transported the following from cars at Boston & Marine wharf to Buoy Depot: 3 whistling buoys, 3 bell buoys, 3 ballast bulls (26"), 3 bell buoy bridles, 6 spare bells, and 6 spare whistles for buoys. Transported 2 gas buoys from Buoy Depot to Boston & Marine Wharf and loaded them on car ready for shipment to be refilled. Made fast to Boston & Marine Wharf for the night at 5:45 P.M.

January 14, . . . stopped at Buoy Depot for gas tank and proceeded east. Relighted Old Man Gas Buoy which was extinguished, took the pressure which showed 9 1/4 ATM. Supplied the buoy with a new tip. . . .

January 16, . . . Sighted a schooner close to Long Island west shore with distress signal flying. Steamed over alongside and it proved to be the schooner *Centennial* of Lubec in route from New York to Lubec coal laden which had struck on John's Island Ledge, disabled his rudder and was leaking considerable. Took her in tow and came to anchor in Burnt Coat Harbor with schooner at 5:00 P.M.

January 25, At Custom house wharf Portland. Unemployed, only necessary ship duty done this day. Gave part of crew liberty in accordance with Inspector's order. Seaman Mabbery J. Cook and Milton Bryant discharged for being absent when it was their watch on board.

February 17, . . . Stopped at Heron Neck Station, Captain Sterling went ashore at the station and found Keepers widow & son in charge of station. The keeper having died Thursday 16. . . . Steamed to Vinal Haven and dropped anchor at 10:30 A.M. Captain Sterling communicated with Light House Inspector by telephone. Underway at 11:25 A.M., made stop at Heron Neck and got widow's name.

February 25, . . . Steamed to Dice Head Light & inspected the station. Keeper Mr. Gott died Feb. 21st. . .

March 3, . . . Steamed to Mount Desert Rock Light Station. Delivered the mail and communicated with the keeper. Could not land furniture on account of rough sea. . . .

April 14, Underway from Port Clyde at 6:00 A.M. Steamed to Franklin Island Light Station and dropped anchor. Landed Mr. Lanabee, his family and household goods. Took onboard Keeper Mr. Sperling, his family of 4 people, and household goods. Underway at 12:30 P.M. Steamed to Castine and made fast to wharf at 5:20 P.M. Landed Mr. Sperling's furniture and made fast for the night at 7:00 P.M.

June 5, . . . Landed 9 bbls water at Mt. Desert Rock, sufficient quantity there now for summer

June 24, . . . Delivered a small lot lumber at Portsmouth Harbor Light and delivered 30 galls mineral oil at Jaffrey & Frost Point Stake Light

June 26, Hauled out on Greens Railway at 10:00 A.M. Employed balance of the day cleaning out chain lockers &

forward collision chamber (getting ready for the survey of the tender to be made by Mr. Gilett & Mr. Savage who commenced their work at 12 noon. . . .)

June 27, . . . Railway crew at work cleaning bottom. Mr. Gilbert & Mr. Savage at work making survey of the tender. Crew employed cleaning out fore hole removing flooring and removing man hole plates to water bottoms.

June 28, On railway at Chelsea, Mass. Mr. Gilbert & Mr. Savage at work making survey of tender. Crew employed cleaning & painting smokestack and painting top of water bottom in fore hole. Railway crew painted bottom one coat of paint.

June 29, On railway at Chelsea, Mass. Mr. Gilbert & Mr. Savage at work making survey of tender. Railway crew painted 2nd coat on ships bottom. Crew employed cleaning off and painting water line and scraping main mast.

June 30, At Chelsea on railway. Messrs. Gillete, Savage & Rowe finished survey of tender at 10 am. Railway crew finished painting 3rd coat on ship's bottom. . . . Left railway at 1 P.M., towed to Bertelseu Petersen Eng. Co. at East Boston. Crew employed laying floor in fore hold storing anchor chains, etc.

June 31, At Bertelseu Petersen Eng. Co. E. Boston. Machinists at work repairing pumps, carpenters laying false forward deck and repairing crew's washroom sink. Crew working at scraping and varnishing foremast and painting

upper deck [Numerous crew members are discharged at their own request]

July 3, At Bertelseu Petersen Eng. Co. E. Boston. Machinists contractors repairing pumps, finished installing new berth in forecastle as per contract. Crew employed painting ship outside above waterline

July 5, . . . All contract work finished at 5 P.M.

July 16, 8 P.M. word received that lobster schooner *Viola Brewer* was ashore on Schoodic Point. Steamed there arriving about 9 P.M. waited for high water and about 12:30 A.M. took strain on hawser and pulled vessel off rocks. Towed her to Winter Harbor where she cast off and proceeded under own engine.

In more recent years, tenders have continued to maintain buoys with occasional visits to light stations to perform maintenance. Their duties have expanded, however, to include search and rescue, icebreaking, military readiness, and law enforcement—a reflection of the expanded mission of the modern U.S. Coast Guard.[85] Coast Guard cutters serving Maine in 2003 were *Abbie Burgess, Bridle, Jefferson Island, Marcus Hanna, Moray, Shackle, Tackle, Thunder Bay,* and *Wrangel.*[86]

Buoy Depots

The first lighthouse depot serving the first lighthouse district was located on House Island, near Fort Scammel in Portland Harbor. There tenders picked up the equipment required for their assignments. The depot also served as a storage facility for spare buoys, coal, and other necessary supplies. The land belonged to the War Department, and in 1873 the Army asked that the depot be removed because the space it occupied was needed for army purposes. The first district inspector indicated that a larger depot was needed:

> Owing to the increased number of Fog Whistles and Buoys in this District the present accommodations are entirely inadequate to the requirements of the District. The coal [shed] holds only two hundred tons of coal and is inaccessible at low water. A proper shed is required which will hold at least eight hundred tons.
>
> The buoy shed is objectionable as to location—it being a long distance from the wharf; the buoys have to be dragged over the rocks, thereby scraping the paint off and otherwise injuring them, especially the nun and can buoys.
>
> The buoy-tender cannot get to the wharf except at high water, and generally has to wait her turn as there are constantly vessels landing materials for the [army] fortifications. In the winter months the Depot is frequently inapproachable on account of ice, and when the tender's crew are at work on the buoys, the most of the time is taken getting them back and forth.
>
> The Inspector has no storehouse, and has only through the courtesy of the Engineer of the district, a place to keep his stores.[88]

PART III: The U.S. Light-House Board (USLHB) Revamps the System

The first district lighthouse depot was relocated on Little Diamond (Hog) Island in Portland Harbor. When completed in 1876, the new depot (facing page) consisted of a wharf and buoy house, coal house, tracks for convenient handling of buoys and sinkers, a custodian's cottage, and water tank. The depot received a blacksmith shop in 1878 and an icehouse in 1879.[87] The depot was taken out of service in the 1930s and sold to a private owner in 1953. (Courtesy of U.S. Coast Guard)

A coal shed was erected on Whitehead Island in 1871. In 1886, Inspector Batcheller recommended that another shed be erected on the lighthouse reservation on Bear Island:

> . . . that a coal shed of a capacity of 300 to 400 tons be built near the wharf at Bear Island Light Station, South West Harbor, Maine.

A supply of coal at this point will greatly facilitate the work of the District. Under the present arrangement it is necessary to take coal from Portland for the extreme eastern fog signals, owing to the want of facilities at Whitehead and its nearness to Portland, that course involves less labor and delay. There is abundant room at Bear Island for a coal shed and for storing buoys, whilst its central location on good harbor renders it a most suitable place for the purpose.[89]

The coal depot completed in 1887 can be seen at left in the above 1935 photo of Bear Island Light Station. (Courtesy of U.S. Coast Guard)

Light stations constructed in the twentieth century

Few lighthouses were built by the U.S. Light-House Board after the turn of the twentieth century. In Maine five new light stations were established— Rockland Harbor Breakwater, Fort Popham, Ram Island Ledge, Isle au Haut, and Whitlocks Mill. They were the last of the traditional lighthouses to be constructed. Maine's first lightship was established in 1903.

Rockland Harbor Breakwater

A variety of aids marked the Rockland Harbor, starting in 1827. As the breakwater was being completed in the harbor in 1899, a permanent light and fog signal station was recommended to mark its end. The first district engineer observed,

The harbor is entered throughout the year by the steamboats of the Boston and Bangor Steamboat Company which during the summer, when dense fogs are frequent, carry large numbers of passengers between Boston and Bangor, touching at Rockland. In summer several other steamers also carry passengers into the harbor. On account of the dense fogs in summer and blinding snow storms in winter, the end of the breakwater should be indicated by a fog-signal. . . .

The harbor of refuge which the breakwater forms will lead any sailing vessels to enter it in the stormy season and they will need ample warning of the location of the end of the breakwater to avoid getting it too close under their lee and the disaster of being carried upon it in blinding easterly and northeasterly snow storms."[90]

The light tower with attached dwelling and fog signal building was established in 1902.[91] (Courtesy of U.S. Coast Guard)

Fort Popham

A wood frame structure on timber legs connected to the shore by a footbridge was erected at Fort Popham in 1903. A keeper's dwelling was erected nearby in 1909. In 1949 the light and fog bell were removed from the structure and a new light and fog bell were installed on the top of the adjacent fort. In 1953 the remaining portion of the station was deeded over to the state of Maine.[92]

Ram Island Ledge

When reporting on the need for a lighthouse on Ram Island Ledge, the First District inspector and engineer indicated that

> . . . there have recently been built at Portland three grain elevators aggregating in capacity 2,750,000 bushels, and the shipments of grain have increased from 1,203,055 bushels in the season of '95 - '96 to 14,128,653 bushels in the season of 1900 - '01. . . . The package freight has also increased in the same time from 24,678 tons in '95 - '96 to 224,550 tons in 1900 - '01.
>
> The large ships engaged in this commerce draw about 30 feet . . . Their course leads them between Ram Island Ledge and Jordans Reef which are three-quarters of a mile apart. But Witch Rock, upon which there are only four fathoms at mean low water, stands about 1,000 yards directly in front of this passage, in the middle of the fairway and in the track of these deep draft ships, to which it is a grave peril; for they cannot take a safe berth from it on either hand without danger from Jordans Reef on the one side or Ram Island Ledge on the other.
>
> Considering the excellence and importance of this port, the class of ships engaged in its growing commerce, and their great peril from these three ledges, in an otherwise excellent fairway, we recommend that a light and fog-signal be established on Ram Island Ledge, to guide ships in safely between Witch Rock and Ram Island Ledge . . . .[93]

The tower was completed in 1905.

In recommending a tower to mark Ram Island Ledge, the inspector and engineer suggested "that the height of the light be such as may be necessary to secure the lantern and the light from injury or from interference by masses of spray and the accumulation of ice."[94] (Courtesy of U.S. Coast Guard)

Isle au Haut

As early as 1837 a petition was submitted requesting a lighthouse on Isle au Haut:

The undersigned Citizens of Maine respectfully represent that the interests of Commerce and Navigation require the erection of a Light House on some suitable point on Isle au Haut to guide vessels into Isle au Haut Thoroughfare Harbor.

Isle au Haut is an outside Island, lying on the border of the Atlantic—is an elevated Island as its name indicates, and is one from which vessels from Penobscot Bay & River outward bound, frequently take their departure; and one which those inward bound to those waters, endeavor to make.

By vessels bound inward this Harbor is much needed especially by those arriving on the coast in the winter season and at night. Having made Saddleback Ledge Light and passed it, a Light is then required to guide them into this Harbor where they may await daylight, as the navigation up the Bay is difficult and dangerous.

Many vessels have been wrecked on this Island and numerous lives have been lost—in one instance the entire crew of a ship and in another that of a schooner.

They therefore pray that an appropriation may be made for the object aforesaid. . . . [95]

The request was ignored until 1902, when the subject was reopened:

Lower East Penobscot Bay and the water seaward for a distance of about 10 miles outside of Saddleback Ledge Light-house are claimed by fishermen to be exceedingly good fishing grounds, and are frequented by fishing vessels ranging in size from 10 to 100 tons burden. Haddock are caught here from March till May, haddock, cod, and hake from May till October, and cod from October till January. The most profitable fishing is during November and December, when northeast snowstorms are apt to prevail, and are often of great severity. The trawls set by fishermen, which often contain several thousand hooks, can not be suddenly left without material loss or disadvantage, and when storms or night

The Isle au Haut Light Station was automated in 1934 and the keepers' houses sold. The dwellings have been used as bed-and-breakfast inn since 1986. The tower was transferred to the town of Isle au Haut under the Maine Lights Program in 1998. (HABS/HAER photo by Richard Cheek, 1991)

PART III: The U.S. Light-House Board (USLHB) Revamps the System

approach the vessels often need to remain on the grounds till the last moment, when it is of the utmost importance that they be able, quickly and with certainty and safety, to make a secure harbor. Isle au Haut Harbor is the best harbor convenient to these fishing grounds . . .[96]

Congress, however, did not authorize the $14,400 required for construction of Isle au Haut Lighthouse until June 1906. The tower was activated on December 30, 1907.[97]

Whitlocks Mill

The first aid to navigation at Whitlocks Mill, on the south bank of the St. Croix River, was a red lantern shown from a tree starting on July 15, 1892. In 1894, the U.S. Light-House Board argued for a more permanent light structure

> . . . to enable the steamers, plying between Eastport and Calais, and especially towboats, to make the difficult turn at the Narrows, a few hundred yards above Whitlocks Mill. The Canadian Government maintains two lights on the left or Canadian bank of the river, and another light was needed on the right or American bank to make the navigation safe at this difficult turn.[98]

Two post lanterns were furnished in 1902. A light tower with a fixed fourth-order light was established in 1910.[99]

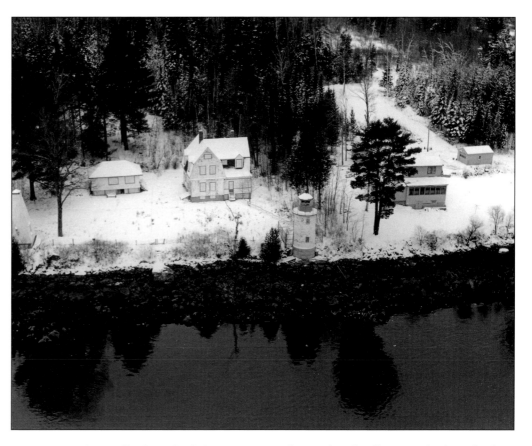

Keeper Frank Ingalls described the Whitlocks Mill station as consisting of

(1) Dwelling: one and a half story building of wood and concrete construction and of Dutch design, containing 7 rooms, 2 hallways and 1 entry with a large cellar and garret. It measures 28 x 30 feet having an outside painted area of approximately 235 sq. yards. (2) Work Shop: One story frame building with 12 foot posts; interior unfinished with an outside painted area of about 120 sq. yards. This building is located close by the dwelling. (3) Light Tower: located on mainland 35 yards distant from the dwelling and classified "Fourth Order Fixed Light." The light surmounts a circular tower of brick exterior and tile interior construction about 30 feet in height and 10 feet in diameter with a total painted area of 150 sq. yards. (4) Oil Supply House: A small building 10 x 12 x 7 ft. of stone (wall) construction with a slate covered wooden roof, having but one door and roof finish painted. Located about 100 yards from light and 65 yards from dwelling.[100]

A fog bell tower was added to the station in 1931. (1975 photo courtesy of U.S. Coast Guard)

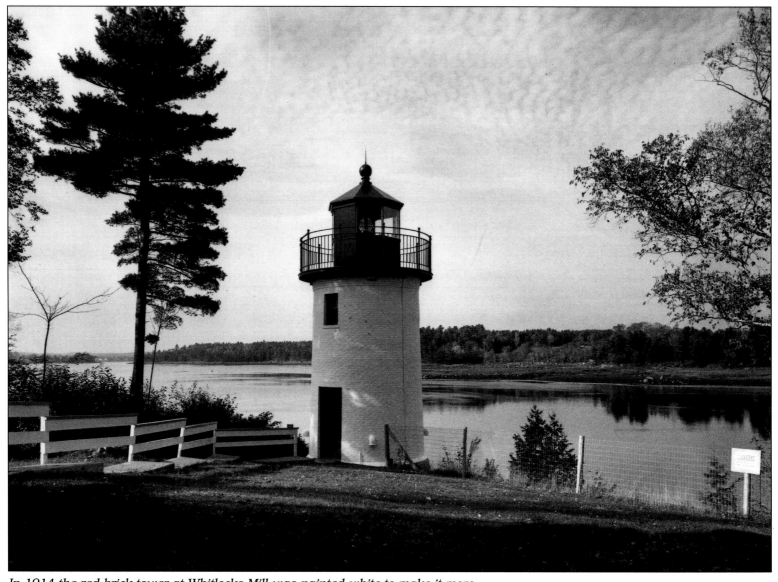

In 1914 the red-brick tower at Whitlocks Mill was painted white to make it more visible. (1963 photo courtesy of U.S. Coast Guard)

　　　　　　　　PART III: The U.S. Light-House Board (USLHB) Revamps the System

Portland Lightship

Lightships were generally placed in locations where a lighthouse could not be constructed. The number of lightships in the United States in 1909 was 56.[101] In pressing the case for a lightship off Cape Elizabeth at the entrance to the main channel into Portland's Channel, Inspector Thomas Perry sent the Board a newspaper article that reported the amount of shipping entering Portland's harbor in 1897: "3,426 schooners, 1,278 steamers, 25 barks, 100 barges, 11 brigs, and 18 sloops."[102]

Lightships were expensive to build and maintain; the one intended for the Cape Elizabeth station required two appropriations totalling $90,000. The wooden lightship, *No. 74*, was placed on station March 7, 1903. Built by contract, the vessel displaced 495 tons, was self propelled and had a steam fog signal. Her coal capacity was 85 tons and fresh water capacity 9,000 gallons. She was built

> . . . with a long forecastle deck and a deck house, in which are located the crew's quarters, the whistling machinery, the upper engine room, and the like. She is propelled by a compound engine . . . . She is rigged with two masts and two try-sail masts and carries a cluster of three lens oil lanterns on each mast. In addition to her steam fog-signal, she has a 1,000-

pound metal bell, a steam capstan, and other modern equipments.[103]

In 1931, Lightship *No. 74* was replaced by Lightship *No. 90*. Lightship *No. 74* was taken to Boston and turned into a relief ship, replacing active lightships when they were taken off their stations for repair or overhauling. The new Portland lightship was fueled by oil rather than coal and offered larger accommodations. No changes were made in the personnel.[104]

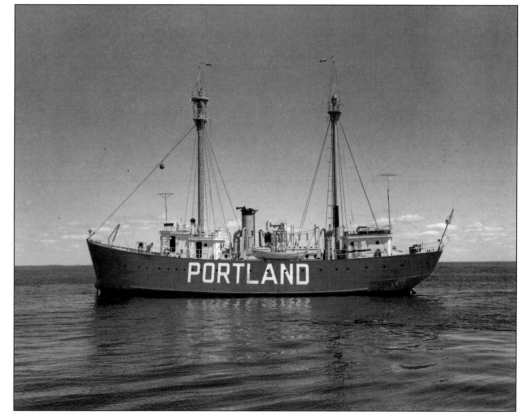

The Portland lightship, shown here in 1969, was the fourth vessel to mark that spot. A different vessel was placed on the station in 1971, and on February 26, 1975, a large navigational buoy (LNB)[105] replaced that lightship. The vessel was moved to assume duties at the Nantucket station, one of three lightships still remaining in active service at that time.[106] (Courtesy of U.S. Coast Guard)

Lifesaving

The U.S. Life-Saving Service was a separate government service established under the U.S. Treasury Department in 1878. In 1915 the Life-Saving Service merged with the Revenue Cutter Service to create the U.S. Coast Guard. Lifesaving stations were often placed near or on lighthouse reservations such as those at Cape Elizabeth and Whitehead Island.

Lifesaving stations were also located at Quoddy Head, Fletchers Neck, Hunniwells Beach, Damiscove (or Damariscove) Island, Cranberry Islands, Cross Island, Wood Island, Great Wass Island, Portsmouth Harbor on Burnt Island, and Isle of Shoals on Appledore Island.[107]

Lighthouse keepers were encouraged to render assistance in saving life and property as long as it did not interfere with their regular duties. Keepers, and sometimes their family members, received commendation when they assisted victims of shipwrecks. On November 20, 1896, Naval Secretary Commander George F. F. Wilde reported that

> . . . the Canadian Government has awarded to Mr. E. H. Pierce and Mr. C. E. Marr, Keepers of the Cuckholds, Me., fog-signal station, two silver watches, in recognition of their services in rescuing the Captain and crew of the Schooner

Aurora of Harbourville, Nova Scotia, on 4 Jan'y, last; and that it is proposed to apply to Congress, at the next session, for permission to enable these persons to accept the testimonials offered.[108]

Two fishermen, John and Ellsworth Gray, assisted the Cuckolds keepers and also received silver watches.

On November 26, 1896, at Moose Peak Light Station, Keeper C. R. Dobbins and his son R. E. Dobbins, at the risk of their own lives, rescued the captain and crew of the schooner *Ashton*. The Canadian government awarded the son a silver "in recognition of the heroic services he rendered."[109]

The Canadian government intended to apply to Congress for permission to award a gold watch to the keeper.

A letter written four years later on May 24, 1900, indicates that C. R. Dobbins finally received the watch for "services rendered in rescuing the shipwreck crew of the British schooner *Ashton*, of Weymoth, Nova Scotia." E. H. Pierce and C. E. Marr received theirs at the same time "for rescuing the shipwreck crew of the British Schooner *Aurora* of Harboursville, Nova Scotia." C. E. Marr was keeper of the Pemaquid Station and Pierce keeper of the Doubling Point Range when the watches caught up with them. Dobbins was still at Moose Peak.[110]

PART III: The U.S. Light-House Board (USLHB) Revamps the System

The lifesaving station on Quoddy Head is pictured in this 1916 postcard. (Courtesy of U.S. Coast Guard)

A lifesaving station was established at Cape Elizabeth (facing page) in 1887. (1940 photo courtesy of U.S. Coast Guard)

Lighthouse tenders frequently went to the aid of distressed vessels. In 1871, Inspector Selfridge reported,

. . . while the *Iris* was lying at Seguin island landing coal, the Revenue Cutter *McCulloch* ran hard and fast ashore in a dense fog, it being at the top of high water.

I happened to be present on the island & upon hearing of the disaster proceeded as soon as possible in the *Iris* to the spot, and after a good pull we were fortunate enough to see her afloat.

As she had been endeavoring in vain for an hour to get off, but for the timely appearance of the *Iris* she would doubtless have been lost.[111]

A shallow ledge named Halfway Rock in Casco Bay posed a hazard for ships approaching Portland, so a lighthouse there was authorized. A granite tower with an illuminating apparatus of the second order was completed in 1871 and the tower lit up for the first time on August 15. The following year Inspector W. H. Mayo wrote Professor Joseph Henry, Chairman of the Light-House Board, as follows:

> Yesterday I learned from Mr. Sterling, principal Keeper of ½ way rock Light House, that on Wednesday the 18th inst. Mr. David Poor, Pilot, left a sea bound steamer 'off the rock' thinking to land there and await the coming of his pilot boat becalmed off Portland Head.
>
> In attempting to land in the face of a dangerous, Swelling Sea, his dory capsized so as completely to cover him, cutting off all means of escape & placing his life in additional peril. Seeing this, the two assistant Keepers, Sylvanus E. Doyle and Horatio G. Cook with considerable heroism lowered the L.H. Boat and Saved the life of Mr. Poor at the risk of their own.[112]

The principal keeper and his two assistants lived in the tower at Halfway Rock (above right). No dwelling was provided on the small rock, only an acre of which was exposed at high tide. The only structures aside from the tower were a boathouse and boat landing. When the boathouse was rebuilt in 1889, it included living quarters in the loft. (1942 photo courtesy of U.S. Coast Guard)

A few months later, *Iris* completed another rescue. Leaving Portland Harbor, the crew spotted

> ...an Hermaphrodite Brig seven miles to seaward flying colors of distress. The weather was cold 10 ° below zero— blowing fresh high sea. The vessel proved to be the *Mary C. Chas* from New York for Portland, eight days east of Cape Cod Light, with all hands except the master & two mates frost bitten & otherwise severely injured by exposure to cold & storms. The three officers above named were exhausted from fatigue and suffering, & the Brig was practically without force. Mr. Day, mate of the *Iris*, with 2 men courageously boarded the Brig in the face of a turbulent sea, and worked her in to smooth water, when the *Iris* took her in tow to the mouth of Portland Harbor, and delivered her to a harbor tug & then the *Iris* proceeded on her course.[113]

Requests for tender assistance became so commonplace that in December 1872, while requisitioning new towlines, Inspector W. K. Mayo suggested that

> ...a charge be made against the owners of the vessels assisted to cover the expense of fuel, hawsers, loss of labor at the buoy depot performed by the *Iris'* crew, etc.
>
> To me it seems just and reasonable that the owners of these vessels who are willing to pay private parties fifteen dollars per

hour for the use of a tug should be called on to pay for fuel, etc., expended by the L.H. Establishment in their behalf.[114]

Perhaps motivated by Mayo's cost-cutting suggestion, Admiral C. S. Boggs issued the following circular in 1873:

The frequent employment of Light-House Tenders in assisting vessels in distress, involving losses of chains, cables, use of fuel, and other expenses to the Light House Establishment, calls the attention of the Board to the necessity of some directions from this office in regard to the matter.

The Board is desirous that the Light House Tenders should do all in their power to save life, but any other assistance must be left in a large degree to the discretion of the officers of the District, they bearing in mind that the special duty of the Tenders is to attend to the Light Houses and Buoys, which service must not under any circumstances be neglected.

Should you be called on to render assistance to vessels in distress, other than relates to the saving of life, a distinct agreement must be made with the owners, captain, or consignees of the vessel, that all expense to the Light House Board will be reimbursed—the agreement to be in writing, or otherwise satisfactory to you; and the amount refunded must include any damage to the Light House vessel incurred in saving or attempting to save property.[115]

Endnotes

[1]According to Charles Lanman, *Biographical Annals of the Civil Government of the United States During Its First Century* (Washington: James Anglim Publisher, 1876), Pleasonton died in office in 1855, having served 38 years as Fifth Auditor of the Treasury.

[2]U.S. Light-House Board, *Laws and Regulations Relating to the Light-House Establishment of the United States*, by authority of the Treasury Department (Washington, D.C.: Government Printing Office, 1880), p. 4. Hereafter titled 1880 *Regulations*.

[3]1880 *Regulations*, pp. 35-40.

[4]1892 *Annual Report*.

[5]1907 *Annual Report*.

[6]1857 *Annual Report*.

[7]W. Branford Shubrick, President; Joseph G. Totten, Brevet Brigadier General; James Kearny, Lieutenant Colonel, Topographical Engineers; F. S. Dupont, Commander, U.S. Navy; and A.D. Bache & Thornton A. Jenkins, Lieutenants, U.S. Navy, "Report of the Light-House Board," January 30, 1852, in *Lighthouse Papers*, p. 628.

[8]Ibid., p. 631.

[9]Ibid., p. 639.

[10]Ibid., pp. 632-633, 635, 645, 647.

[11]1854 *Annual Report* and Candace Clifford, editor, *1994 Inventory of Historic Light Stations*, National Park Service, National Maritime Initiative (Washington, D.C.: Government Printing Office, 1994). See <www.cr.nps.gov/maritime/ltsum.htm>.

[12]James Rodgers to Pleasonton, August 3, 1842 (NA, RG 26, E 17F (NC-31): "Miscellaneous Letters Received (Alphabetical), 1801-52").

[13]Duane to Henry, April 23, 1873 (NA, RG 26, E 24).

[14]Naval Secretary Commander R. D. Evans, January 26, 1889 (NA, RG 26, E 23).

[15]Chairman of the Committee on Lighting to Henry, September 7, 1874 (NA, RG 26, E 9).

[16]Shubrick, et al., "1852 Report of the Light-House Board," in *Lighthouse Papers*, p. 692.

[17]Keeper's journal, Goose Rocks Light Station (NA, RG 26, E 80).

[18]Commander Oliver A. Batcheller to Vice Admiral Stephen C. Rowan, Chairman, Light-House Board, March 2, 1886 (NA, RG 26, E 24 or Letterbook 643).

[19]1890 *Annual Report*.

[20]Ibid.

[21]Keeper's journal, Lubec Channel Light Station (NA, RG 26, E 80).

[22]Ibid.

[23]1890 *Annual Report*.

[24]Millis to First District Engineer, May 8, 1896 (NA, RG 26, E 23).

[25]Naval Secretary Commander George F. F. Wilde to First District Engineer, March 20, 1897 (NA, RG 26, E 23).

[26]Peter Dow Bachelder, *The Lighthouses & Lightships of Casco Bay* (Portland, Maine: The Breakwater Press, 1975) pp. 66, 69.

[27]1901 and 1902 *Annual Reports*.

[28]Congressman N. Dingley to Commander Thomas Perry, First District Inspector, February 11, 1898 (NA, RG 26, E 24 or Letterbook 1163).

[29]1875 inspection report.

[30]1891 *Annual Report*.

[31]Inspector quoted in letter from Engineer Secretary Major F. U. Farquhar to First District Engineer, December 3, 1881 (NA, RG 26, E 23).

[32]1882 *Annual Report*.

[33]1875 *Annual Report*.

[34]J. L. Davis, Chairman of the Committee on Location, to Henry, November 18, 1876 (NA, RG 26, E 9).

[35]Chairman of the Committee on Engineering to Chairman, USLHB, October 6, 1882 (NA, RG 26, E 9).

[36]1891 *Annual Report*.

[37]1890 *Annual Report*.

[38]1893 *Annual Report*.

[39]1895 *Annual Report*.

[40]Engineer Secretary Major G. H. Elliott to General J. C. Duane, March 8, 1872 (NA, RG 26, E 23).

[41]Colonel John Wilson, Chairman of the Committee on Engineering, to USLHB, January 20, 1896 (NA, RG 26, E 9).

[42]Engineering Secretary Captain John Millis to First District Engineer, September 18, 1896 (NA, RG 26, E 23).

[43]1880 *Regulations*, p. 38.

[44]Nathaniel Niles to Secretary of the Treasury Samuel Ingham, September 18, 1829 (NA, RG 26, E 17F).

[45]Winslow Lewis to Stephen Pleasonton, August 26, 1841 (NA, RG 26, E 17G).

[46]Ibid.

[47]1857 *Annual Report*.

[48]Holland, *America's Lighthouses*, p. 18.

[49]*Lighthouse Papers*, pp. 712-713.

[50]U.S. Light-House Board, *Organization and Duties of the Light-house Board; and Regulations, Instructions,*

Circulars, and General Orders of the Light-house Establishment of the United States (Washington, D.C.: Government Printing Office, 1871), hereafter referred to as the 1871 *Regulations*, p. 61.

[51]Duane to Henry, February 4, 1873 (NA, RG 26, E 24 or Letterbook 318).

[52]Unpublished 1848 annual report (NA, RG 26, E 6).

[53]Johnson, pp. 23, 54, 61.

[54]Duane to Henry, December 3, 1873 (NA, RG 26, E 23 or Letterbook 337).

[55]Pleasonton to Ilsley, June 1, 1820 (NA, RG 26, E 18).

[56]Collector Solomon Thayer to Pleasonton, July 12, 1827 (NA, RG 26, E 17C).

[57]Jewett to Pleasonton, March 9, 1850 (NA, RG 26, E 17C).

[58]Attachment to letter from Shubrick to Secretary of the Treasury William P. Fessenden, January 28, 1865 (NA, RG 26, E 46 (NC-31): "Correspondence of the Light-House Board, 1851-70").

[59]Ibid.

[60]1866 *Annual Report*.

[61]1872, 1875, 1876, 1880, and 1882 *Annual Reports*.

[62]Engineer Secretary Major O. M. Poe to Duane, May 7, 1869 (NA, RG 26, E 23).

[63]Engineer Secretary Major F. W. Farquhar, to First District Engineer, September 19, 1881 (NA, RG 26, E 23).

[64]Engineer Secretary Major D. P. Heap, to First District Engineer, September 11, 1886 (NA, RG 26, E 23).

[65]Engineer Secretary Major James F. Gregory to First District Engineer, July 6, 1889 (NA, RG 26, E 23).

[66]Engineer Secretary Captain John Millis to First District Engineer, August 1, 1895 (NA, RG 26, E 23).

[67]1876 *Annual Report*.

[68]1889 *Annual Report*.

[69]1890 *Annual Report*.

[70]Form 60, corrected to May 1, 1935 (NA, RG 26, E 63, (NC-31): "Descriptive List of Lighthouses 1858-1889, 1876-1939").

[71]1888 *Annual Report*.

[72]W. W. Duffield, Chairman of the Committee on Lighting, to USLHB, November 6, 1895 (NA, RG 26, E 9).

[73]Joseph Farwell, Master, Steamer *Daniel Webster*, to Light-House Inspector Lieutenant W. B. Franklin, September 12, 1853 (1853 *Annual Report*).

[74]Ralph Eshelman, National Register nomination for Manana Island Fog Signal Station, 1998.

[75]"Personnel Classification Board, Form No. 14—Field Questionnaire" (NA, RG 26, E 111 (NC-31): "Record of Reclassification of Light-House Keepers Salaries, 1922-28").

[76]Amy K. Marshall, "A history of buoys and tenders," *Commandant's Bulletin*, November 1995, pp. 3-4.

[77]1859 *Annual Report*.

[78]1869 *Annual Report*.

[79]1875 inspection report.

[80]1893 *Annual Report*.

[81]Ibid.

[82]1882 *Annual Report*.

[83]1897 *Annual Report*.

[84]Deck logs for *Lilac*, 1910-1912 (NA, RG 26, E 328 (A-1): "Buoy Tender Logs, 1873-1941").

[85]Candace Clifford, *U.S. Coast Guard Cutter Fir (WLM-212): A Lighthouse/Buoy Tender for the Pacific Northwest*, Historic American Engineering Record, National Park Service, 2001.

[86]U.S. Coast Guard First District Units found at <www.uscg.mil/dl/roles/units.htm>.

[87]1874, 1875, 1877, 1878, and 1879 *Annual Reports*.

[88]W. N. Allen to Henry, September 9, 1873 (NA, RG 26, E 24 or Letterbook 337).

[89]Batcheller to Rowan, April 26, 1886 (NA, RG 26, E 24 or Letterbook 643).

[90]First District Engineer Stanton to USLHB, September 16, 1899 (NA, RG 26, E 24 or Letterbook 1317).

[91]Ted Panayotoff and Courtney Thompson, *The Lighthouse at Rockland Breakwater* (Rockland, Maine: The Friends of Rockland Breakwater, 2002).

[92]Disposal file for Fort Popham Light (NA, RG 26, E 99 (A-1): "Board of Survey - Real Property, 1946-74").

[93]First Lighthouse District Inspector Greenfief A. Merriam and Engineer William F. Stanton to USLHB, April 3, 1902 (NA, RG 26, E 48 (NC-31): "Correspondence of the Light-House Board, 1901-10," File # 3979).

[94]Ibid.

[95]C. J. Abbott of Castine to Honorable T. I. D. Fuller, House of Representatives, December 12, 1837 (NA, RG 26, E 45).

[96]1902 *Annual Report*.

[97]National Register nomination.

[98]1894 *Annual Report*.

[99]Personnel Classification Board Form No. 14—Field Questionnaire (NA, RG 26, E 111).

[99]1906 *Annual Report*; First District Inspector indicates the light is to be lit "about January 31st, 1910" in a letter to the USLHB, January 10, 1910 (NA, RG 26 E 48, File # 2612).

[101]CWO E. B. Paradis, Release No. 169-75-3, February 21, 1975, from First District Coast Guard District Public Affairs Office, Boston, Massachusetts.

[102]Perry to USLHB, January 12, 1898 (NA, RG 26 E 24 or Letterbook 1163).

[103]1903 *Annual Report*.

[104]Author unknown, "New Lightship Due Today Ousts Old No. 74, Off Cape since 1903," *Courier-Gazette*, Rockland, Maine, February 16, 1931; courtesy Ken Black.

[105]Large Navigational Buoys perform all the functions of lightships at half the expense, without risking anyone's life.

[106]Paradis, Release No. 169-75-3, February 21, 1975.

[107]Ralph Shanks and Wick York, *The U.S. Life-Saving Service: Heroes, Rescues and Architecture of the Early Coast Guard* (Petaluma, California: Costano Books, 1996), p. 27.

[108]Naval Secretary Commander George F. F. Wilde to First District Inspector, November 20, 1896 (NA, RG 26, E 23).

[109]Wilde to First District Engineer, March 7, 1897 (NA, RG 26, E 23).

[110]First District Inspector Commander James K. Cogswell to USLHB, May 24, 1900 (NA, RG 26, E 24 or Letterbook 1283).

[111]C. K. Mayo to Henry, December 21, 1872 (NA, RG 26, E 24 or Letterbook 318).

[112]Selfridge to Henry, August 23, 1871 (NA, RG 26, E 24 or Letterbook 318).

[113]Mayo to Henry, February 1, 1873 (NA, RG 26, E 24 or Letterbook 318).

[114]Mayo to Henry, December 26, 1872 (NA, RG 26, E 24 or Letterbook 318).

[115]Circular from Naval Secretary Admiral C. S. Boggs to Duane, January 6, 1873 (NA, RG 26, E 23).

PART IV. Keepers: Who They Were, How They Lived, What They Said

Keeper appointments

After 1852 the United States Light-House Board restricted the appointment of keepers to "persons between the ages of 18 and 50, who can read, write, and keep accounts, are able to do the requisite manual labor, to pull and sail a boat, and have enough mechanical ability to make necessary minor repairs about the premises, and keep them painted, whitewashed, and in order."[1] "Men of intemperate habits, and those who are otherwise mentally or physically incapable of performing the duties of light keepers, must not be nominated for appointment."[2] Initially superintendents of lights were charged with paying salaries and disbursing other funds, as well as nominating light-keepers. This responsibility was eventually transferred to the district inspectors.

Inspectors were well qualified for promoting keepers because they could assess their performance and competence during inspection visits.

Principal keepers were generally promoted from the ranks of assistant keepers. There was a hierarchy of stations, and many keepers started out at smaller, less attractive stations and worked their way up through the system.

In cases where more than one man was competing for an appointment, the candidate often garnered support through local petitions or a letter from his Congressman. Politics often influenced keeper appointments. After Democrat Franklin Pierce won the 1852 presidential election, ousting the former Whig administration, 23 keepers were removed from their posts at Maine lighthouses, including John Grant, keeper at Libby Island Lighthouse.[3] Grant would later receive the keeper appointment at Matinicus Rock, replacing Abbie Burgess's father. (Abbie is discussed later.)

In one case the record shows that keepers were expected to donate money as a sign of party loyalty. On August 6,

1880, Thomas Day, keeper at Seguin Island Lighthouse, wrote the inspector, "I understand that the Keeper of Boon Island Light is removed for not paying money for Republican Campaign expenses. Will you be kind enough to inform me of the fact, as myself and my two asst. have been asked for $79 for campaign expenses." The inspector was at a loss as to what to do and was "of the opinion that these poor people ought not to be expected to contribute so largely from their meager pay."[4]

Keepers were encouraged to cultivate the land on the lighthouse reservation and were forbidden to engage in any business that interfered with their presence at the station or with the proper and timely performance of their duties. Keepers were not allowed to take in boarders, nor were they given pensions or compensation for injury. In 1883 male keepers were issued uniforms consisting of a coat, vest, trousers, and a cap in a dark indigo blue color. "It is believed that uniforming the personnel of the service, some 1,600 in number, will aid in maintaining its discipline, increase its efficiency, raise its tone, and add to its esprit de corps."[5] A regulation apron was issued for inside cleaning and a brown working suit for outdoor work.

Keepers were expected to keep their stations in good repair. Daily logs reveal the many tasks required to keep their light stations neat and functioning. The Light-House Board furnished carpenters for major construction projects; lampists and machinists oversaw the installation and major repairs of the illuminating apparatus and fog signals. All other maintenance and upkeep was the responsibility of the keepers. An 1873 circular admonished "that if the keepers do not keep their iron windows in good working order, or if they break glass in their dwellings or towers and do not replace it, they should be reported to the Board for dismissal. Keepers who do not know how to set common window glass should also be reported."[6]

Avery Rock (below) was a small, one-family offshore station that was not deemed as attractive as some of the other family stations in Maine. It was the second assignment for keeper Elson Small and his wife, Connie, who described their life there in her book, The Lighthouse Keeper's Wife.[7] *She preferred Avery Rock to her husband's first assignment as assistant keeper at Lubec Channel Light, where he rotated two-day shifts with head keeper Loring Myers and spent his off-duty days on shore with Connie, as there was no accommodation at Lubec Channel Lighthouse for families. (Courtesy of U.S. Coast Guard)*

St. Croix River Light Station (facing page) was Elson Small's last post. He had been principal keeper at Seguin Island, with two assistants working under him, before moving to St. Croix River. This was wife Connie's favorite assignment. Here they had access to the mainland and enough cultivable land to raise a cow and plant a garden.[8] (1946 photo courtesy of U.S. Coast Guard)

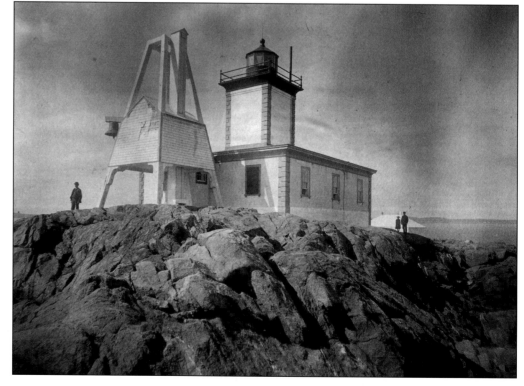

PART IV. Keepers: Who They Were, How They Lived, What They Said

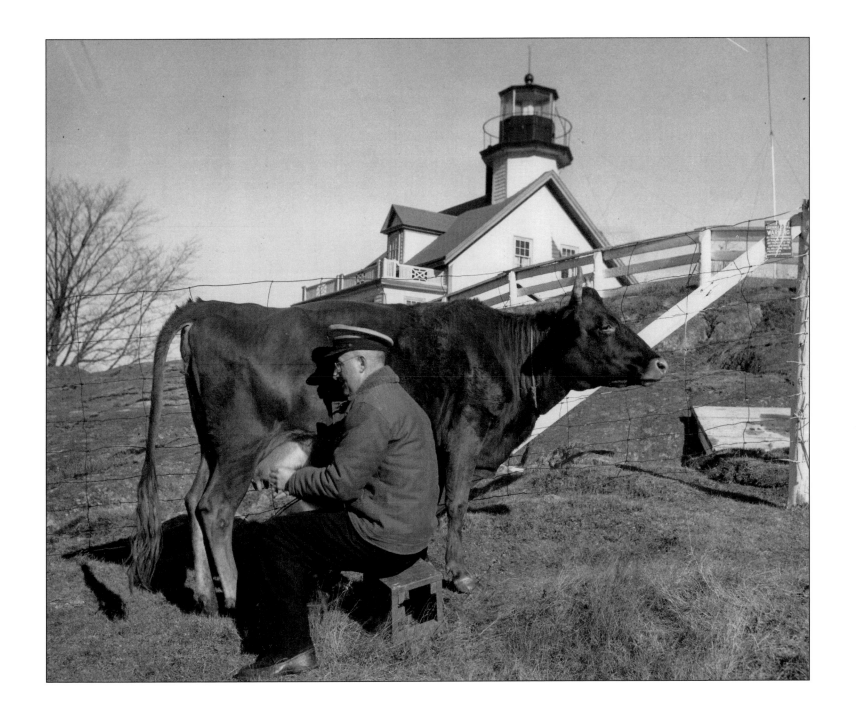

Maine Lighthouses: Documentation of Their Past

Keeper Arthur Beal in his Lighthouse Service uniform with his wife (right) during their tenure at Whitehead Island Light Station ca. 1940. (Courtesy of David Gamage)

Keeper George Woodward's wife and child (below) at Owls Head Light Station. (Courtesy of U.S. Coast Guard)

PART IV. Keepers: Who They Were, How They Lived, What They Said

DETERMINING A KEEPER'S SALARY

The U.S. Light-House Board developed criteria for determining a keeper's rate of pay. According to an 1872 circular,

> . . . It is believed that some of our Light-Keepers with facilities for gardens, fishing, etc., and stations in proximity to school and church, etc., get in some instances more pay than those who have not these advantages.
>
> In making the investigation you will please to take into consideration the order of the light; the rank of the keeper, that is whether he is principal, first or second Assistant Keeper . . .. You will also take into consideration the peculiar situation of each Light-House; the area and character of the public ground around it, and whether it is suitable for cultivation and grazing or otherwise; the facilities for fishing; the facilities for procuring supplies for the families of the Keepers; the sizes and character of the dwellings; whether there are steam or other fog-signals worked by machinery at the stations; the exposure to weather in attending on or getting to and from the lights; and the dangers to life in necessarily crossing waters between the lights and the main-land or the offices of the Superintendent of Lights.[9]

In addition to a salary, the Board supplied keepers at some very isolated stations with the following provisions:[10]

Beef	200 pounds	Potatoes	4 bushels
Pork	100 pounds	Onions	1 bushel
Flour	1 barrel	Sugar	50 pounds
Rice	25 pounds	Coffee	24 pounds
Beans	10 gallons	Vinegar	4 gallons

In the 1890s the USLHB favored increasing the keepers' pay in isolated locations rather than providing rations.

Records required of lighthouse keepers

Like most government agencies, the Light-House Board gradually deluged its employees with paperwork. A keeper had to submit monthly reports on the condition of the station and make explicit specifications for any needed repairs. Expenditures of oil, etc., and salary vouchers were to be submitted quarterly. Property returns were submitted annually and receipts kept for extra supplies and for their delivery. The keeper signed a receipt for all station property when he took charge.

Keepers forwarded to the district inspector reports of shipwrecks, any damage to station or apparatus, and any unusual occurrence. Keepers were expected to keep a daily-expenditure book, a general-account book, and, after 1872, a journal in which the principal keeper recorded "The visits of the Inspector or Engineer, or of the lampist or machinist, and an account of any work going on or delivery of stores . . . as also any item of interest occurring in the vicinity, such as the state of the weather, or other similar matter. The books must be kept in ink, with neatness, and must always be kept up to date."[11]

In 1872 the Light-House Board sent out "twenty-four fog signal record books for the purpose of recording the duration of fog, quantity of fuel consumed, etc., at West Quoddy Head, Petit Manan, Matinicus, Whitehead, Monhegan, Cape Elizabeth, Portland Head, ..."[12] The inspector was instructed that

> You will forward by mail without delay one of these books to each station where there is a fog-signal using a steam or hot-air engine, and direct the principal keeper to be careful to keep a full and complete record of the quantities called for as indicated by the headings of the columns.
>
> With the books are sent you a lot of blank forms, 30 of which you will send with the record book to each fog-signal station, and instruct the keeper that on the first of each month, he will make duplicate copies of the record of the preceding month on these forms, and forward one to the Engineer and the other to the Inspector of the District.
>
> You will on the receipt of the monthly reports see that they are copied into your own record book, and will then forward a condensed report of all the Stations in your District to the Light House Board.[13]

The inspector was instructed to compare the reports of each station with former reports and those of other stations "to the end that you may see that there is the utmost economy of fuel with efficiency of service."[14]

The *1880 Laws and Regulations Relating to the Light-House Establishment of the United States* listed 68 different types of forms used in managing the Lighthouse Service.

Light-House Board personnel

Inspectors visited the stations in their districts quarterly to report on needed repairs, renovations, and improvements, and the condition of the station, lantern, illuminating apparatus, and related equipment. It was the inspector's job to make sure the keeper understood the printed instructions for operating all equipment and other attendant duties. The inspector also reviewed the keeper's journal and records relating to expenditures, shipwrecks, and vessels passing. The inspector assessed the "attention of the keeper to his duties, and his ability to perform them well."[15] Both inspectors and engineers had authority to dismiss a keeper or other employee found in a state of intoxication.

Engineers superintended the "construction and renovation of the fixed aids to navigation in their respective districts."[16] The engineer or the inspector was responsible for acquiring information on the ownership of any potential site and reporting these details to the Board along with information about the topography of the

Along with the daily logs, some keepers kept a "journal of shipwrecks." At Goat Island Light Station, this journal indicated 46 shipwrecks on the rocks around Goat Island between November 1865 and January 1920. Of the 46, 28 vessels were a total loss. Fortunately, of the 229 men crewing these vessels, not a single life was lost. An entry dated March 26, 1876, describes the fate of the cargo schooner E.E. Stimpson *bound for Portland:*

> In a heavy S.E. gale and bad sea this vessel went ashore on S.W. Point of Folly Island and went to pieces in less than two hours. Nothing of any consequence saved. Upon seeing vessel ashore, got boat off with difficulty, it being low water. But upon reaching Folly Island found the men had saved themselves by swinging ashore on the peak downhaul. Took them to Goat Island and cared for them. Went back with Captain and assisted him to save his nautical instruments, charts and a few other things. Light seen by all on board two hours before she struck.[17]

Despite the abundance of shipwrecks at this location, the 1875 inspection report indicated that "None but fishing smacks can use the harbor of refuge, so called, here," and recommended the light be transferred to Cape Neddick.[18] (Courtesy of U.S. Coast Guard)

PART IV. Keepers: Who They Were, How They Lived, What They Said

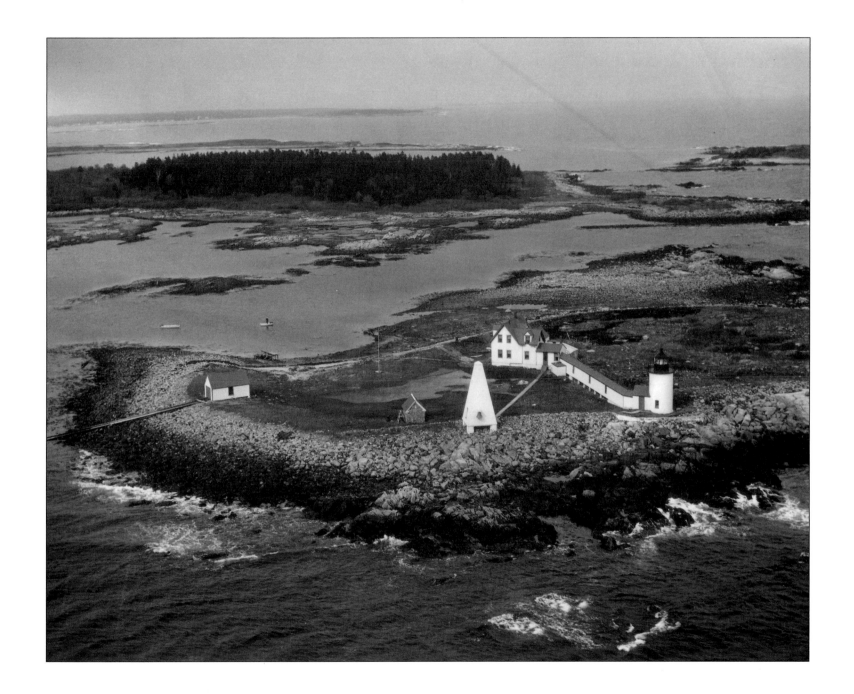

Maine Lighthouses: Documentation of Their Past

site and the potential light's relationship with other lights and the water or hazard it was marking. Engineers were instructed to inspect all materials and supplies to make sure they were in conformance with contracts. When a tower was nearing completion, the engineer notified the superintendent of lights or inspector so that he could nominate the authorized number of keepers.[19]

In 1896, lighthouse service employees were classified within the federal civil service system. When the U.S. Coast Guard took over the administration of lighthouses in 1939, the current keepers were given a choice of staying as civil service employees or enlisting in the Coast Guard. Eventually the post of civilian keeper faded into history. Coast Guard personnel followed a career path that included many different types of assignments, of which lighthouse keeping was only one. In the 1970s it was Coast Guard policy to rotate lighthouse keepers every two years. By 1990 all U.S. stations but one, Boston Harbor, were automated and the traditional keeper obsolete.

Instructions to keepers

In the first half of the nineteenth century, keepers were given minimal instructions. The major concerns of the administration, aside from keeping a good light, were that the keeper keep good records of the oil expended at his station, and that he remain sober. Several early keepers addicted to drink had caused all kinds of problems. After the lighthouses were fitted up with Winslow Lewis's patented reflectors and lamps, a form was issued in 1813 to guide keepers in tracking their annual oil usage, supplies on hand, and repairs needed.

In discussing the appointment of Rufus Dunning to be keeper at the nearly completed Indian Island Lighthouse, Collector Luther Jewett gave reasons for his recommendation:

As it is important to have good and worthy persons appointed to take charge of Light Houses and especially such persons, who make no use of ardent spirits as a drink, I would respectfully recommend the appointment of said Dunning and for these reasons: He never makes use of ardent spirits as a drink—He has been long at sea and Knows by experience the value of a good light—He is recommended by Ship Owners and Ship Masters, and has always sustained a good reputation. . . .[20]

As the number of lighthouses increased, so did the need for more formal instructions for their keepers. In April 1835, when the number of lighthouses in the country had grown to 177,[21] Secretary of the Treasury Levi Woodbury wrote,

. . . the propriety of issuing a general letter or circular to each Lightkeeper, whether of House or Boat, instructing him in regard to the time of making light in the evening,—to his attention to the Light during the night, by trimming it, etc.,—to a judicious economy in the use and application of the oil, so as to produce the best light at the smallest expense,—to the necessity of strict care in respect to the cleanliness, order and safety of the lamps, reflectors, lens & other machinery, and the importance of a careful super-vision and preservation from fire and depredation of the property of the United States under his charge. The general course to be pursued in his sickness or absence, and in case of accidents might also be usefully prescribed. The sale of ardent spirits should be forbidden on the premises of the United States, and civility should be enjoined as a duty to strangers wishing to examine the Lights, and, in case of shipwrecks near, every practical effort required to be made to render reasonable and efficient relief, and all due vigilance exercised to detect and expose every breech of the revenue laws in his neighborhood.[22]

PART IV. Keepers: Who They Were, How They Lived, What They Said

Acting upon the Secretary's suggestion, Pleasonton issued the following instructions.

INSTRUCTIONS TO THE KEEPERS OF LIGHT HOUSES WITHIN THE UNITED STATES

1. You are to light the lamps every evening at sun-setting, and keep them continually burning, bright and clear, till sun-rising.

2. You are to be careful that the lamps, reflectors, and lanterns, are constantly kept clean, and in order; and particularly to be careful that no lamps, wood, or candles, be left burning any where as to endanger fire.

3. In order to maintain the greatest degree of light during the night, the wicks are to be trimmed every 4 hours, taking care that they are exactly even on the top.

4. You are to keep an exact amount of the quantity of oil received from time to time; the number of gallons, quarts, gills, etc., consumed each night; and deliver a copy of the same to the Superintendent every 3 months, ending 31 March, 30 June, 30 September, and 31 December, in each year; with an account of the quantity on hand at the time.

5. You are not to sell, or permit to be sold, any spirituous liquors on the premises of the United States; but will treat with civility and attention, such strangers as may visit the Lighthouse under your charge, and as may conduct themselves in an orderly manner.

6. You will receive no tube-glasses, wicks, or any other article which the Contractors, Messr. Morgan & Co., at New Bedford, are bound to supply, which shall not be of suitable kind; and if the oil they shall supply, should, on trial, prove bad, you will immediately acquaint the Superintendent therewith, in order that he may exact from them a compliance with their contract.[23]

7. Should the Contractors omit to supply the quantity of oil, wicks, tube-glasses, or other articles necessary to Keep the lights in continual operation, you will give [the Superintendent] timely notice thereof, that he may inform the Contractors and direct them to forward the requisite supplies.

8. You will not absent yourself from the Lighthouse at any time, without first obtaining the consent of the Superintendent, unless the occasion be so sudden and urgent as not to admit of an application to that Officer; in which case, by leaving a suitable substitute, you may be absent for the space of twenty-four hours.

9. All your communications intended for this Office, must be transmitted through the Superintendent, through whom the proper answer will be returned.

(Signed) S. Pleasonton, *Fifth Auditor and Acting Commissioner of the Revenue*   *April 23d, 1835*[24]

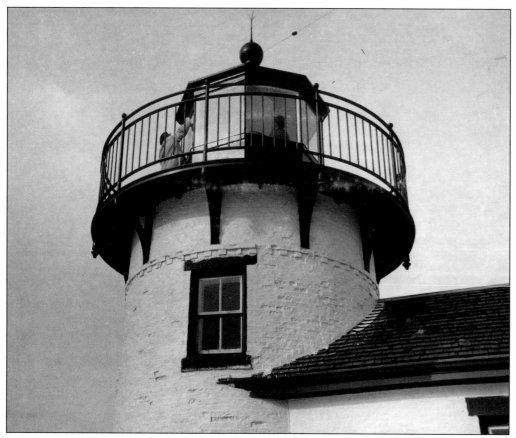

In this 1946 image, Mrs. Andrew W. Kennedy, wife of the Coast Guard keeper at Bear Island Lighthouse, gives the windows of the lantern their daily cleaning. (Courtesy of U.S. Coast Guard)

After 1852 the Light-House Board insisted on a much more structured approach for administering lighthouses. The Board issued rules and regulations for the overall management of the lighthouse system and detailed instructions to the individual keepers for operation of the lights. From the start the Board stressed the importance of the written instructions; the 1852 report said that "Inspectors and light-keepers should be provided with printed instructions, in the form of manuals of instruction, as well as those necessary to guide them in the policing of the establishments, similar to those provided for inspectors of light-houses in France and Great Britain."[25] The instructions to keepers and other Light-House Board employees were expanded with each printing.

The 1881 *Instructions to Light-Keepers* began, "The keeper is responsible for the care and management of the light, and for the station in general. He must enforce a careful attention to duty on the part of his assistants; and the assistants are strictly enjoined to render prompt obedience to his lawful orders." Absences had to be communicated to those left in charge and reported to the inspector. "Light-keepers may leave their stations to attend divine worship on Sundays, to procure needful supplies, and on important public occasions."[26]

Watches must be kept at all stations where there is an assistant. The keeper on watch must remain in the watch room and give continuous attention to the light while he is on duty. When there is no assistant, the keeper must visit the light at least twice during the night between 8 p.m. and sunrise; and on stormy nights the light must be constantly looked after.[27]

A keeper was expected to use strict economy in the use of his supplies: "He must be careful to prevent waste, theft, or misapplication of light-house property." Quantities of oil and other supplies used each day were to be recorded.[28]

Light-keepers must not engage in any traffic on light-house premises, and they must not permit it by any one else. They must not carry on any business or trade elsewhere which will cause them to be often absent from the premises, or to neglect, in any way, their proper duties.[29]

Visitors to a light station were to be treated courteously and politely, but not allowed to handle the apparatus or carve anything on the lantern glass or tower windows. An 1845 report by Collector John Anderson noted that he "found Owls Head Light in good condition except the glass in the lantern. Several panes were cut and scratched by visitors names." The keeper was directed to "knock out these panes and set new glass" and was admonished "that such marring of the property, if suffered while in his charge, would be good cause for removal."[30] The *Instructions* also noted that intoxicated visitors were to be removed "by the employment of all proper and reasonable means."[31]

Keepers were not to change the colors of towers or buildings without written orders. The colors and configuration of stations were noted in the *Light Lists* to aid mariners in establishing their location during daylight hours. All parts of the station, including bed chambers, were to be neatly kept. "Untidiness will be strongly reprehended, and its continuance will subject a keeper to dismissal."[32]

Shipwrecks were to be reported promptly to the inspector. "It is the duty of light-keepers to aid wrecked persons as far as lies in their power." Precautions had to be taken against fire; fire-buckets were to be kept filled and ready. Burning mineral oil, or kerosene, was to

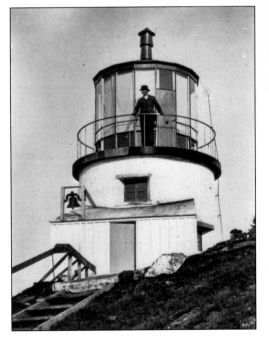

be extinguished with sand or ashes rather than water.[33]

Boats were furnished at stations where they were "necessary for communication with the mainland, to obtain household supplies, etc." They were to be used only for light-house purposes; "the boats must not be used for freighting, wrecking, fishing with seines, ferrying, or for carrying goods or passengers for hire."[34]

Keepers were encouraged to "consider the care of the light and the light-house property their paramount duty, beyond any personal consideration."[35] With few exceptions, keepers took their jobs very seriously. Knowing that lives depended on their attention and efficiency in keeping their lights and fog signals operating, most keepers were vigilant in tending these aids however extreme the weather.

A visitor at Owls Head Light Station takes in the view. Note the curtains sheltering the lens and lamp from the sun. (Courtesy of Ken Black, Shore Village Museum)

Family stations

Browns Head Lighthouse (facing page) was always a family station with a lone keeper serving there. Alonzo Morong, who was appointed keeper on May 1, 1918, described his duties in 1928:

> At sunset I light my lamp in the tower as an aid to mariners, which is kept burning until sunrise of the following day.
>
> I then clean and trim my lamp and have everything in readiness for the next night.
>
> This station is what is known as a 'one man' station and claims as near my constant attention as it is possible to give.
>
> At night when I light my light I do not retire until I am satisfied that all is well in the Lighthouse and its sur-roundings.
>
> Should the weather be thick, day or night, I have to start the fog signal, which is run by winding up a weight, which starts an automatic clock. This signal is a machine bell and is struck at intervals of twenty seconds each, a single and then a double blow. I keep this signal sounding until the weather clears.
>
> I also am requested to do all I can without interfering with my other duties, toward the saving of life and property.
>
> At the end of each month, I make a monthly report of my station and send it to the District office; and at the end of the fiscal year I also submit a report for the year passed.
>
> As a rule I take a vacation each year from active duties of fifteen days duration, all my other absences from

A section of the keepers' instructions was devoted to the "Care of Lights and their Appurtenances," which included detailed instructions on the care of the optics. The keepers were to hang lantern curtains each morning and to wear a linen apron to protect the lens "from contact with the wearing apparel." The lens and lantern glass were to be cleaned daily. Rouge was used to polish the lens and "rotten-stone" to shine the brass. Keepers were "forbidden to use any other materials for cleaning and polishing than those supplied by the Light-house Establishment." The revolving clockwork and carriage rollers were to be kept properly oiled. Keepers had to cut replacement glass for the lantern when necessary.[36]

Whitehead Island Light Station (above) with curtains sheltering the lens in the lantern. (Courtesy of U.S. Coast Guard)

my station are routine absences to get mail and supplies.[37]

Keeper Morong depended on his family to help in the continuous operation of his station. In 1926, his log reported that his wife took care of the light and other station duties while he was sick for several weeks. (Courtesy of U.S. Coast Guard)

Log accounts of Burnt Coat Harbor Light Station

Entries in the Burnt Coat Harbor keeper's log began in April 1874. Keeper F. A. Allen made entries only on days with events or weather worth noting.[38]

April 3, 1874, Received this Book from Capt. Johnston.

April 10, Heavy Easterly Gale, large quantity of snow fell, stopped snowing in the afternoon, wind canting to the N.E.

April 20, Cleared away the rocks from the landing and built some fence.

April 26, Easterly Gale. Several boats sunk in the Harbor. One vessel came in with loss of mainsail.

April 28, Whitewashed both towers outside and the kitchen overhead.

Station maintenance dominated Keeper Allen's logbook.

May 5, Made a gate; the schooner (U.S.), Capt. Green, came in the Harbor.

May 15, Cleaned out the two 50 Gall[on] oil tanks.

May 29, Painted the oil tanks, whitewashed the oil room.

Occasionally an unusual occurrence brought a change of pace.

June 6, The Buoy broke away off Hay Island Ledge, towed it into the Harbor.

June 9, Discovered the Buoy was gone off Heron Island Ledge.

But then back to housekeeping duties:

June 11, Painted the 100 gall. oil tank.

June 15, Whitewashed the wood house outside.

June 24, Painted the window frames of the lantern room outside with white paint.

June 25, Painted the inside of little tower.

July 9, Painted the tower floor service table and steps.

July 11, Painted the pedestal in the little tower.

July 18, Painted the upper room floor in the rear tower.

August 4, Whitewashed the outside of the little tower.

August 17, The chimney on the little light broke and smooked up the lenses.

August 18, Three Government men came to board while they put a hole for a spindle [a type of buoy] on Gang Way Ledge.

August 19, U.S. Schooner *Wave*, Capt. Green, came in the Harbor landed a water tank.

September 7, Our well all dried up, had to boat water acrost the Harbor.

September 10, Capt. Allen, lighthouse Inspector, visited the lights; he came on the Steamer *Iris*, Capt Johnston.

September 11, Prepared ½ Bushel Lime for whitewashing.

September 17, U.S. Schooner *Wave*, Capt. Green, came in the Harbor to set a spindle on Gang Way Ledge.

September 20, Whitewashed rear tower.

September 22, Helped Capt. Green set the spindle on Gang Way Ledge.

September 23, Helped Capt. Green plumb the spindle on Gang Way Ledge.

September 26, Foggy throughout these 24 hours. Today made some stairs to go up into the Ell chamber.

October 9, At 5:30 P.M. U.S. Steamer *Iris*, Capt. Johnston, came in the Harbor landing a cooking range and coal tar; the lampist Mr. Foster examined the lights.

October 22, Commenced to tar the rear tower steps but found it too cold.

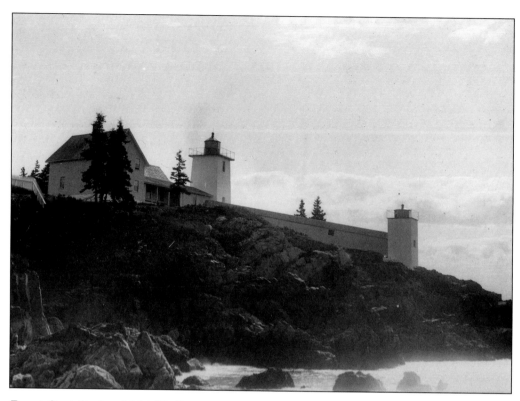

Burnt Coat Harbor Light Station was established on Swans Island, a large island of about 7,000 acres and, in the nineteenth century, a source of granite and a center for fishing and lobstering. The Light-House Board in 1870 submitted an estimate of $10,000 "for the establishment of two small lights to mark the approach to, and serve as a range for entering this important harbor of refuge at night, when threatened with such weather as to make it necessary to seek a safe anchorage. This harbor is commodious and safe, and is distant 36 miles from the nearest place of safe anchorage on that coast."[39]

This new station was completed and lighted for the first time on the 15th of August, 1872. Both of the [range] lights are white, the rear, fourth order dioptric, 75 feet above sea-level; the front, fifth order dioptric, 42 feet above sea-level, and are 100 feet apart, on a course NE 3/4 N. The towers are of brick, square in plan; the keeper's dwelling is of wood, and all of the buildings are white. The station is located on the north side of the entrance to the harbor.[40]

(National Archives photo # 26-LG-1-54 (above) and drawing (facing page) from RG 26)

PART IV. Keepers: Who They Were, How They Lived, What They Said

November 2, Finished coal taring the rear tower steps.

November 13, Had to boat water from across the Harbor; no water in tank and the well dry.

November 15, Commenced to take down the lamps in the morning on account of cold weather.

November 16, Had to boat water.

A heavy gale in late November did damage to local shipping at Burnt Coat Harbor. The fishing schooner *Express of Gloucester* lost her mainmast head. Keeper Allen boarded and took her into the harbor. On December 16 it was so cold that he "had to pack the tubes to keep the oil from getting cold." On December 21 he took the altitude of the sun to check the time and found his clock was two minutes fast. On January 29 he received mail after a 20-day lapse.

February 9, N.W. Gale, very cold weather at 2 A.M. So cold could not keep the light burning; had to take them down

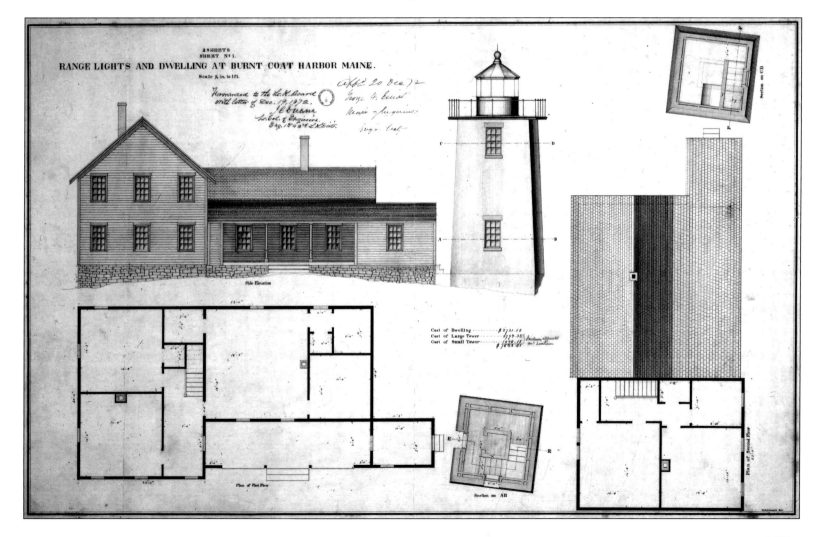

and heat them on the stove and set them a going again with hot oil.

February 10, Still cold; had to keep a regular watch to keep the light burning. The Harbor all closed up with ice to the extent that one could walk to Brooklin on the ice.

In June 1875 all of Keeper Allen's family were sick with measles. Keeper Allen was replaced by William N. Wasgatt in January 1876. Wasgatt recorded a number of tragedies at Burnt Coat Harbor:

July 11, 1876, A sad accident. Friday afternoon about four o'clock Mr. Cutler and wife of Boston was here on a visit. Mr. Cutler and wife and my two daughters in the lighthouse boat and the boat was capsized and Mrs. Cutler was drowned.

July 5, 1880, A vessel wrecked on Johns Island Reef at one o'clock A.M. It was foggy, the name was *Malanta of Corning* bound for Boston loaded with Railroad Sleepers, one hundred and six (106) tons register. There was a crew of five men, none was lost. The wreck was sold at auction as it lay on the rocks. The proceeds was about ($400) four hundred dollars. Saved a large part of the cargo and the sails & anchors. The vessel was said to be seaworthy at the time of the disaster.

March 7, 1882, A vessel wrecked on Black Ledge at 1 o'clock P.M. in a thick snowstorm. Name: *J.W. Sawyer* of Portland Me, bound for Portland from fishing banks loaded with fresh fish. One

hundred and fifteen tons register. Was a crew of fifteen men, three was lost, the remaining twelve brought to Swans Island. The vessel was a total loss.

James H. Orcutt, who took charge as keeper on November 11, 1886, also recorded wrecks:

November 13, 1887, At 7 P.M. the American Schooner *Christina Ellsworth* was working into the Harbor struck bottom on Brimstone Island, rolled down, upset stove set vessel on fire and was a total loss.

January 27, 1888, The British Schooner *Riverside* drifted down the bay and went ashore on West end of Harbor Island at 12 o'clock today. She was abandoned by crew with loss of both anchors and chains, sails blown away and flying jib boom gone, cargo of turnips from St. Andrews N. B. for Boston.

February 23, 1889, Fishing Schooner *Gardner W. Tarr*, Capt J. T. Barnett, dragged her anchor and went ashore on Harbor Island; was assisted off the 25th by People of Swans Island.

After pages and pages of weather reports the inspector admonishes the keeper to track of the work done on the station.

Keeper Roscoe Chandler took charge on February 1, 1932, and wrote, "I [Chandler] have very bad distress in stomach. Same old trouble." That same month, the inspector ordered Chandler

to clean up his station. Chandler wrote in his log:

Sweeping down tower; putting glycerine on windows, cutting up trees that blowed down, repairing and nailing boards on picket fence, putting glycerine on windows, sweeping up boat house, polishing brass in tower, cleaning lens, scraping on kitchen floor, cleaning and polishing steel under lens, polishing the extinguisher, scraping on floor, scraping loose paint off ceiling in kitchen.

February 11-12, ... not able to do any work on account of stomach trouble ...

In the July 1940 log, Keeper Chandler crossed out "Department of Commerce" and wrote "Treasury Department U.S. Coast Guard." He entered the Coast Guard as a BM1 (Boatswain's Mate First Class).

Keepers at Eagle Island

John Ball, a former ship captain, took over as keeper at Eagle Island on May 11, 1883. He replaced A. P. Sweetland, who had been keeper since November 1871. Keeper Sweetland took sick on March 15, 1883, and one of his children wrote in the keeper's journal: "The keeper (father) is sick, had Dr. here from Castine brought by the Revenue Cutter, *Levi Woodbury*." After visits from three different doctors, Sweetland died of heart disease on April 18, 1883. His remains were taken to Camden for burial on April 19.[41]

In the mid-1800s, Bangor served as one of America's leading lumber ports; between 1835 and 1885, more than eight billion board feet of lumber were shipped out of Bangor and the area.[42] To guide ships into the Penobscot River and on to Bangor, a lighthouse was established on the east end of Eagle Island at the eastern entrance to Penobscot Bay in 1838. Although the tower was modified in 1858 to accommodate a Fresnel lens, the original tower (above) survives today. (Courtesy of U.S. Coast Guard)

John Ball had served as keeper for 15 years when he was replaced by his son Howard, who also served 15 years. John remained at the station until his death at age 82. Sickness and death were a continual theme at this lighthouse. In July 1902, Keeper Howard Ball reported several visits from Dr. Noyes and Dr. Wasgatt of Stonington to care for seven-year-old Agnes. Agnes died on July 7 and was buried in Hancock. On July 15, 1903, the doctor was sent for to tend Mrs. Ball. Her condition was serious, and they "left the station at 1 o'clock P.M. to carry wife to the E.M.G. Hospital to have an operation performed for appendicitis." On February 1, 1910, son Elmer was sent to the Waldo County Hospital. Keeper Ball was called to his side on February 16; on February 22 Elmer died, and Keeper Ball returned to Eagle Island on February 23.[43]

Tragedy struck again in January 1913 when Keeper Ball caught pneumonia after assisting a fishing vessel during a storm. He died within a week and was buried at Hancock.[44]

Edward S. Farren was appointed keeper in March 1913. His term ended when he was transferred to the Fort Point Light Station in 1919. He was replaced by Charles W. Allen, who kept a very detailed log of his activities on Eagle Island. One of Allen's first projects was to clean up the wood shed and to fill it with wood he sawed on a sawing machine. He also cleaned out the hen house and worked on his boat. As spring approached, he prepared his garden for planting and cleaned up the grounds, carting away brush and burning dead grass. In May, Allen planted oats, peas, and potatoes, as well as a flower garden. He whitewashed the tower and cellar walls and painted the tower dome and dwelling. Painting continued through the summer months. On May 17 Allen noted the boats heading off to begin the fishing season. In addition to fish, Allen ate clams and lobsters. He also kept pigs, which he slaughtered and prepared for salting.[45]

Keeper Allen and his family often entertained friends and family and sometimes went visiting off the Island. During the summer, he recorded visitors calling at the station. July duties included mowing; August meant getting in the hay, hauling in the oats, and blueberrying. School began on August 25. Potatoes were dug, apples gathered, and winter cabbage collected in early October. By mid-November, it was time to put on the outside windows. On November 27 Allen reported, "Elsie was married Thanksgiving, went to wedding reception in evening."[46]

In January 1920, Keeper Allen reported killing all his roosters and dressing them as well as spending a week cutting ice. Then seasonal duties began again with cutting and hauling wood in February. Year-round duties included cleaning brass, hauling coal, and performing general maintenance on all station buildings and implements.[47]

On August 4, 1920, Keeper Allen took his wife to Northwest Harbor. The change in penmanship in the log makes it apparent that Mrs. Allen had been recording the log entries. She returned on August 21 with a baby boy. On August 26, Allen recorded 50 callers at the station. On February 8, 1922, he took Beulah to school in New Hampshire. In March, many family members, including Allen himself, came down with flu. On July 14, 1922, Allen noted that a sea plane passed over the island. On April 6, 1923, the Allens listened to the first radio concert on Eagle Island. In June, the Allens' baby boy underwent an operation and died a few weeks later. After burial in Stonington on June 29, Allen noted "A month full of sorrow for us all" and pasted the child's obituary in the logbook: "Allen—Eagle Island Light Station, June 27, Erland, son of Mr. and Mrs. Charles W. Allen, aged 2 years, 10 months, 20 days." At the end of December, Allen concluded the year, stating, "1923 at a close after bringing deep sorrow to us all."[48]

Beginning in 1926, Allen recorded that he and his family "Went to Church by

PART IV. Keepers: Who They Were, How They Lived, What They Said

Charles W. Allen (above) was a career lighthouse keeper. He was appointed second assistant keeper at Boon Island in 1907.[50] Here he is pictured at Marshall Point, where he served from 1933 to 1946. (Courtesy of St. George Historical Society)

radio." In September he took daughter Viola away to begin school. In September 1927, Allen's wife and children moved to Deer Isle for the school year, although they returned for visits on many weekends and keeper Allen occasionally joined them for meals. A new baby arrived on April 4, 1928. During Mrs. Allen's trips off the island, her husband said he performed the housework and cared for the baby.[49]

More planes were noted in 1930, and on August 17 one actually landed on the island. That Christmas, mail was dropped to the station from a flying machine. On August 19, 1931, Allen received word that he was to be transferred to Doubling Point Light Station. He was replaced by Frank Earl Bracey, Jr., who had previously served at Seguin. Bracey kept the Eagle Island station from 1931 to 1945.[51]

Keepers on Curtis Island

In 1875, Curtis Island was described as "about 7 acres, rocky with spruce trees and grass" with areas devoted to a garden and corn. The "tower is stone, octagonal sheathed outside with shingles whitewashed." A steamboat company had given the keeper a horn to use in foggy weather.[52] In October 1882, the inspector provided a small hand bell to ring in case of fog.[53]

In 1889, the 1835 rubble masonry dwelling was replaced by a frame house built on the same foundation.[54] According to the May 2, 1889, log entry of Keeper Henry Wiley, Captain Nickerson, the lighthouse inspector, arrived on the lighthouse steamer *Myrtle* with men and materials to build a new dwelling house, barn, boathouse, and boat. On June 1, Keeper Wiley reported that the new house would be plastered soon, that the trimmings on the barn were finished, and that the boathouse and slip were about half-finished. On June 27, the work completed, the crew left the station for Boston and Portland. Seven years later, Captain Nickerson returned on *Myrtle* with material for a new tower. On May 11, 1896, the lantern was removed from the old tower and the light was exhibited that night from a temporary tower 40 feet east of the old one. On June 24 Keeper Wiley reported, "The masons and machinists got through with their work today & left the station for their homes; the carpenters left the station Monday morning for Southport." One month later, on July 24, Wiley received a notice from the inspector that the [fourth-order] lens would be "moved to and exhibited from the new tower on or about the 30th and to notify the Dept. when the provisions of the order are carried out." On July 30, with the paint still drying on the new tower, the light was exhibited. On September 5, 1896, Captain Nickerson arrived on *Myrtle* with a new fog bell

Today the well-protected harbor at Camden is a haven for recreational and pleasure craft. In the nineteenth century the harbor served two major Maine industries—lime and shipbuilding. Originally called "Negro Island," Curtis Island[55] was located on the south side of the main entrance to Camden Harbor, on the west side of West Penobscot Bay. The first lighthouse (left), located at the south end of the island, was under construction in 1835 when its first keeper, Henry K. M. Bower, was hired to "care for the oil and other public property at the Lighthouse, until the latter shall be finished and lit up."[56] Keeper Bower was also given permission to cut down trees on the island for wood and to cultivate any land that was suitable.[57] Completion of the lighthouse was delayed until the spring of 1836. (National Archives photo # 26-LG-4-58) Curtis Island Light Station (above) in 1892. (Courtesy of U.S. Coast Guard)

and materials for a new bell tower. Two days later the log reported that "Henry Wiley, Keeper of this station died this day at two o'clock A.M." John F. Wiley took over as interim keeper until Howard M. Gilley was transferred from his post at Deer Island Thorofare Light to Curtis Island, arriving on October 8, 1896.[58]

Forty-five years at Marshall Point Light

Charles C. Skinner was appointed keeper of Marshall Point Light on September 1, 1874. He remained at that post until May 7, 1919—a record 45 years of service at a single station. Four years into his tenure, Skinner noted in his log on March 12, 1878, that "Lampist Johnson was here today to change the lamps so as to use kerosene oil, but the lamps not fitting the lens, had to postpone the change. They left a barrel of kerosene oil from the steamer *Myrtle*." Johnson returned on April 16 and installed kerosene lamps that fit.[59]

Skinner noted many strandings in the area of his station. On October 28, 1884, "A fin-back whale stranded on Mosquito Island last night. Sixty seven feet in length." On February 10, 1886, "Steamer *Cambridge* was wrecked on Old Man Ledge at 4:45 A.M. Passengers and crew all saved & landed on Allen Island where they were taken off by Steamer

Dallas this forenoon and taken to Rockland. The *Cambridge* is a total loss, is fast breaking up." On February 11, 1886, "there are some forty small schooners and from three to four hundred men at the wreck of the steamer *Cambridge*, saving what freight they can. Estimated that there was $100,000 worth on board."[60]

On April 1, 1887, "Captain Ambrose Heal of schooner *Leaping Water* arrived at this place today. He says after the schooner struck Old Gilley that they took to the boat and having lost their oars, were blown to sea; but they managed by the aid of a piece of board to steer the boat so as to land on Matinicus Island. One of the men was

Marshall Point (below) before a new keeper's dwelling was built in 1895. The tiny building at right was the "privy." The larger building behind it was a workshop. Captain Skinner made shoes there. After the main house was struck by lightning in 1893, this workshop was moved to a location near the entrance to the grounds, and the family lived in it until the new dwelling was completed. (Courtesy of St. George Historical Society)

quite badly frozen. There were three men besides the Captain."

On January 21, 1889, Skinner noted,

Blew most a gale from NE during last night and snowed. Is more easterly today; blowing a gale with snow and sleet. Sea is very rough. At high water the sea would clash against the glass of the lantern and would toss rocks weighing tons about near the base of the tower; has not been such a sea on the point the past fifteen years.[61]

On September 20, 1892, Skinner noted receiving a "Circular from Secretary of the Treasury relative to burning any bedding, garbage or other articles that may be washed ashore from vessels sailing from foreign ports infected with cholera."

On April 4, 1898, a signal tower was erected at the station and "a representative of the New England Telephone Co. here hiring men to dig holes for telephone poles." Apparently instructions for the signal tower were relayed by telephone. On February 18, 1902, Skinner noted, "Hurricane signal ordered up last night, but lines were down and did not get message until today."[62]

Captain Charles C. Skinner (left) was keeper at Marshall Point Light Station for 45 years (1874-1919). This new keeper's dwelling (below) on Marshall Point was completed on November 2, 1895. Earlier that year, Keeper Skinner recorded in his journal "Heavy thunder showers passed over here at 1 o'clock this morning. The dwelling house at this station was struck by lightning and one chimney, the roof, one window, and three rooms badly shattered, lightning entered from rooms besides the cellar, no one seriously injured. Two other houses between this and the village were damaged by lightning." Although repairs were made to the old dwelling, orders were received on July 19 to vacate the old dwelling and on July 23 workers began to tear it down. (Photos courtesy of St. George Historical Society)

PART IV. Keepers: Who They Were, How They Lived, What They Said

Character building at Egg Rock

Egg Rock Light Station, situated on a rock island at the entrance to Frenchman Bay, was built in response to the increasing maritime traffic in the bay caused in part by the growth of summer tourism in and around Bar Harbor. In 1875, the year of the station's construction, the inspector reported that "the Island (or Rock) has about 5 acres at low water and 2½ at high water—highest point at Station say 35 feet. About ½ an acre has light soil, the rest rock."[63]

The first entry of the keeper's log at Egg Rock Light Station indicated that Ambrose J. Wasgatt came to the station on September 25, 1875. On November 1 he wrote, "Light was shown from this station tonight; the light is red & should be seen a distance of fourteen miles."[64]

The following spring Wasgatt's log entry for March 21 indicated a

> Gale of wind from South East; the sea washing all over the Island, washing the boat house away with coal & provisions in the same, washing away the bell house, breaking machinery to the bell & moving the bell tower thirty feet to the N.W., breaking in the windows on the southeast side & flooding the dwelling house with water to such an extent that the oil butts was moved from three benches, also two doors broken upon on the inside of the house, the island being swept of anything movable.[65]

The 1876 *Annual Report* noted the same storm: "During a gale on the 21st of March, 1876, the sea washed over the rock, carrying away the fuel shed and moving the bell-tower some 30 feet. The windows of the dwelling were broken in on the sea-side, and the dwelling flooded to such an extant that the oil-butts were moved from their benches."

Bad weather frequently prevented the keeper from leaving the island. In November 1884 the keeper reported, "this has been the roughest month I have seen for the past nine years. I have only been away from the station three times during the month of November."[66]

Another storm was reported on December 28, 1887: "East to S.E. with heavy gale rain & snow and large sea at 11:45 P.M. Sea breaking all over the Rock, breaking the side of Bell Tower, breaking machinery and moving tower off of butments, washed away bridge and parts of boathouse and flooding same. Out house and hen house and in fact everything moveable was washed away."[67]

On October 24, 1894, Keeper Lewis F. Sawyer described a shipwreck:

> At about 8 P.M. the fishing schooner *Amy Hamsen* of Boston Mass., Capt K. S. Gayton, ran ashore on the rocks about ½ mile S.W. from this station, remained there until about 4 A.M. of the 23rd & then floated off, filled & sank. The crew of 18 left in their dories & reached Bar Harbor in safety, saved nothing but their clothing.[68]

Sawyer's son, Herber, succeeded him as keeper when Sawyer was transferred to Bear Island in November 1899. (The assistant keeper position Herber had held was abolished.) On Christmas Eve, the younger Sawyer discovered wreckage "about 1/4 mile S.W. from Light which on investigation proved to be broken deck plank, spars and cordage of pinky *Julia Ann*, a total wreck, nothing was seen or heard from her at the station, so nothing being known of fate of crew or cause of wreck . . . ." A few days later the owner of the vessel arrived to investigate and they determined "that she probably struck ½ mile S.W./W. from Light, her two dories were completely smashed. By this and by position of anchors & cables no attempt was made to save themselves (i.e. the crew) or the schooner crew . . . undoubtably drunk."[69]

Heavy seas on the night of January 29, 1900, "broke in boat house by breaking in shutter at foot of doors, and washed away some loose articles around wood pile . . . but did no further damage beyond washing away some wood piled up above ordinary tide way." At midmorning on March 2 the sea broke in boat house with that and succeeding ones completely washing it to pieces so that by 12 n., nothing but the roof remained on the beach, all its contents gone including boat compass and some stores, saving the station boat and one belonging to myself (the keeper) have secured them as well as circumstances permits ... From 10:30 A.M. to 12:30 P.M. sea very heavy coming up around house and bell tower but did no damage there, also washed away platform in front of oil house. Saved most of the material belonging to the War Department, putting same in their building.[70]

The keeper noted at the end of the log for March 1900, "This has proved to be an exceptionally blowy and rough month. One gale and heavy sea succeeding another in quick succession, especially the high tide and heavy sea of the 2nd inst. being the worst for 24 years as the 'Records' of the station shows." In 1901, the keeper complained of perpetual leaks, "water standing on floor of watch room, on tower stairs and on floor of narrow hall connecting S.E. and S.W. sleeping rooms; the water in the hall coming in over door connecting this (hall) with room at base of tower.

Also new chimney leaks in S.E. sleeping room."[71]

On September 26, 1901, keeper Sawyer "received notice on this date that on or about October 15, 1901, the characteristic of the Light at this station will be changed from fixed red to flashing red every five seconds, and the intensity from a fifth to a fourth order, with a request to notify the Inspector's Office when the changes are carried into effect." On October 1, the tender *Myrtle* landed the material and on October 14, Machinist Clifford installed the new fourth-order apparatus. The new light went into commission on October 18; Machinist Clifford stayed on station until October 24. The keeper's trials with the new equipment began immediately. On October 25, he reported that "During the first part of the [previous] night the 'Light' was erratic, but soon got it in order." On October 26: "During the first part [of the night], the light was difficult to run correctly overall, I hardly leaving it until 12, turning the lens by hand a large part of the time. It has been giving more or less trouble every night since being put in operation."

On October 27, Keeper Sawyer reported, "Have succeeded in getting the light apparatus in good running order." The next night he tried adding another weight to the clockwork

Egg Rock Light Station was substantially altered around 1899; the roof was raised to add a second story. (Courtesy of U.S. Coast Guard)

mechanism which controlled the revolution on the lens, providing a temporary fix.

The lens continued its erratic behavior until on November 9, the keeper discovered

the lens badly cracked in several places, the longest one in an irregular form extending nearly from bulls eye to frame, the other extending through one segment. Visited the lantern at 8:00 P.M. 11:30 and 12:00, going up with the second lamp to change; a few minutes later, just as I started from the watch room for lantern, I heard something crack sounding like metal falling & striking metal, so suspect that is what it was, for on reaching the lantern, I quickly noticed it. The light was burning normal & I can't account for or see any cause for breakage. Have informed the Inspector and Engineer by letter of the fact, sending the letter by Mr. Bunker (a lobster catcher).[72]

On November 17, a lampist named J. H. Johnson and two machinists arrived to look over the lens. Apparently they found nothing inherently wrong, but the keeper continued to have problems with it. On January 1, 1902, he reported,

On visiting the light at 4:40 A.M. found the lens stopped by the appearance of the weights; think that it had been stopped about 1 hour. Visited it during the night at 8:15 & 11:30 P.M., 1:00 & 2:00 A.M. being in excellent order. Put on an additional weight making it work all right

with the same number (i.e. 6) of weights; is working in good order now (7 P.M.)[73]

On February 3, the keeper "made a thorough overhauling of Illuminating Apparatus, finding it all in good order, with the exception of connecting shaft showing wear, where ball bearing plates strike it, thus showing some side motion, yet showing no apparent reason for lens slowing down or stopping." He checked again on April 12 and "found no reason for stoppage."[74]

Some of his frustrations may have been relieved with notification on May 12 that an assistant keeper had once again been assigned to his station. On July 1, Clifford M. Robbins and family arrived. In late October, Robbins was transferred and on November 2, Stephen F. Flood arrived to take his place.[75]

The lens continued to stop periodically and the keeper concluded it was "unreliable." On January 6, 1903, a mechanical problem of a different sort arose when the wire on the fog bell broke and put the bell out of commission. Until the machinist arrived to fix the problem ten days later, the fog bell had to be rung by hand. In May 1904, the fog bell was replaced with a Daboll trumpet operated by steam. On July 9, the inspector instructed the keeper to put the new signal into operation. On July 10, the keeper reported, "Put trumpet in operation this

A.M. to see if it would work properly. Found that valve to reed box too tight; after running a few minutes, the lever that operates the valve broke thus making the trumpet useless. Valve would not open or close automatically." On July 11, the keeper notified the inspector and engineer of his difficulties; by then he had put the bell back in operation.[76]

On January 7, 1905, the keeper reported, "Sea coming up over plank walk and a small quantity going in whistle house through crack in door. Plank walk would have washed away had it not been fastened. Found that the leak in dwelling comes in through the roof. From about 10:30 A.M. to 12 noon, could not get trumpet to blow, finally putting in a spare reed, which in so doing let water out of horn (or trumpet) which probably was the trouble."[77]

The keeper and his assistant received salary increases that went into effect January 23, 1905. Sawyer's additional $24 brought his annual salary to $624. Flood received an $80 increase, bringing his salary to $480. In late August, Flood transferred to the station at Whitehead; his replacement, John E. Parrington,[78] arrived with his family on the tender *Geranium* on September 28.

In December 1905, Keeper Sawyer reported that the kerosene oil was of such poor quality that the "lamps will

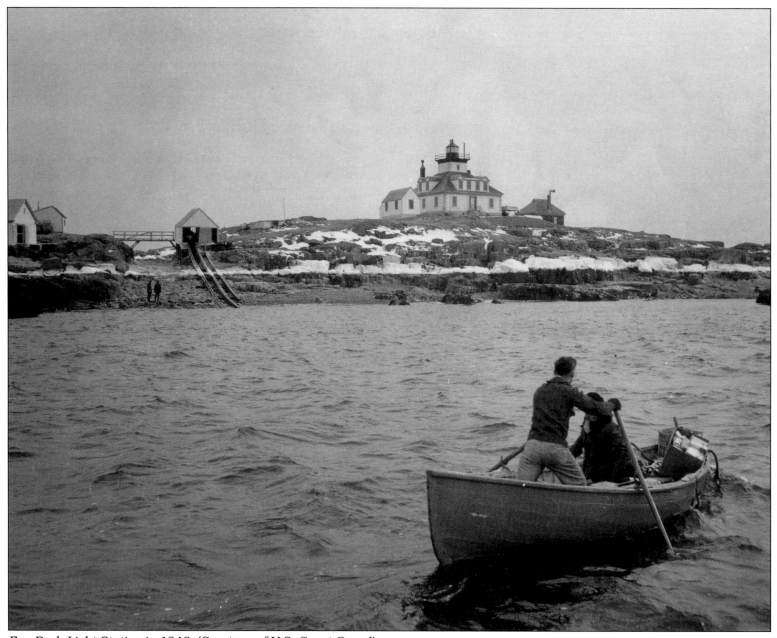

Egg Rock Light Station in 1946. (Courtesy of U.S. Coast Guard)

PART IV. Keepers: Who They Were, How They Lived, What They Said

not burn more than two hours before getting low." He could not see any difference, however, in "the running of engines to fog signal." The fog signal acted up again on February 6, 1907:

> This day we have overhauled air compressor to right engine, taking out piston, all valves, cleaning and adjusting them, running engine to try its working which it does not do sufficiently, only pumping about ½ its usual quantity of air but enough to run the 'whistle'. Engine does not start up good, can find no apparent cause for either not working properly.[79]

On February 1, 1908, Keeper Sawyer described another storm:

> Very strong S.E. gale snow & rain. 7 P.M. to 11:30 very heavy sea washing completely over the Rock breaking in the two (2) shutters and one (1) window and one pane of glass from the other window on seaward side of whistle house continually flooding the same, the water coming in around window, door, and through water exhaust pipe trench. The drip pans and other small articles were floating around, also ripping off shingles of hip, washing away ladder & box the weights run down in to bell tower, washing away sink drain, 20 ft. of railing to plank walk, water conductor of S. side of dwelling, moved privy nearly down to boathouse, washed away platform and walk at boathouse and slip, wood & some lumber belonging to the keeper and lumber belonging to Uncle Sam. In fact everything moveable was washed away. Also

raised up one stringer of boat slip 8 inches for a distance of about 50 ft. Keeper on duty in whistle house. Asst. left at 8 A.M. for Bar Harbor to obtain mail, supplies and medicine, no chance to return.[80]

On July 27, 1908, the keeper reported a visit by the lighthouse tender *Mayflower* with Oscar S. Straus, Secretary of Commerce and Labor, and Rear Admiral A. Marix, Naval Secretary of the Light-House Board, on board. "Station was inspected by the Admiral who seemed pleased with the condition of the station, saying it had a very neat appearance." The keeper also filled a Board member's request for fish bait.[81]

In October 1909, Assistant Keeper Parrington requested a transfer to Whitehead Island Light Station and received it. Frank B. Ingalls was his replacement. In March 1911, the keepers faced a serious water shortage, requiring them to boat water from Bar Harbor to fill their cisterns and run the fog signal.

Keeper Sawyer did not indicate whether it was with relief or sadness that he received his transfer to Bear Island Light Station, which took effect March 1, 1912.[82]

Lighthouses as tourist attractions

On May 21, 1821, a number of owners of coasting vessels and Boothbay Harbor town officials presented a petition to the local customs collector: "The undersigned persons, interested in the navigation of Boothbay harbour, beg leave respectfully to represent that they have considered the subject of a site for a light house at Boothbay and are of opinion that Burnt Island near the enterance of said harbour is the most eligible situation for a light house."[83] Boothbay Harbor was a busy fishing port in those days. The petition was granted and the tower was built on Burnt Island that year.

On October 17, 1821, Collector Ilsley reported to Fifth Auditor Pleasonton that the tower at Burnt Island would soon be ready for lighting. "Mr. [Winslow] Lewis is now fitting the Light Houses with Lamps, Reflectors, etc., and will have them completed in a few days, and at the same time will have them furnished with Oil."[84] Joshua B. Cushing was appointed the first keeper. He lit the lamps in the lantern on November 9, 1821.[85]

The frontis of the first Burnt Island logbook was inscribed, "Journal of passing events at the Burnt Island Light Station commenced July 1, 1872 by James A. McCobb Light-Keeper."[86] James

McCobb was a descendant of the prominent family that led the settlement of Boothbay Harbor in 1729.[87]

Almost immediately, on July 7, Keeper McCobb wrote of the "many strangers looking around the station." By 1872 Maine had become a popular summer resort for people who could afford to build cottages there, as well as for patrons who stayed at pleasant onshore resorts. Resort promoters used the term "exclusive" to indicate that their wealthy clientele would have no contact with the middle- and lower-class tourists who took day trips to the beaches or bought tickets on excursion boats.[88] The steamship companies, however, saw a growing market of less affluent day-trippers, who enjoyed cruising among the many islands and stopping to picnic and walk about. A lighthouse was splendid entertainment —a novelty, and a tour of the premises cost nothing. The 1853 *Instructions for Lighthouse Keepers of the United States* stated that the keeper

> is expected to be polite to strangers, in showing the premises at such hours as do not interfere with the proper duties of his office; it being expressly understood that strangers shall not be admitted to the

Steamer Sebenoa *(facing page) of the Eastern Steamship Company. (Courtesy of Maine Maritime Museum, Bath, Maine)*

In 1857 the wooden keeper's dwelling at Burnt Island (below) was replaced by the one-and-a-half-story cottage in the photograph. The Lewis lamps were replaced in 1858 with a fourth-order Fresnel lens.[89] The station is shown here ca. 1859. (Courtesy of Ken Black, Shore Village Museum)

PART IV. Keepers: Who They Were, How They Lived, What They Said

light-room after sunset. Not more than three persons shall have access to the light-room at one and the same time during the day, and no stranger visiting the light-house shall be permitted to handle any part of the machinery or apparatus.

On July 4, 1874, McCobb again noted the "many strangers around visiting the station. Many yachts—both steam and sail, carrying excursions from island to island in the outer harbor during the day."

He repeated his comments on July 23:

Many strangers visiting the station to see the light, it being something new to most of them. Three boats a day from

Bath to Squirrel Island, making their trips with passengers. From six to eight steam boats per day are passing this station, showing the increasing importance of a light station at this place, and also that some fog signal should be established here.

The following summer McCobb's comments were in the same vein:

June 24, 1875, Many strangers from abroad tenting about on the Islands and visiting from place to place.

June 26, Many strangers visiting the station to see the light, Harbor and Bay full of pleasure yachts the whole day through . . .

July 8, Many strangers visiting the station to see the light. Quite good sort

of people. Many steamers now moving about us. Two boats a day now from here to Bath.

July 15, Hottest day of the season. . . . Sailing parties in all directions about the Harbor. Many of them visiting this station to see the light. . . .

July 17, . . . Many strangers around. Mostly pleasure parties. Three steamers a day now from Boothbay to Bath passing this station each way besides a fleet of fishing steamers running to Maddox's Porgie Factory.

When summer came around again in 1876, the visitor influx continued. Not many days passed before the steady flow of visitors began to tell on Keeper McCobb:

August 13, 1876, Dry hot weather continues. All who can are leaving the cities and country back of us and coming to the sea shore to enjoy the sea breezes. Very many are visiting this station daily. Some days more than one hundred have called and in fact so many that they are becoming a real burden, taking up half my time to wait upon them.

The Fourth of July was apparently quieter than usual in 1877, but by July 14 hot weather had set in.

Samosset House, Mouse Island, full of company, said now to be doing a rushing business. Pleasure seekers running to this place and to that place to find where the most fun is, and the most amusement located and though not much fun for them here at the station, yet we get as

Burnt Island Light Station in 1885. (National Archives photo # 26-LG-1-48)

PART IV. Keepers: Who They Were, How They Lived, What They Said

many of them as we want and in fact, a few more.

July 22, . . . Much company around visiting the station. Some days occupied most of my time not engaged in work about the light house in waiting upon them. Sometimes almost make themselves troublesome.

On August 6 Keeper McCobb repeated this complaint and added,

sometimes I almost wish those summer resorts had been in Tophet [Tibet?] before they were located so near this station.

August 17, . . . Many strangers visiting the station. Shall be truly glad when it is time for them to leave here and go to their homes for at times they do trouble me very much.

The Fourth of July in 1878 "passed off pleasantly. . . Stayed at home all day waiting upon company most of the time who had come on to see the place. "

On July 19 James McCobb celebrated his 62nd birthday.

July 31, Dog days has set in in good earnest. . . . Much company about us now, a little more than we want of strangers coming by night as well as by day to see the station and lantern of Light House, and wanting too to see the light after it is lighted up at night, though in that they have not yet succeeded for no one has yet been inside of Lantern after dark except myself or one of my family to look after the light since I have been at the station, neither will I allow it otherwise.

By August 29 his patience had run out:

. . . Much company here today to see the Light House and to make themselves troublesome generally as they could. Wish the Board would issue one more regulation, and that would be that no more strangers could be admitted into the lantern under no consideration.

His sigh of relief can almost be heard on September 9:

Cool pleasant Sept weather. Strangers who have been stopping through the hot weather on the Islands around us have nearly all left. The cool weather has

Fort Point Light Station was another popular summer tourist destination in Maine. Many escaped hot cities to enjoy the cooler climate along the coast. A large hotel named Wassawinkeag, "birthplace of seals," was built 50 feet north of the Fort Point Light Station. An 1875 inspection report noted that the resort boasted 100 rooms and that excursionists "travel and walk over the grounds"of the light station, leading the inspector to suggest that it be enclosed by a fence. On June 7, 1898, the keeper at Fort Point reported, "Alarm was given at 10 P.M. that the Fort Point Hotel was on fire. The building fell at 10 minutes of 11 P.M. It was totally destroyed."[90] (National Archives photo # 26-LG-2-14B)

started them, and the keeper of this station is much pleased with the change the cool weather has brought about.

McCobb extols an unusually cool June in 1879:

Summer company not so plenty as usual and that is pleasing to the keeper. Would rather have cold rough weather than so much rough company.

By the end of July, the weather had turned fine.

Much company, mostly strangers coming to the station and this time quite civil. Hope they begin to think about other folks has rights as well as themselves.

By September 6 he was feeling cranky again. By late September, his patience had given out:

. . . summer company have now all left the Island and gone to the D—— for anything I care. Wish they might stay away and not trouble us anymore. Am fond of company; still would much rather a large portion of pleasure seekers in summer would stay away.

By 1880 his annoyance was beginning to tell on Keeper McCobb:

August 5, . . . Much company around. Twelve boats with from three to twelve persons in each have landed on the Island today to see and inspect the Light House, all strangers, and to make themselves generally troublesome. Do wish that Government would stop all strangers from landing at the station, they are

perfectly horrid. They are a nuisance all through. May be found fault with for speaking so of them but can't help it.

August 8, Strangers came to station today to look through the Light House but it was not opened to them, nor has it been for last two years or more on Sundays to visitors. So much company around, feel as if I would like to have Sunday to myself. They do not appear to like it. Many of them acting as if I was here just [to] wait upon them and for nothing else. More and more of them coming every year to the islands. Soon will have to have regular hours of the day for company to be admitted.

James McCobb obviously took great pride in his light and was very conscientious about his duties. His wife had died in March of 1877, and McCobb must have found the loneliness very trying. On October 7, 1880, he "sent his resignation to the Superintendent of this L.H. District to take effect soon as his successor can be appointed. Owing to poor health, the keeper does not at all times feel able to do the duties required of him at the station. He feels the importance of a good light in all kinds of weather."[91]

Increased visitation became a problem at other lights as well. Eventually the Light-House Board issued more precise instructions, as follows:

INSTRUCTIONS TO KEEPERS: VISITING HOURS AT THE LIGHT STATIONS IN THE FIRST LIGHT HOUSE DISTRICT:

Sunday. On Sundays the light and tower will be closed to all visitors.

Visiting Days. Visitors will be admitted to the light on Tuesdays and Fridays of each week.

Hours, Summer. Visiting will be from 9 A.M. to 12 N., and from 1 P.M. to 6 P.M., June 1 to Sept. 1.

Hours, Winter. Visiting hours will be from 9 A.M. to 12 M., and from 1 P.M. to 4 P.M., Sept. 1 to June 1

Keepers are instructed that due regard should be observed for visitors who may come from long distances, and in such cases, they are hereby authorized to make reasonable exceptions in carrying out these orders, except on Sundays, when the light and tower will be closed to all visitors.

Visitors will not be allowed to enter the lens of a 1st, 2nd, or 3rd order light.[92]

Education at lighthouses

Schools were built in towns in the first half of the nineteenth century, and Maine's first teacher institutes were organized in 1847. Tax support was provided to schools after 1868. But because lighthouses were not located in towns, few lighthouse children had any schooling in the early days other than that provided by their parents. An 1839

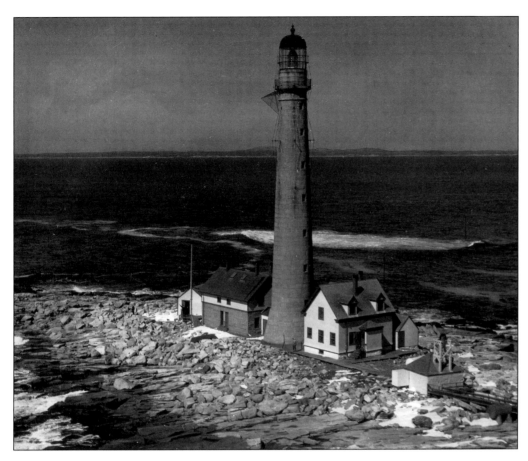

Boon Island in 1944 (Courtesy of U.S. Coast Guard). After education was made compulsory, families on many offshore stations had to make arrangements for their children to live on the mainland during the school year. According to the keepers' column in the Rockland Courier-Gazette, February 6, 1932:

> Assistant Keepers Batty and Dalzell have their families with them this winter, but Keeper H. I. Hutchins has to keep bachelor's hall during the nine months of the school year. Mrs. Hutchins lives at York Beach with the four children in order that they may attend school. The three Batty children are at present boarding with their aunt and going to school at Portland. Needless to say, there is a grand reunion about June 10, as soon as the schools close for the year. Last summer there were 18 of us on the island. Were the days happy? We're telling you![94]

Unpredictable weather would sometimes delay school as it did many other types of trips on and off Boon Island Light Station.

> . . . Keeper Hutchins' wife and children, Second Assistant Gray's wife and children, and Florence and Thornton Batty [First Assistant's children] were awaiting smoother weather so they could go ashore for the beginning of school.
>
> Schools began the 12th of September. Day after day went by, with no chance of getting off the slip. Great white rollers were chasing each other across the slip, the only place where the boats can go off or on the station.[95]

letter to the Secretary of the Treasury is particularly interesting:

> Mr. William Perry, Keeper of the Light at Marshals Point, Maine, has requested me to make the inquiry of you, whether there is any objection to his teaching a small school in the school district where the light is situated, &, I believe in sight of the Light House. It is a day school, & will engage Mr. P. not over six hours each day. I believe Mr. Anderson has told him that, if the Light is in every respect well kept, he could see no objection to his teaching the children in that district. Mr. Perry, being a very prudent & cautious man, wished me to obtain also your opinion. It was the wish of the persons residing in the district that Mr. P. should teach the school.[93]

In the second half of the nineteenth century a handful of light stations provided facilities for teaching keepers' children. Whitehead had its own schoolhouse, and Keeper Isaac Grant taught the children on the island in the

1870s. Later the island school was discontinued.[96] Many stations, however, were located a long distance from regular schools.

In 1898, Fred W. Morong, Keeper of Libby Island Light, requested permission to trade positions with the keeper at Little River, Roscoe G. Johnson, so that his "family of boys" could benefit from better schools. Johnson, who had previously served at Libby Island, favored the exchange because it would bring him a larger salary and place him nearer to his home.[97]

The keeper at Eagle Island Light Station reported to the *Rockland Courier-Gazette*, June 25, 1938:

School here closed June 17 after a successful term taught by Miss Edith Farnsworth. The closing exercises at the schoolhouse were very pleasing. Several from Sunset attended. An interesting contest was carried on between Eagle and Sunset schools. Public school scholarship pins were awarded the winners. Miss Farnsworth went last Saturday to her home at Hull's Cove.[98]

In 1938, special legislation was passed providing for the transportation of keepers' children of school age.[99]

Notable Keeper Marcus Hanna at Cape Elizabeth

Stories of heroism in the line of duty have become an integral part of lighthouse lore. Marcus Hanna, the keeper appointed to Cape Elizabeth light in 1873, was already a hero. Hanna's father was keeper of the light on Franklin Island when Marcus was born in 1842. He spent his first 10 years at that light before he went off to sea. When the Civil War broke out, he did a tour in the U.S. Navy, then joined the 50th Voluntary Infantry of

PART IV. Keepers: Who They Were, How They Lived, What They Said

Marcus Hanna (above) (Courtesy of U.S. Coast Guard)

In 1873 Marcus Hanna became the principal keeper at Cape Elizabeth (facing page). The following year, two new cast-iron towers were completed and the old masonry towers torn down. (National Archives photo # 26-LG-1-62-A2)

In August 1997, the U.S. Coast Guard launched the 175-foot buoy tender USCGC Marcus Hanna *(right), one of the* Keeper *class of tenders, homeported in South Portland, Maine. (Courtesy of U.S. Coast Guard)*

Massachusetts. His bravery under fire while getting water for his company earned him the Congressional Medal of Honor. At war's end he married and spent four years in Bristol, Maine, piloting a small tender supplying a fish market. In 1869 he secured the keeper's position at Pemaquid Light. He and his wife taught at a local school during the winter.[100]

Hanna was transferred to serve as head keeper at Cape Elizabeth in 1873. In January 1885 a fierce midnight gale drove the schooner *Australia* onto the rocks below the lighthouse, again tapping Hanna's willingness to risk his life to save others. In the dim morning light his wife glimpsed the masts of the stricken vessel. The only two survivors, Irving Pierce and William Keller, had tied themselves in the rigging of the foundered ship. Hanna crawled down over the icy rocks as near to the surf as he dared and repeatedly threw a line weighted with a piece of scrap to the stranded mariners. A wave washed over the rocks and engulfed him. He fell, dropping the line. The line had reached the nearer man, who tied it under his armpits. Hanna was able to get another hold and pulled Pierce to shore through the surf. Repeated casts finally reached Keller, whom Hanna, half frozen, valiantly hauled ashore. Fortunately, help arrived just then to carry the three wet and frozen men into the fog signal building and thaw them out.[101]

Following the rescue Inspector A. H. Crowninshield stated that

> . . . The gale which was raging at the time was one of the severest that has been experienced in this vicinity in many years; as it was accompanied by a blinding snowstorm and a temperature as low as from five to ten degrees below zero. . . . I

would respectfully recommend that the Board would express to Mr. Hanna its commendation of his services and of the assistant Keepers who assisted him on this occasion.[102]

Several months later, the U.S. Life-Saving Service awarded Marcus Hanna the Gold Lifesaving Medal.[103] On July 18, 1885, First District Inspector A. H. Crowninshield

> . . . presented the gold medal awarded to Mr. Marcus A. Hanna, Keeper of Cape Elizabeth Light Station . . . Some forty persons, including the Collector of the Port, the Postmaster and other Government officials were invited to witness the ceremony, which was held on board the Light House tender "Iris." The party having assembled on board, I proceeded to Cape Elizabeth, where Mr. Hanna and his assistants were taken on board; and the medal presented with suitable remarks by myself. Refreshments were then served, and the party returned in the tender to the city.[104]

The wreck of *Australia* became additional ammunition in the argument for a lifesaving station on Cape Elizabeth, which was established in 1887.

Keeper dismissals

Although many keepers were replaced with political appointees when administrations changed in Washington, some keepers were removed for neglecting their duties or for cheating the government. Early keeper fraud generally involved the expensive oil or other supplies furnished to each station.

In 1804 Jonathan Delano replaced John Polerecsky as keeper of the Sequin Island Lighthouse. Delano had been at his station for several decades when, in 1825, Collector Isaac Ilsley reported,

> I have lately been informed that Jonathan Delano, Keeper of Seguin Light House had fraudulently disposed of Lamp Wicks from that establishment, the evidence of the fraud is in the affidavit of Lewis Demot herewith enclosed, and which I believe to be true. The Wicks are now in this Office and are good and not damaged, or refuse as said to be by Spencer, son of the Keeper.
>
> About two years since complaints were made of the fraudulent conduct of Mr. Delano, the particulars of which are contained in eighteen depositions, transmitted with my letter to you the 20th December 1822.
>
> It will be seen by the Annual Statement of the two last years, that the consumption of Oil at Seguin Light House with 14 lamps has been 167 Gallons more than consumed at Portland Head Light House with 15 lamps all lit

up in both light Houses. It would appear from this difference in the consumption that the oil must have been wasted or improperly disposed of at Seguin, of this however I have no other evidence than the Keepers returns.[105]

Ilsley attached Demot's statement regarding the disposal of the wicks.

> I, Lewis Demot of Scarborough in the State of Maine, testify and say, that on the 24th April last I was on the Island of Seguin, and at the Light House, and went into the Dwelling House with the intention of selling to the family some tin ware; while in the house trading with the woman (whom I supposed to be the Light House Keeper's Wife) for some of my tin wares, for which she was to pay in rags and truck in the house, I observed her cutting up with her scissors some Lamp Wicks, I told her she need not do that, for I should sell them all together at the Paper Mills, and there was no necessity for cutting; Spencer, her son, then brought forward a parcel of lamp wicks; about thirty six dozen, said they were refuse, and gave them to his mother to sell. She then weighed them and sold them to me for three cents a pound. Mr. Delano the Light House Keeper was present all this time, heard the conversation and saw the disposition of the lamp wicks, and made no objections to the sale of them. The same thirty six dozen of lamp wicks I now have and are here produced.[107]

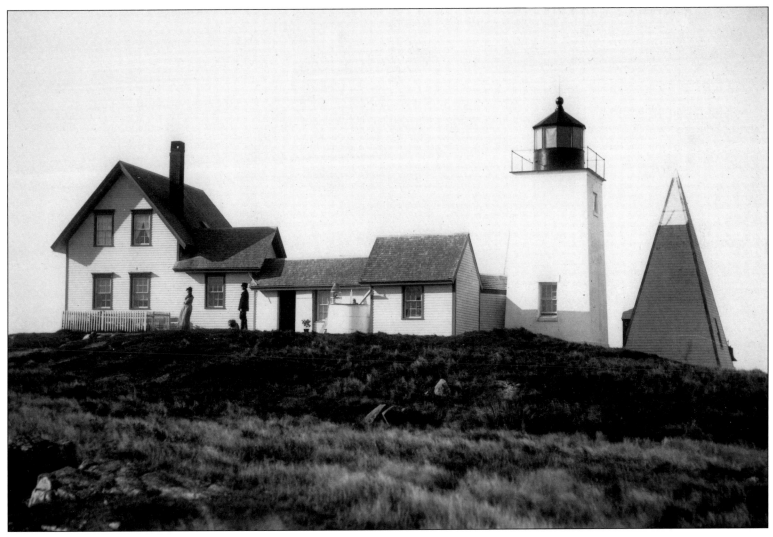

The Light-House Board was able to track its keepers through regular inspections. Inspectors generally submitted reports of incompetence or inappropriate behavior that led to keeper dismissals. On July 18, 1872, Inspector Selfridge wrote Light-House Board Chairman Joseph Henry:

I would recommend very strongly that new Keepers be appointed for Nash's Island Light . . . The Keeper . . . has been there seven years & yet he has no Knowledge of the regulations, is shiftless and indifferent. He acknowledged that contrary to express regulations he was in the habit of lighting his light with matches. His light has been out more than once. In February last for an hour or more, and he asked the Keeper of Narraguagus light not to report it . . .[106]

(Nash Island Light Station in National Archives photo # 26-LG-4-22)

On March 2, 1825, Jonathan Delano was replaced with John Salter.[108]

Indifference to duty was also the complaint against the keeper of the Grindle Point Lighthouse. Inspector Mayo reported,

. . . I had been watching the light during the night for two hours—it burned dimly all that time and at 3 a.m. had not the brilliancy of an ordinary family lamp, at four miles distance. The entire service of this lamp by Mr. Gilkey, the principal keeper, is faulty, he manifests no interest in his duty—talks much and from his own story to me I judge that he spends most of his time at the Grocery and post office. He was going to those places when I landed; but seeing the Inspector's boat returned. I found the "Morning Routine" neglected & that it was habitual for him to do this. . . . the personal appearance of Mr. Gilkey and the look of the Government property under his charge convince me that Mr. Gilkey is an unfit man for the post of Light House Keeper, either principal or assistant. I therefore recommend his removal.[109]

Several other keepers were found wanting in October 1872. First Assistant Keeper E. B. Davis at Monhegan was absent from his watch in the lantern on the evening of October 17, and apparently made a habit of such absences.[113] Mayo recommended the dismissal of Keeper Enoch Dyer at Cape

Untidiness or neglect of the station property was also cause for dismissal. Inspector Batcheller reported that during a regular inspection, he found the Goat Island Light Station (above) "in indifferent condition in regard to neatness and the dwelling absolutely dirty from top to bottom. I pointed this out to the Keeper and warned him that he must do better." On the next inspection, Batcheller

. . . found the whole station in a very untidy and dirty condition. Although it was 10:30 a.m. when I landed, the curtains had not been hung and the lantern and tower had not, apparently, been swept or dusted for weeks. The lens was covered with lint and dust, the reflector was dirty and the plate glass of the lantern was streaked with dirt and spotted with fly specks and paint. The lamps and covered way only were in fair condition.[110]

(Courtesy of U.S. Coast Guard)

In some cases a keeper was not dismissed for untidiness but was transferred to a less appealing station. Inspector James K. Cogswell reported,

At my inspection of West Quoddy Head Light Station, Maine, . . . I found the station in an unsatisfactory condition.

In the whistle house the boilers were stained with dirt and dusty, the steel rods of the engines were somewhat rusty and covered with dust.

The paint work of the interior of the tower showed neglect, and in the lantern room the lens was dusty, brass work greasy, and greasy rags about. The walks, and fence about the grounds, were in poor condition.

During the past year the dwelling was enlarged, but neither the keeper or assistant occupy their parlors, except the assistant who uses his as a store-room for unused furniture.

I desire to bring to the notice of the Board that West Quoddy Head is the only station in the district which seems to be neglected. Moreover, the station is a most desirable one, being on the main land and within easy communication of South Lubec, which may possibly account for the keeper's neglect.

I consider that West Quoddy Head station should have a keeper who would be a good example to his assistant, and under the circumstances, I respectfully suggest the following change:

That John W. Guptill, Keeper of West Quoddy Head, be transferred to Avery Rock, and that Warren A. Murch, Keeper of Avery Rock, be transferred to West Quoddy Head, as Keeper.

Mr. Murch has had experience with steam boilers of fog signals at Libby Islands, and is a good carpenter, and also neat and careful about his duties.[111]

When the tender arrived at West Quoddy Head (below), Keeper Guptill declined to be transferred and tendered his resignation, stating, "after being in the service more that seventeen years and seven of them at Averys Rock I cannot go there again . . .."[112] (Courtesy of U.S. Coast Guard)

Elizabeth, indicating that a simple scolding would not "correct the abuses there practiced and stimulate him to the performance of his duties . . . he has not character enough for correction. He must have things his own way, and throw aside the printed instructions and derisively receive those from the Inspector."[114]

Inspector Mayo was zealous in weeding out ineffective keepers. The keeper at Tenants Harbor, John A. Farnham, was reportedly "negligent in his duties and has been so for some time. The condition of his charge is faulty and he is quite lazy and disobedient to the Rules, etc."[115] In this case, Mayo recommended that E. B. Davis (mentioned earlier) be transferred from Monhegan to take Farnham's place. Davis must have somehow redeemed himself after his earlier infraction.[116]

Elderly keepers were tolerated unless they were not able to effectively perform their duties. Inspector Mayo recommended the removal of the keeper of Negro Island Light Station as he "is an old man who has served the light for eleven years: but if the condition of the light as I found it is the best he can do, & he assures me it is, he has outgrown his usefulness. The light was very dim at 2 A.M. & I learn is habitually so."[117]

Unapproved absence from the station was grounds for dismissal. Inspector Mayo reported

> . . . that Mr. Sylvanus E. Doyle, assistant Keeper at Halfway Rock absented himself without leave from his station and in disobedience of orders from the principal Keeper to return. This conduct of Mr. Doyle left the principal Keeper on the Rock alone, from about February 6 to March 5th 1873. Mr. Doyle plead sickness as an excuse for not returning, but there is proof that Mr. Doyle was in good health, and was in Portland in the meantime. Mr. Sterling the principal Keeper, wrote me that Mr. Doyle gives him a great deal of trouble.[118]

Female keepers

Although 140 women served as principal keepers at American lighthouses between 1776 and 1939, only three of those women were appointed in Maine. Most female keepers were the wives or daughters of keepers who had died while in service. Family members were generally familiar with the tasks necessary to keep a light, and thus were natural candidates for assistants and/or replacement keepers. After a keeper's death, women family members often kept the light until a replacement keeper could be found and were sometimes offered a permanent position when there was no other source of livelihood.[119]

Betsy Humphrey generally received good reports on her conduct as keeper on Monhegan Island. In 1872, Inspector Mayo wrote,

> In forwarding the report of inspection of Manheigan Light House, etc., . . . I desire to commend to your notice the principal Mrs. Betsey Humphrey for the assiduous care she takes of the interests committed to her charge. Although there are some irregularities at this station which have required the Inspector's correction, yet this station is in very good order and is creditable to Mrs. Humphrey.[120]

Despite the praise, gender bias persisted. The inspector did not consider Humphrey competent to take on scientific experiments:

> I have rec'd 2 sets Meteorological Instruments from the Board which I was instructed to transmit to the Keepers of Mt. Desert & Manheigan Lights. But inasmuch as the Keeper of Manheigan is a woman and her assistant a very illiterate person, and the Keeper at Mt. Desert not a suitable man to make the required observations, I would respectfully recommend that the Keepers of Matinicus & Boon Island make the observations, who are intelligent men.[121]

One of Humphrey's assistants had charge of the fog signal, which was under her jurisdiction until it became an independent station in 1876. She may have found supervising the men under

PART IV. Keepers: Who They Were, How They Lived, What They Said

her rather daunting. In 1872, Inspector Mayo wrote:

> In conversation with Genl. Duane, this morning, he united with me in recommending the dismissal of Mr. Addison F. Brackett, asst. light Keeper at Manheigan, in charge of the fog whistle . . . for general unfitness ans'ing principally from laziness and ill-adaptation. The man, I understand is a fair black-smith with some leaning to machinery, but is too indolent to provide for himself and cannot manage public property. Good men, residents of the island, can be found very readily, who will identify themselves with the work & not complain.[122]

Brackett was subsequently discharged.

In 1875, the assistant in charge of the fog signal was James Marston. According to the 1875 inspection report,

> . . . all in the family take care of the light in foggy weather in July and August when it is scarcely sun, while Marston has the Fog signal to run. The Keeper was told that at night the two assistants should be at Signal. The Station on Monheigan (at Light) is in very good order, but the Fog Signal and dwelling for Assistant on Mananas Island are in a dirty condition. A change should be made here and two men to take care of it in foggy times. Mrs. Humphrey says her son assists her, but this Station, including fog Signal on Mananas, ought to have a man Keeper who could give his attention to both light and Signal.[123]

In 1880, Betsy Humphrey died and Sidney G. Studley took her place as principal keeper. Betsy's son, Frederick F. Humphrey, then 37, was appointed Studley's assistant and served in that position until his death in 1901.

The next woman to receive a principal keeper appointment in Maine was Melissa Holden, who replaced her husband, Samuel, at Deer Island Thorofare in 1874. Samuel Holden, a Civil War veteran, received his appointment in 1868. Upon his death, the appointment went to his widow, who held it for two years. In 1875, the inspector reported that Mrs. Holden had "five children, the eldest a boy 13 years old. The Station is in a neglected state."

Mrs. Betsy Humphrey assumed the head keeper position on Monhegan Island upon the death of her husband, Joseph, in 1862. Betsy had seven living children when she became keeper. Two of her sons, Edward and Albert, were away fighting in the Civil War. In May 1864, son Albert died in battle.[124] Humphrey's logs indicate that she was assisted by Sidney G. Studley and that they alternated watches.[125] What the logs do not show is that Studley was her son-in-law and lived with her daughter Ellen in a separate dwelling. (Ca. 1859 photo courtesy of U.S. Coast Guard)

Located on Mark Island, Deer Island Thorofare Light Station was first lit in 1858 to enable vessels to cross Isle au Haut Bay.[126] Keeper Melissa Holden discontinued the light each winter when ice prevented shipping. (Courtesy of U.S. Coast Guard)

Cleanliness and neatness are strangers to it. If no improvement, the Keeper should be removed. Her husband died March '74 of sore throat."[127]

The 1875 inspection report also refers to a female assistant keeper at Portland Head Light. "The Station is not kept in as good order as it should be. The assistant is a woman. Where there is a fog Signal, the Stations are not as efficient when women are Keepers or assistants. No woman should be at such a Station."[128]

Isaac H. and Abbie Burgess Grant

The name of Abbie Burgess, who was born in 1839 on Matinicus Island, "has become legendary in the Penobscot Bay region of mid-coast Maine."[129] In 1856, when she was 17 years old, Burgess kept the light on Matinicus Rock through a month-long gale for her keeper father, who had gone to Matinicus Island for medicine and supplies and was unable to return.

Burgess's own words have come down to us in a letter to a friend:

PART IV. Keepers: Who They Were, How They Lived, What They Said

The new dwelling was flooded and the windows [shutters] had to be secured to prevent the violence of the spray from breaking through. As the tide came, the sea rose higher and higher, till the only endurable place were the lighttowers. If they stood, we were saved, otherwise our fate was only too certain. . . . we were without assistance of any male member of our family. Though at times greatly exhausted by my labors, not once did the lights fail. . . .

You know the hens were our only companions. Becoming convinced, as the gale increased, that unless they were brought into the house they would be lost. . . . seizing a basket, I ran out a few yards after the rollers had passed and the sea fell off a little, with the water knee deep, to the coop, and rescued all but one. It was the work of a moment, and I was back in the house with the door fastened, but none too quick, for at that instant my little sister, standing at the window, exclaimed, "Oh, look there! The worst sea is coming!" That wave destroyed the old dwelling and swept the Rock.[130]

In 1860 Abbie's father, Samuel Burgess, lost his keeper position to a Republican appointee, but Abbie stayed on to help the new keeper, Captain John Grant. She fell in love with his son, Isaac H. Grant, then first assistant keeper, and married him in 1861.

Abbie and Isaac Grant remained on Matinicus Rock until 1875, when they and their four children were transferred

to Whitehead Island Light, near Spruce Head, Maine.[131] Abbie was appointed Isaac's assistant on June 2, 1875.

On August 7, 1881, Isaac Grant too rose to hero status in

. . . a remarkably prompt and gallant rescue. At about 8 o'clock in the morning of that day two men, named Thomas Wilson and John Lynch, mate and seaman on board the schooner *Vicksburgh*, of Bangor, Maine went out in a yawl from their vessel, which was at anchor in Seal Harbor. There was a dense fog, a strong breeze, with frequent squalls and a heavy sea, and at 9 o'clock, when the boat had been absent from the vessel an hour, and was about a mile to the eastward of

A Coast Guard keeper-class tender, named in honor of Abbie Burgess (above), serves out of Rockland, Maine. (1997 photo courtesy of U.S. Coast Guard)

Whitehead light-house, she suddenly capsized.

The men contrived to get astride the bottom, and clung to the keel, but were repeatedly torn off by the violent seas, although they often managed to regain their position. Their cries for help were drowned out by the roar of the waves, and the dense fog prevented alike their being seen from or seeing the shore. In this pitiable condition of suffering and struggle they continued for three hours, a strong current caused by the ebb-tide

Abbie and Isaac Grant served at Whitehead (above) until 1890, when her failing health led them to resign. She died two years later. Isaac then became storekeeper of the U.S. Lighthouse Service lamp shop in South Portland—a position he held until 1910. He lived until 1918. (Courtesy of David Gamage)

PART IV. Keepers: Who They Were, How They Lived, What They Said

meanwhile bearing them out to sea, and the prospect of being lost rapidly becoming imminent, when the fog fortunately lifted and disclosed them to the keeper of the light-house as they tossed, clinging to the yawl's bottom, far out on the rough waters.

Keeper Grant acted at once with admirable forethought and energy. He dispatched his daughter [Mary, age 12-13] with the alarm to the keeper of the life-saving station, about a mile away, and while the girl sped on her errand launched his own boat, with the aid of his son Frank [a surfman from the life-saving station], and put out to the rescue. So stormy was the sea after getting past the lee of the light-house that he was forced to throw over sail and ballast to keep the boat from swamping. He soon found that the nearest way to the perishing men was across a dangerous shoal, and time being precious, he risked this peril, and after a hazardous pull came up with the sufferers, who by this time were so helpless that they had to be lifted into the boat. They were in a frightful condition, exhausted, benumbed with cold, their trouser-legs chafed off at the knees by the abrasions of their struggles in keeping their hold of the boat's bottom, and the skin and flesh excoriated for spaces each as large as a man's hand, forming ghastly wounds.

The keeper of the life-saving station [Horace Norton] soon came up in a boat better than that by which the rescue had been effected, and to this they were transferred and taken to the light-house,

where their hurts were bandaged [with strips of a sheet of Abbie's] and every attention was bestowed upon them. The silver medal of the Life-Saving Service was bestowed upon Mr. Grant in recognition of his humane and gallant service upon this occasion.[132]

Gunfire at Portland Head

Many lighthouses, including Portland Head, were built near military installations. On January 19, 1898, Inspector Perry reported

. . . that the battery of high powered guns now being mounted in the emplacements at Portland Head by the United States Military Authorities for the defence of Portland Harbor is so far advanced that it is expected to have all finished and ready for use early next summer.

As it will be desirable then, and is probably anticipated by the army officials, to have target practice with these guns and to continue it at intervals, it becomes necessary now in the interests of the Light House Establishment to consider what effect the firing of these guns will have upon the lantern, lens, etc., of the Portland Head Light House, which stands so near any possible line of fire from this battery to a target at sea, that it appears possible serious injury would be done to the lantern and lens unless some provision is made to prevent it.[133]

The first test of the 10-inch guns took place on August 10, 1898. Keeper Joshua

F. Strout reported the outcome in his logbook: "This day target practice with the big guns at Portland Head Battery. 8 panes glass broken in Dwelling and 16 in barn, 1 in oil house. No damage done to the lantern or lenses in the Lt House. The plastering in kitchen broken."[134] The district engineer had taken precautions to protect the lens by wrapping it with "bed clothing" and wedging the pedestal with wood. He also arranged that two panes in the lantern be left open, along with the tower windows and doors, and the windows of the signal house, dwelling, and outhouse.[135]

Although further precautions were taken to protect the window glass, the damage continued. On October 12, 1900, the keeper reported, "This P.M. Target practice at Ft. Williams, 16 panes of glass broke in dwelling" and on September 24, 1902, "Gun practice at Fort Williams and the concussion having broken some 25 panes of window glass, also some yards of plastering taken off in dwelling."[136]

Strout wrote a more enthusiastic entry regarding his military neighbors on August 26, 1903: "This A.M. the Man of War maneuvering fleet made descent on the Forts at this harbor—a grand display" and on August 27, "The war vessels made another attack on Portland Forts this afternoon."[140]

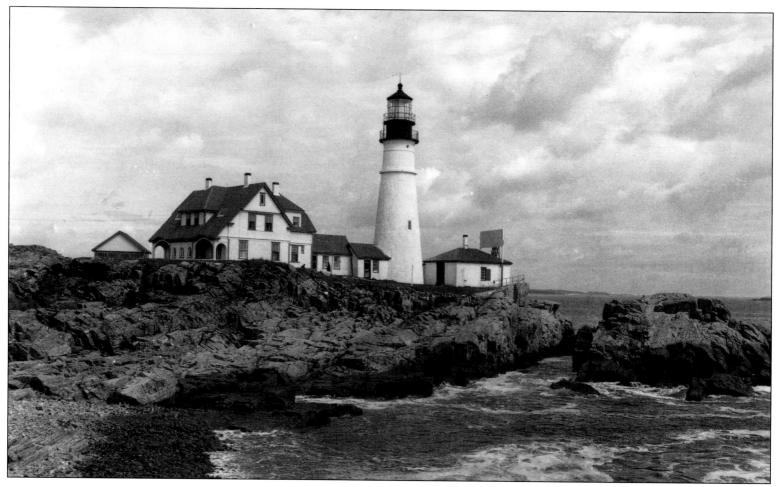

References to the guns near Portland Head Light Station continued for decades. On November 8, 1908, "the emissions from guns opened up roof of oil house and destroyed chimney on fog signal house."[137] In 1915 consideration was given to relocating the station but it was found impracticable and "from the mariners' viewpoint very undesirable":

The station is situated between the sea and the batteries, which extend a considerable distance on either side, so that nothing would be gained by moving to any point within that area, and to move the station inland to the rear of the batteries, necessarily a considerable distance, would, of course, very much impair its usefulness.[138]

On September 18, 1916, "A shot from one of the guns knocked off a piece from the overhang on the lantern deck." A 1941 entry indicated that personnel from the fort did sometimes take responsibility for the damage. After the December 8, 1941, entry—"Fired 12 in. guns, finished at dusk, broke quite a few windows"—the keeper indicated on December 9 that "Carpenters from Fort taking measurements of windows for glass."[139] Portland Head Light Station is shown here in 1940. (Courtesy of U.S. Coast Guard)

PART IV. Keepers: Who They Were, How They Lived, What They Said

Keeper compatibility

As technology at light stations became more complex, the tradition of family members performing all the duties faded and assistant keepers began to be assigned to major stations. In making those assignments, the Light-House Board had no way of knowing whether keepers, living in isolated locations and close quarters, could get along with each other. Not all of them did.

Recruits for duty on Cape Elizabeth were hard to find, and harmony among the men was not easily achieved. In 1872 the district inspector wrote the chairman of the Light-House Board regarding assistants Allan Gatehill and James Low:

> There has been constant quarreling between these men for a long time, and from all that I can learn, Gatehill has generally been the aggressor. . . .
>
> The charge of rendering false account of expenditure of oil was made by Gatehill to my predecessor & found by him to be groundless. . . . I found that it was merely based upon the fact that more oil was expended during Low's watch than in Gatehill's. It was doubtless owing to a better light having been given to correspond with the increased expenditure. Gatehill did not charge that oil had been sold, or given away, or in any manner disposed of. I am satisfied that these charges are frivolous and originate more from hostility towards Low than from any desire to protect the public interest, &

respectfully recommend that Gatehill be dismissed.[141]

Maine elections in 1880 brought more personality clashes at Cape Elizabeth. Head Keeper Marcus Hanna gave his assistants permission to go ashore to vote, assuming they would go when they were not on watch. Hanna later accused his second assistant keeper, Charles Chase, of leaving the watch room at the fog signal unattended and going ashore when he should have remained on duty.

> I left the station to go to the polls at 7 ½ a.m. Meeting Mr. Chase at the polling place (7 miles away) two hours later, and feeling that he was neglecting his duty, I hastened back to the station, arriving at 10 a.m. and found that it had been foggy since 8 ½ a.m. I immediately started fire at the Fog-signal; Mr. Chase returning and relieving me at about 11 o'clock.
>
> I further charge Mr. Chase with malicious falsehood, dishonesty and insubordination.
>
> . . . the antagonism which he has manifested toward me renders him of little account to me or the Station as an Assistant Keeper save that of taking a turn on watch, and his presence here is a constant menace and embarrassment to me . . . I respectfully request that he may be discharged.[142]

Hanna went so far as to level formal, notarized charges of insubordination against Chase, to which Chase replied,

"You cannot have me removed; you may do your worst." In further correspondence with the inspector, Hanna called Chase "an unmitigated liar."

> I beg to respectfully submit that Mr. Chase instead of frankly and manfully acknowledging his errors, has endeavored to twist and distort my instructions to him so as to make it appear that he has done nothing wrong.[143]

Charles Chase's letters to the inspector (who had originally supported his appointment) were barely literate, which makes one wonder whether he could follow instructions.

> When I was in your office I said that this would hapen, now it hear come. I no there has been threcerry [treachery] used, but I shal go by the law if you think that I am bad let me no at once.[144]

Chase claimed that Keeper Hanna gave him permission to go to the town hall to vote, agreeing that fog was unlikely. "The sun was shininge and we could see all of five miles. I do my duty prompt and do not trouble him in enny form."[145] In spite of his protests, Chase was removed.

In 1886 Inspector Batcheller wrote the Light-House Board chairman about further trouble at Cape Elizabeth:

> I regret to have to report a serious quarrel between the Principal and 2nd Asst. Keeper . . . which resulted in an assault by the latter. The altercation

commenced about a trivial matter and, had there not been bad feeling already existing between the parties, would probably have resulted in nothing but words. . . .

The 2nd Asst. Keeper Mr. Hiram Staples complained to the Principal Keeper Mr. Marcus Hanna, that certain repairs, which he could not make himself, were needed and that the Principal Keeper had not asked to have them made by the L.H. Inspector or Engineer.

The Principal Keeper admits saying "anyone but a jackass could make the repairs himself." The Asst. claims he said "anyone but a d——d jackass," etc.

Whichever statement is correct, the Asst. responded by knocking the Principal Keeper down and, according to the latter, followed the blow with further blows and kicks. This the former denies but admits the first blow.

The Principal Keeper claims that the Assistant was under the influence of liquor, which the latter denies, and I could find no evidence beyond the Principal Keepers statement to sustain the charge. My investigation convinced me that the interests of the service imperatively demand that a change be made at this station as early as possible.[146]

The Inspector recommended that Staples be dismissed from the service and that Hanna be reprimanded "for the undignified and improper part in the quarrel."

Hiram Staples wrote in his own defense that "Mr. Hanna is not liked by the people of this vicinity on account of his mean disposition, and he has quarreled with nearly all of his assistants, which shows that he is a disagreeable man to deal with. I have done my duty always and have tried to please Mr. Hanna in many ways, but I think he is the meanest, most contemptible specimen of the man that I have met."[147]

A further letter from Keeper Hanna to Inspector Batcheller adds that "Mr. Staples is known to be cruel and abusive in the treatment of his own wife. Myself and wife, also members of the 1st Assistant's family, have been eye and ear witnesses to unseemly family brawls between Staples and his wife since they have lived at this station. Mrs. Staples has on several occasions come to my house and with tears streaming from her eyes, related her abusive treatment by her husband."[148] Not a matter of a keeper's job performance, but certainly affecting the harmony of a multiple-keeper station. Staples was dismissed.

Inspector Batcheller wrote Vice Admiral Stephen C. Rowan, USLHB Chairman, in January 1888, ". . . I have visited Cape Elizabeth Lt. Station to investigate a verbal report of the principal Keeper against the 1st Assistant of neglect of duty and insubordination."

It appears from this report that the principal Keeper thinking that glycerine had not been applied to the plate glass of the lantern of the Western light when it should have been, posted the circular from this office in regard to its application, in the watch room of this tower.

The 1st Assistant claims that glycerine had been applied, but not according to the circular, as up to the time it was posted, he had not seen it. He took it down and put it in the watch book as a matter of convenience. When the principal Keeper heard of this, he ordered it returned to the place he had posted it, and this the 1st Assistant refused to do and so admitted to me. He however expressed his regret for this and promised that nothing of the kind should occur again. . . .

The 1st Assistant then made complaint of "offensive manner and spying" against the principal Keeper, to which he replied that this would compel him to make a further charge against the 1st Assistant . . . . related to events which transpired prior to the matter of the glycerine circular, and which had been held in reserve to meet any complaint the Assistant might make.[149]

What sort of men do these records describe? Keeper Marcus Hanna had an outstanding Civil War record and was extolled for his daring rescues of shipwrecked mariners. But clearly the men working together in very close quarters at his station were incompatible.

Cape Elizabeth (below), with its twin towers placed 923 feet from each other and a steam fog signal installed in 1869, required first one, then two, then three assistants. In fact, the first assistant keeper after 1870 was paid more than the other assistant and was to be a "practical engineer, having a knowledge of steam and machinery."[150] In 1881 head keeper Marcus Hanna requested that the salary differential be ended because all three assistants were assigned to tend the fog signal. (National Archives photo # 26- LG-1-61)

A similar personality conflict arose at Halfway Rock in Casco Bay, a three-man station with no families in residence. Two keepers were always on the station, with the third on leave on the mainland.

In October 1885 the district inspector wrote to the chairman of the Light-House Board in Washington to explain a letter written by G. H. Toothaker, former principal keeper at Halfway Rock, to the Board. Mr Toothaker, who had received his assignment on the inspector's

recommendation, complained about his replacement "allowing his light to go out, as well as for other irregularities." The inspector explained the chain of events leading to Toothaker's resignation:

Some 18 months ago Mr. Holbrook, then 1st Asst. Keeper . . . came to my office and reported to me that when he and Mr. Toothaker were alone on the Rock (the 3rd Keeper being absent), Mr. Toothaker would often refuse to speak to him for a week or ten days at a time without any

In 1867, the Committee on Lighting reported,

> . . . Halfway Rock in Casco Bay lies in the direct course of British navigation to Portland, that a light upon it would be a safe guide which is much needed for clearing the dangers of Bulwark Shoal, and would moreover be the best possible guide to the entrances of the safe harbors of Broad Sound and Harpswell Roads, both of which have an easy inner communication with Portland.[151]

The third-order lens was lit on August 15, 1871. (National Archives photo # 26-LG-1-62)

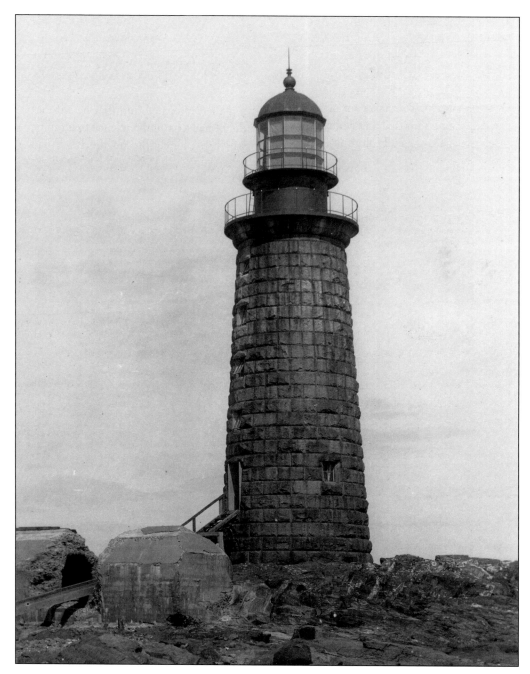

PART IV. Keepers: Who They Were, How They Lived, What They Said

apparent reason whatsoever. The place was lonely enough of itself, and to be deprived of the company of the only other person there seemed, unless good reasons existed, an improper state of affairs. . . . I called upon Mr. Toothaker for an explanation, and he admitted that while he had nothing against Mr. Holbrook, or any cause to complain of his conduct, still there were times when he, Mr. Toothaker, was moody and did not care to speak to any person. I informed him that this could not go on . . . and he promised that in the future he would not refrain from speaking to Mr. Holbrook, etc. but nevertheless he did continue to refuse to speak to Mr. Holbrook, until last spring Mr. Holbrook reported to me that Mr. Toothaker, he believed, was at times out of his mind, or on the verge of so being. Also that Mr. Toothaker, while in a rather excited state, had taken the boat early in the morning and left the station, going to his home at Harpswell some seven miles distant; and doing this on two occasions, . . . leaving Mr. Holbrook alone at the station.

Finally, Mr. Holbrook informed me that he was afraid to remain longer at the station with Mr. Toothaker, as he believed Mr. Toothaker, while in an excited state, might attack him, and that he ought to resign. I at once visited the station and repeated to Mr. Toothaker the report that Mr. Holbrook had made to me, and Mr. Toothaker admitted that it was true, that he had left the station . . ., that he did get

into a queer state of mind at times, due he believed to his residence of 13 years on that lonely station; and he also admitted to me that his grandmother died insane.

I then informed him that he without doubt had a natural tendency to insanity, which his lonely life on the Rock had aggravated—that if he lived on shore where he could associate and live among his neighbors & friends, he might overcome it; but I thought he certainly would go crazy if he remained there longer, as I believed he was on the verge of insanity. I then informed him that I could not take the responsibility of his remaining there longer—that if he did, there might be a tragedy, and that if he did not resign, I should be obliged to ask the Board to remove him. Thereupon Mr. Toothaker resigned.[153]

Toothaker wrote the Board again in February 1886 accusing Keeper Holbrook of having been absent without leave and abusing the President of the United States. Inspector Batcheller investigated and reported to the Board that Holbrook denied the charges. The inspector also pointed out that the charges should have been made at the time and not months after Toothaker had resigned his position.[154]

In 1887 problems arose among the keepers at West Quoddy Head.

Inspector Batcheller wrote the chairman of the Light-House Board in July that

the Keeper of West Quoddy Head Light Station made a report against the Assistant Keeper in which, without making any specific charges, he said, "I do not feel safe with him." This taken in connection with a rumor which subsequently reached me of a knockdown fight between the Keepers led me to fear that matters were in very bad shape there.[155]

The inspector investigated:

I found there was no serious difficulty whatever—only a wrangle about family matters, and neither Keeper had any complaint to make against the other so far as their duties were concerned. . . . I, however, warned both Keepers that wrangling would not be tolerated and that if they could not live together peacibly, I should recommend the Board to take serious action . . . .[156]

A great deal of the inspector's time must have been absorbed in correspondence over such peccadillos—all of it hand-written by a clerk, with a second copy made for the files.

The problem between the keepers at Moose Peak Light on Mistake Island in Eastern Bay was less easily solved. In December 1887 Inspector Batcheller wrote the chairman:

I investigated a report made by the Asst. Keeper . . . that the conduct of the Principal Keepers family toward him and his family was such that he would have to resign. . . .

It appears . . . that the wife of the Principal Keeper and his grown up daughters habitually use the vilest possible language not only to him and his family, but to the Principal Keeper himself, and to visitors.

The Principal Keeper admits this, though he claims that no visitor has been insulted at the station. He stated that there was no place where he could have peace except in the tower and that lately his wife had taken to coming there. . . .

The Principal Keeper . . . has always kept a good light. He is however utterly unable to controll either his wife or his grown-up daughters, nor can he give any assurance that if they are removed from the station, they will not return and again make trouble. . . .

I am therefore reluctantly compelled to recommend that the services of Mr. Tho. E. Dodge, keeper of Moose Peak Light Station, be dispensed with.[157]

Dodge was replaced by Charles E. Dobbins, who was his assistant. (National Archives photo # 26-LG-3-70)

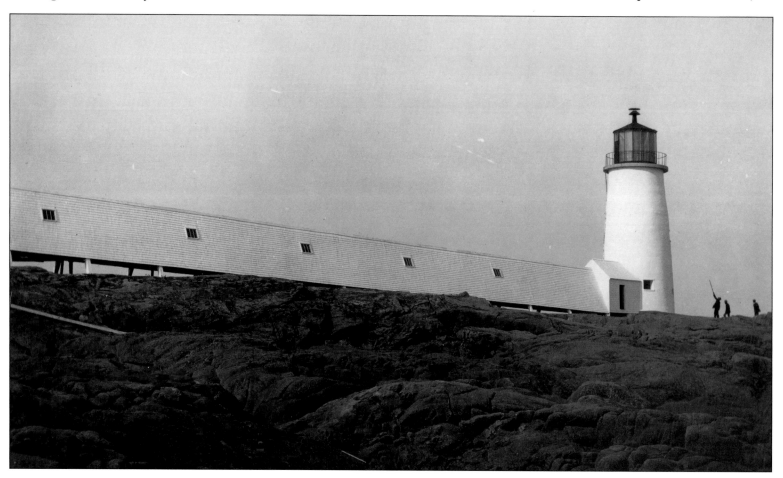

PART IV. Keepers: Who They Were, How They Lived, What They Said

Endnotes

[1] Johnson, pp. 102-103.

[2] 1880 *Regulations*, p. 53.

[3] "Light House Keepers," *Portland Daily Advertiser*, April 26, 1853.

[4] Thomas Day, keeper of Seguin Lighthouse, to J.S. Skerrett, August 6, 1880, attached to letter to John Rodgers, August 9, 1880 (NA, RG 26, E 24 or Letterbook 502).

[5] 1885 *Annual Report*.

[6] Circular from Engineer Secretary Major G. H. Elliot to General. J. C. Duane, December 2, 1873 (NA, RG 26, E 23).

[7] University of Maine Press, 1999. •

[8] Small, *The Lighthouse Keeper's Wife*, pp. 34, 43, 76, 112.

[9] Circular from Naval Secretary Admiral C. S. Boggs to Duane, August 1,1872 (NA, RG 26, E 23).

[10] "Allowances for Provisions," 1883 amendment to the 1881 Instructions.

[11] U.S. Light-House Board, *Instructions to Light-Keepers*, July 1881 (Washington, D.C.: Government Printing Office, 1881), p. 9. Hereafter referred to as 1881 *Instructions*.

[12] Circular from Elliot to Duane, July 24, 1872 (NA, RG 26, E 23).

[13] Ibid.

[14] Ibid.

[15] 1871 *Regulations*, pp. 54-55.

[16] Ibid., p. 57.

[17] Quoted in Tom Bradbury, "The Guardian of the Harbor," Kennebunkport Conservation Trust fall/winter 1993 newsletter.

[18] 1875 inspection report (NA, RG 26, E 9).

[19] 1871 *Regulations*, pp. 57-58.

[20] Jewett to Pleasonton, July 22, 1850 (NA, RG 26, E 17C).

[21] This number refers to the number of lights (including lightships), not stations, i.e., twin lights were counted twice. "Number of Light-Houses and Floating Lights in the United States, from the Year 1817 to 1841, both inclusive (corrected list)" (NA, RG 26 E 6).

[22] Woodbury to Pleasonton, April 4, 1835 (NA, RG 26, E 17K).

[23] Several years later, Pleasonton struck out No. 6 and modified No. 7 to replace "Contractors" with "Superintendent."

[24] NA, RG 26, E 18.

[25] *Lighthouse Papers*, p. 717.

[26] 1881 *Instructions*, p. 5.

[27] Ibid.

[28] Ibid.

[29] Ibid., p. 6.

[30] Anderson to Pleasonton, August 28, 1845 (NA, RG 26, E 6).

[31] 1881 *Instructions*, p. 6.

[32] Ibid.

[33] Ibid.

[34] Ibid., p. 7.

[35] Johnson, p. 106.

[36] 1881 *Instructions*, pp. 7-9.

[37] Personnel Classification Board, Form No. 14—Field Questionnaire (NA, RG 26, E 111).

[38] Keeper's journal, Burnt Coat Harbor Light Station (NA, RG 26, E 80).

[39] 1870 *Annual Report*.

[40] 1873 *Annual Report*.

[41] Keeper's journal, Eagle Island Light Station (NA, RG 26, E 80).

[42] "Eagle Island" under Notice to Keepers in *The Keeper's Log*, summer 1991, p. 32.

[43] Keeper's journal, Eagle Island Light Station (NA, RG 26, E 80).

[44] Ibid., and D'Entremont web site, "New England Lighthouses: A Virtual Guide" at <www.lighthouse.cc/eagleisland/history.html>. The log makes no mention of assisting fishermen but records sickness, death, and burial.

[45] Keeper's journal, Eagle Island Light Station (NA, RG 26, E 80).

[46] Probationary appointment form dated May 29, 1907 (NA, RG 26, E 48, File # 10582).

[47] Keeper's journal, Eagle Island Light Station (NA, RG 26, E 80).

[48] Ibid.

[49] Ibid.

[50] Ibid.

[51] Ibid.

[52] 1875 inspection report (NA, RG 26, E 9).

[53] Keeper's journal, Curtis Island Light Station (NA, RG 26, E 80).

[54] 1889 *Annual Report*.

[55] In 1934 the name was changed from "Negro" to "Curtis" in honor of Cyrus H. K. Curtis.

[56] Pleasonton to Joseph Hall, December 18, 1835 (NA, RG 26, E 18).

[57] Pleasonton to Chandler, October 5, 1835 (NA, RG 26, E 18).

[58] Keeper's journal, Curtis Island Light Station (NA, RG 26, E 80).

[59] Keeper's journal, Marshall Point Light Station (NA, RG 26, E 80).

[60] Ibid.

[61] Ibid.

[62] Ibid.

[63] 1875 inspection report (NA, RG 26, E 9).

[64] Keeper's journal, Egg Rock Light Station (NA, RG 26, E 80).

[65] Ibid.

[66] Ibid.

[67] Ibid.

[68] Ibid.

[69] Ibid., entry for December 28, 1899 (NA, RG 26, E 80).

[70] Keeper's journal, Egg Rock Light Station (NA, RG 26, E 80).

[71] Ibid.

[72] Ibid.

[73] Ibid.

[74] Ibid.

[75] Ibid.

[76] Ibid.

[77] Ibid.

[78] Also spelled "Purrington."

[79] Keeper's journal, Egg Rock Light Station (NA, RG 26, E 80).

[80] Ibid.

[81] Ibid.

[82] Ibid.

[83] Petition dated May 21, 1821 (NA, RG 26, E 17C).

[84] Ilsley to Pleasonton, October 17, 1821 (NA, RG 26, E 17C).

[85] Ilsley to Pleasonton, November 24, 1821 (NA, RG 26, E 17C).

[86] Keeper's journal, Burnt Island Light Station (NA, RG 26, E 80).

[87] "Highlights of Boothbay History" at <www.boothbayharbor.com/visitor_history.asp>.

[88] Dona Brown, *Inventing New England: Regional Tourism in the Nineteenth Century* (Washington, D.C.: Smithsonian Institution Press, 1995), p. 174.

[89] 1858 *Annual Report*.

[90] 1875 inspection report (NA, RG 26, E 9).

[91] Keeper's journal, Burnt Island Light Station (NA, RG 26, E 80).

[92] Loose sheets found in keeper's journal, Negro Island (Curtis Island) Light Station (NA, RG 26, E 80).

[93] Albert Smith to Secretary of the Treasury Woodbury, December 14, 1839 (NA, RG 26, E 17F).

[94] Reprinted with permission from the *Courier-Gazette*, Rockland, Maine.

95October 22, 1932, issue; reprinted with permission from the *Courier-Gazette*, Rockland, Maine.

96Interview with David Gamage, Whitehead Island resident and grandson of former lighthouse keeper Arthur Beal, September 2001.

97Perry to USLHB, April 20, 1898 (NA, RG 26, E 24 or Letterbook 1163).

98Reprinted with permission from the *Courier-Gazette*, Rockland, Maine.

99U.S. Department of Commerce, *Annual Report of the Secretary of Commerce*, 1938, p. 129.

100CWO Al Primm, "Marcus Hanna, 1842-1921, Medal of Honor—1895, gold Lifesaving Medal—1885," U.S. Coast Guard Historian's web site <www.uscg.mil/hq/g-a/awl/bclass/wlm/Marcus.htm> and report and testimony from the First District Inspector, March 11, 1885 (NA, RG 26, E 24 or Letterbook 615).

101Ibid.

102Commander A. J. Crowninshield to Rowan, February 13, 1885 (NA, RG 26, E 24 or Letterbook 615).

103Primm article indicates he received the medal on April 25, 1885. The 1885 Annual Report gives the date as June 23, 1885.

104Crowninshield to Rowan, July 20, 1885 (NA, RG 26, E 24 or Letterbook 643).

106Selfridge to Henry, July 18, 1872 (NA, RG 26, E 24 or Letterbook 318).

105Ilsley to Pleasonton, January 28, 1825 (NA, RG 26, E 17C).

107Ibid. Attached statement of Lewis Demott, dated January 6, 1825, and recorded by James Boyd, Justice of the Peace, Portland.

108Ilsley to Pleasonton, March 10, 1825 (NA, RG 26, E 17C).

109Mayo to Henry, October 21, 1872 (NA, RG 26, E 24 or Letterbook 318).

110Batcheller to Henry, August 8, 1887 (NA, RG 26, E 24 or Letterbook 721).

111Cogswell to USLHB, April 29, 1899 (NA, RG 26, E 24 or Letterbook 1219).

112Guptill to First District Inspector, May 25, 1899 (NA, RG 26, E 24 or Letterbook 1219).

113Mayo to Henry, October 21, 1872 (NA, RG 26, E 24 or Letterbook 318).

114Mayo to Henry, October 22, 1872 (NA, RG 26, E 24 or Letterbook 318).

115Mayo to Henry, October 24, 1872 (NA, RG 26, E 24 or Letterbook 318).

116Mayo to Henry, November 4, 1872 (NA, RG 26, E 24 or Letterbook 318).

117Mayo to Henry, October 21, 1872 (NA, RG 26, E 24 or Letterbook 318).

118Mayo to Henry, March 19, 1873 (NA, RG 26, E 24 or Letterbook 318).

119Mary Louise and J. Candace Clifford, *Women Who Kept the Lights: An Illustrated History of Female Lighthouse Keepers* (Alexandria, Virginia: Cypress Communications, 2000).

120Mayo to Henry, October 14, 1872 (NA, RG 26, E 24 or Letterbook 318).

121Selfridge to Henry, February 27, 1872 (NA, RG 26, E 24 or Letterbook 297).

122Mayo to Henry, November 8, 1872 (NA, RG 26, E 24 or Letterbook 318).

1231875 inspection report (NA, RG 26, E 9).

124Sandra M. Clunies, personal communication, September 2, 2003.

125Keeper's journal, Monhegan Island Light Station (NA, RG 26, E 80).

1261855 *Annual Report*.

1271875 inspection report (NA, RG 26, E 9).

128Ibid.

129Frederick C. Hart, Jr., "Keepers of the Matinicus Light: Isaac H. and Abbie E. (Burgess) Grant and their Families" in *The New England Historical and Genealogical Register*, Volume 150, October 1996/Whole Number 600, p. 391.

130Segments of Abbie's letter are quoted in several sources, including Clifford, Ross Holland, Robert Carse, and Edward Rowe Snow.

131A detailed description of the Whitehead Light Station can be found in the fall 2000 issue of *The Keeper's Log*, entitled "Whitehead Light Station" by David A. Gamage. Gamage also has an article entitled "White Head Light Station: Childhood Memories" in *Lighthouse Digest*, August 2000.

132U.S. Life-Saving Service, *Annual Report of the Operations of the U.S. Life-Saving Service for the Fiscal Year ending June 30, 1882* (Washington, D.C.: Government Printing Office, 1882), as quoted by David Gamage in his lighthouse research. Information in brackets from Hart, p. 409.

133Perry to USLHB, January 19, 1898 (NA, RG 26, E 24 or Letterbook 1163).

134Keeper's journal, Portland Head Light Station (NA, RG 26, E 80).

135Thomas Perry to USLHB, September 1, 1898 (NA, RG 26, E 24 or Letterbook 1219).

136Keeper's journal, Portland Head Light Station (NA, RG 26, E 80).

137Ibid.

138Inspector Sherman to Commissioner of Lighthouses, August 7, 1915 (NA, RG 26, E 50 (NC-31): "Correspondence of the Bureau of Light-Houses, 1911-39," File # 665).

139Keeper's journal, Portland Head Light Station (NA, RG 26, E 80).

140Ibid.

141Inspector A. E. K. Benham to Admiral Shubrick, July 14, 1872 (NA, RG 26, E 24 or Letterbook 297).

142Hanna to Skerrett, September 14, 1880 (NA, RG 26, E 24 or Letterbook 502).

143Hanna to Skerrett, September 23, 1880 (NA, RG 26, E 24 or Letterbook 502).

144Chase to Skerrett, September 23, 1880 (NA, RG 26, E 24 or Letterbook 502).

145Ibid.

146Batcheller to Rowan, January 8, 1886 (NA, RG 26, E 24 or Letterbook 643).

147Staples to Batcheller, January 5, 1886 (NA, RG 26, E 24 or Letterbook 643).

148Hanna to Batcheller, January 6, 1886 (NA, RG 26, E 24 or Letterbook 643).

149Batcheller to Rowan, January 12, 1888 (NA, RG 26, E 24 or Letterbook 721).

150Hanna to District Inspector G. S. Skerrett, February 14, 1881 (NA, RG 26, E 24 or Letterbook 502).

151Benjamin Pierce, Chairman for the Committee on Lighting, to USLHB, March 15, 1867 (NA, RG 26, E 23).

152Batcheller to Rowan, December 8, 1887 (NA, RG 26, E 24 or Letterbook 721).

153Crowninshield to Rowan, October 13, 1885 (NA, RG 26, E 24 or Letterbook 643)

154Batcheller to Rowan, February 23, 1886 (NA, RG 26, E 24 or Letterbook 643).

155Batcheller to Rowan, July 2, 1887 (NA, RG 26, E 24 or Letterbook 721).

156Ibid.

157Batcheller to Rowan, December 8, 1887 (NA, RG 26, E 24 or Letterbook 721).

Part V. Lighthouses under the Bureau of Lighthouses, 1911-1939

In 1911 the U.S. Bureau of Lighthouses was created to streamline and simplify the administration of the Lighthouse Service. The eight-member U.S. Light-House Board was replaced by a Commissioner of Lighthouses. George R. Putnam, an experienced engineer from the Coast and Geodetic Survey, was appointed to head the bureau and remained in charge for 25 years. He sought to promote a professional service with advancement based solely on merit, free of political influence. He kept his headquarters staff small and decentralized authority to district superintendents, who were "given a wide responsibility in maintaining the lights, buoys and signals and . . . [were] held responsible for results . . . "[1]

Putnam's new bureau, commonly referred to as the Lighthouse Service, was located in the Department of Commerce. The Lighthouse Service used the same organizational practices as the Light-House Board. The military officers who served as inspectors and engineers, however, were replaced with civilians and the inspector position was retitled "superintendent."

New technology, adopted gradually over the first half of the twentieth century, provided new types of aids to navigation and changed the character of lighthouse keeping. Electricity was extended to the entire lighthouse network, and it made the lights both brighter and far easier to tend. By 1938 electricity was used for "43 percent of lights on fixed structures. . . . The great increase in this form of illuminant has accounted for the substantial reductions in almost all other forms."[2] Automation of lights began to make keepers redundant. More buoys and minor aids were added to the system.

Near the end of the Bureau's administration of lighthouses in 1938, the total number of aids to navigation in the United States was 28,758. Fog signals at light stations and on lightships decreased by 3 percent, due almost entirely to the discontinuance of secondary, and often hand-operated, fog signals at stations and their replacement by more effective fog signals on buoys placed closer to the track of vessels.[3]

The total personnel of the Lighthouse Service as of June 30, 1938, was 5,189, including 1,177 light keepers and assistants; 1,895 officers and crews of lightships and tenders; 113 Bureau officers, engineers, draftsmen, district superintendents, and technical assistants; 186 clerks, messengers, janitors, and office laborers; 144 depot keepers and assistants, including laborers; 1,243 laborers, etc., mostly employed on a part-time basis; and 431 field force employees engaged in construction and repair work.[4]

Introduction of radio

Invention of the radio was an enormous boon to mariners. With the ability to communicate with land and other vessels, mariners could send distress calls and share weather forecasts and notices of new wrecks, moved buoys, or defects in aids to navigation.[5] Lighthouse keepers greatly appreciated radios because they brought instructions, news of the outside world, and entertainment to lonely stations.

The first radio beacons, installed after 1921 to allow navigators to pinpoint their position, must have seemed almost miraculous. "Only the radio signal penetrates the fog and rain which may blot out a light . . . it alone is unaffected by the roar of the storm which drowns the sound of the most powerful [fog] signal."[6] Marine radio beacons were non-directional—the signal was sent to the whole horizon. The first signals used were short and distinctive for each station. Sending minutes were alternated and frequencies varied so that signals would not interfere with each other. Ships needed only a simple direction-finder or radio compass to pick up the signals.

The first radio beacon in Maine was authorized for the Portland Lightship *No. 74* in 1925; the Bureau did not receive the first record of transmissions until early 1927.[7]

Ships bound for Portland, from points along the coast or from across the Atlantic, invariably set their courses by the lightship. Steamers equipped with radio compasses pick up their first signals from the little ship sometimes as far as 500 miles away. The radio beacon of the lightship is transmitted in group flashes of one dot and two dashes for 60-second periods, followed by periods of 120 seconds of silence. The radio beacon is flashed from 5:30 to 6 and 11:30 to 12 every morning and at the corresponding hours every evening, fair weather or foul.

When the Portland-bound steamers are within 50 miles of the lightship, they pick up submarine signals with their under-water receivers. Sent out by means of a deep-toned submarine bell lowered some 30 feet below the lightship and rung every 33 seconds in foggy, rainy, or otherwise overcast weather, or whenever the visibility is less than five miles. The bell is tolled seven times, following by four addition strokes, spelling out 74—the official number of the lightship.[8]

The second radio beacon in Maine was placed on Mount Desert Rock in 1931 and sent out a signal each hour for fifteen minutes. A newspaper account noted that the signal was particularly useful for navigation in foggy weather.[9] West Quoddy Head got a radio beacon in 1932 and was synchronized with the other two Maine stations. Although the keepers were responsible for the radio beacons at their stations, their operation was practically automatic.

The operating schedule in clear weather follows: On the 31st minute of the hour, Mount Desert Rock starts the schedule, the radiobeacon transmits the International code letter "B" for that minute, followed in order by West Quoddy Head transmitting the letter "Y" and the Portland lightship follows with the letter "K". Therefore, each station transmits one minute and is silent two minutes. These stations transmit in that order for the full third quarter of each hour. In foggy weather continuous operation is in order in the same manner as above.[10]

In 1938 a radio beacon was installed at the fog signal station on Manana Island.

. . . Roughly, the device operates as follows: Blasts from a large horn and a dash from the radio transmitter on the Island are emitted at the same instant. The radio dash arrives at the receiver on the ship at almost the same instant that it was transmitted. The person on board the ship knows, when he receives the dash, that the horn has just been sounded. Since sound waves travel very much slower than radio waves, the sound will not reach the ship for a number of seconds. By dividing the number of seconds between the time the dash was first heard and the time when the horn was first heard by the known velocity of sound, a mariner can easily figure out to

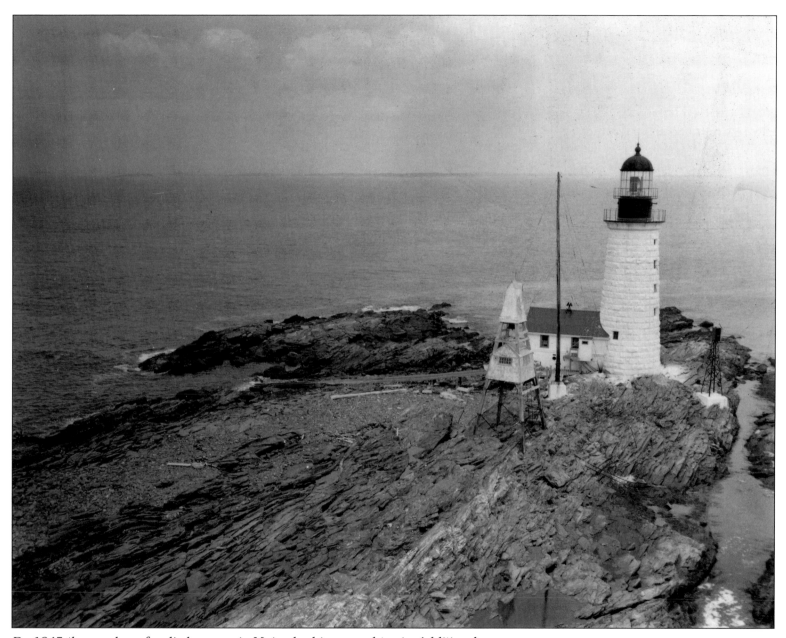

By 1945 the number of radio beacons in Maine had increased to six. Additional stations had been installed at Matinicus and at Halfway Rock (shown here in 1945). (National Archives photo # 26-S-398)

within a thousand feet or less how near he is to Manana Island.[11]

In 1938, the grand total of all radio beacons was 133. "There is indication that the present-day needs of shipping for major radio navigational facilities are now well served, particularly as respects those radiobeacons which have a purpose similar to the great landfall lights, in the recently decreased rate of expansion in this field."[12] By 1945 the total number of radio beacons had increased to 185.[13] The development of LORAN[14] during World War II made it possible to ascertain a ship's position precisely so that visible landmarks were no longer needed.

Flying Santa

In the early days of aviation, pilots, like mariners, often used lighthouses to track their location. Lacking sophisticated navigational equipment, they sometimes relied on lighthouses to set their course in stormy or inclement weather. One such pilot, Captain William H. Wincapaw, a native of Friendship, Maine, flew a variety of aircraft, including amphibious planes, around the Penobscot Bay area. In 1929, Captain Wincapaw, flying blind in a snowstorm and low on fuel, spotted the gleam of Dice Head Light, which led him safely home. To show his appreciation to the hardworking keeper,

that Christmas he dropped gifts to light stations in the Rockland area and began the tradition of the Flying Santa.[15]

The packages containing newspapers, magazines, coffee, candy, and other items were so well received and the keepers and their families were so appreciative that Wincapaw expanded the tradition to include light stations not only in Maine, but all over New England. After a few years, Wincapaw was assisted by his son, Bill, Jr., and

Keeper Arthur B. Mitchell of Fort Point Light, Stockton Springs, expressed his appreciation to Captain Wincapaw:

We thank you for remembering us again this year. The bundle of papers and magazines landed very near our mail box. Our dog was the first to hear the sound of the motor and then we all rushed out in time to see the plane circle over the reservation and go sailing down over the Penobscot again. We all join in wishing you and yours the happiest New Year ever.[16]

Photo of Fort Point Light Station in 1975. (Courtesy of U.S. Coast Guard)

eventually by one of Bill's teachers, Edward Rowe Snow. Snow had an avid interest in lighthouses and maritime history and would later become a well-known author. When Captain Wincapaw was transferred to Bolivia in 1938, Snow carried on the tradition, assisting with the flights until 1980. In 1981, the Hull Lifesaving Museum in Hull, Massachusetts, stepped up to continue the Flying Santa visits. The tradition has endured to this day. Every year members of the Friends of Flying Santa helicopter to New England Coast Guard stations and distribute gifts to children up to 10 years old.[17]

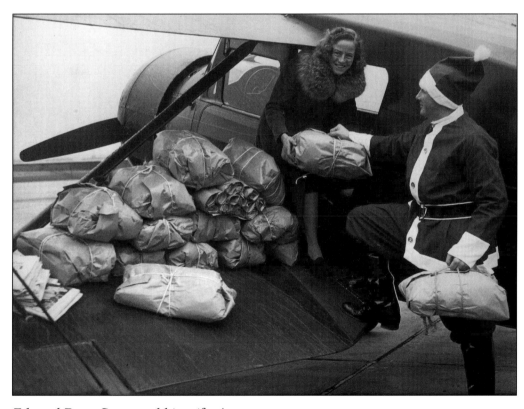

Edward Rowe Snow and his wife, Anna Myrle, load gift packages to be distributed through Flying Santa. (Photo from the collection of Edward Rowe Snow, courtesy Dolly Snow Bicknell)

Lobster fishing

Many lighthouse keepers fished and hunted near their stations. Duck and lobster were staples in their diet. Keeper Herber Sawyer at Egg Rock reported that 40 lobster traps belonging to him and his assistant were smashed up in a storm.[18] Other keepers recorded the fluctuating price of lobsters in their logbooks. Some offshore keepers got to know the lobster fishermen and depended on them to carry messages back and forth to the mainland.

Lobster fishing was a large industry in Maine; the 1910 catch of lobsters amounted to nearly 20 million pounds at a value of over two million dollars.[19] Some lobster fishermen saw the keepers as competition. In 1911, the lobster fishermen of Casco Bay put together a petition asking that the employees of the U.S. Lighthouse and Life-Saving Services

. . . refrain from the lobster fishing business other than to supply their own individual needs. . . .

Each year these government employees encroach more and more upon the waters where we make our bread and butter, extending their traps in all directions and making it necessary for us to go farther and farther off shore with all the attendant loss of time and gear that results.

Many of these lighthouse employees make a regular business of lobster fishing, monopolizing the most convenient and most prolific fishing grounds. In many instances they operate fully as many if not more traps than we regular fishermen do and pull their traps from motor boats and carry their catches to market in the same daily manner that we do. They also have the great advantage of being directly on the lobster fishing grounds enabling them to watch [for] lulls in bad weather and haul when conditions do not allow the regular fishermen to visit their own traps. . . .[20]

Inspector Jno. McDonald investigated the extent of lobstering by the keepers in the vicinity of Casco Bay and concluded that "The petition is exaggerating and misleading. . . . the natural inference is that the lobster fishermen on the coast of Maine only make their 'bread and butter,' while as a matter of fact, their business is lucrative, and their profits far greater than those of any lighthouse keeper."[21]

The principal keeper at Ram Island Ledge Light Station responded to the inspector's inquiry:

. . . During the past six years, (nearly) in which this station has been in my charge I have never owned or hauled a lobster trap, I have no time and do not care to fish. My time is occupied in and around my station, and I prefer to be a light-house keeper rather than a fisher-man. The two occupations do not go well together.[22]

Based on the inspector's recommen-dation, Commissioner Putnam concluded,

. . . the small amount of lobster fishing done by lighthouse keepers on the Maine coast is not of sufficient importance to justify this privilege being withdrawn from them, and the Bureau does not deem it advisable to issue orders prohi-biting them from lobster fishing, when it does not interfere with their work at the station.[23]

The Great Gale of January 27-28, 1933

The *Courier-Gazette*, Rockland, Maine, published reports from keepers in the area.

Great Duck

What a sea and what a surf! . . . It is impossible to describe the height of the seas and surf but we will give you some idea of the damage it did. The island was divided during the high tide, and the drift wood on one side went across to the other side. The place where this happened is about a quarter of a mile wide, so you can imagine what the seas were like. The graveyard was washed away, small trees along the shore were seen drifting off, and large rocks were taken from their places and put upon the banks. The boathouse was surrounded by water but no damage done to it.

Now Old Man Winter has blanketed us with snow so everything is beginning to look like winter again.[24]

Two Bush

The big storm of Jan. 27-28 brought our first snow and the highest tide in my recollection. Our power dory and all of the boats had to be hauled well up on the grass ground. Little Two Bush was submerged, and the pond is full of salt water, and the black ducks had to vacate as there was no place for them to drink.

The keepers at Saddleback Ledge (right) reported that on January 27-28, 1933,

. . . we certainly got a good washing. The seas smashed in the boathouse doors which had a 4" x 4" bar across them, then a brace from the center of the bar to the wench, broke both of them, threw the doors and a 130 gallon kerosene tank up to the wench, where they became wedged between the boats, tore off about eight square feet of clapboard from the northeast side of the house, ripped up some of the shingles on the roof and the water came in over the keeper's and first assistant's room; also ripped shingles from our coal bunker, took about 80 feet or more of our boat slip, and we cannot use the liberty boat until the slip is repaired. It parted our tele-phone cable close to the Ledge, and broke the wire rope stay to the masthead. Seas striking the side and roof shook the building so the stove rattled.[25]

(1951 photo courtesy of U.S. Coast Guard)

Maine Lighthouses: Documentation of Their Past

The Cuckolds

The northeast gale of last weekend raised havoc at this station. The bulkhead was broken down by the seas and driven into the east side of the house, breaking out all windows but one on the lower floor and also broke through the thick wall in the dining room, flooding the rooms all day with water. The keepers made temporary shutters and put on the windows toward night when the tide was low and they could work without being washed over by the seas.

For two days and nights the heavy seas pounded the house and everything in the rooms were wet with salt water before they could be removed. Clapboards and shingles were torn from the buildings, the back porch washed away, the kitchen door broken and one end of the fuel house was smashed. The middle section of the flat slip went adrift, and many other damages resulted. Although no injury was done on the keeper's side of the house, the rooms were flooded with water. Some concern was felt for the safety of the whole house before being able to get shutters up again, as there seemed danger of the seas smashing the partitions. We are waiting anxiously for the breakwater to be replaced, as a southeast gale would do more damage even than a northeast wind on the eastern side of the dwelling house.

The experience was rather a hectic one for Earle Macauley of Boothbay Harbor, who was substituting for Assistant Keeper Seavey. We had no radio service as the salt water caused a short circuit to the batteries, and having no telephone, we were entirely marooned. For a couple of hours West Cuckholds was completely covered. Our postmaster at Newagen said there had never been anything like it here for 40 years . . .[26]

Boon Island

The storm was very bad out here on our little island. We saw it coming, so to speak, and put things in under cover, boats in the boathouse, etc., and closed all the doors tightly. But we did not expect such a deluge. At one period of the storm we fully expected the houses to be stove in by the heavy seas which pounded them.

However, they did not break in, for which we are thankful. A rock weighing several tons was thrown up on the walk by the tower. The walk going from the double house door to the boathouse was picked up and thrown several feet up to a sandbox the children played in last summer. The boathouse was a boiling mass of water, around it, under it, and in it. It trembled and lifted up, but as each roller receded, it settled down again, and is still here at this writing, though somewhat battered and worse for wear.

In fact, the whole island is much the worse for wear. . . . The slip was washed away in a bad rough spell before this storm. The cable to the telephone went out of order the first day of the storm. We hope it will be fixed soon. To sum it all up, we were not battered as much as some of the stations, but bad enough. The water was at one time up to the window sills on the double house. Keeper Gray had to watch his chance to dash out to the engine house and back. The engines have to be oiled every half hour— and they have to run from 2 a.m. until 12 or 1 p.m. in order that the light may run at night.[27]

Grindle Point

The recent northeaster did considerable damage to the road leading to the lighthouse, making an island of the point on which the lighthouse is, for a few hours.[28]

Spring Point Ledge

As we have a good harbor, we were not affected much by [the storm] except that we were marooned off here with a small supply of food, therefore our stomachs gave us the most trouble. It is our custom to go ashore daily for fresh home cooked food, so as the duration of the storm extended beyond that of an ordinary one, we were on the rocks for eatables. And although the senior keeper, Mr. Wilson, is nearing the age of 70, he still has his childish desires for milk and must have at least one quart a day. By the time the storm was over, he was very near weaned. But our wives were eager to see us and had a large supply of food awaiting, so we made up for all that we had lost.[29]

Modern conveniences

Electricity not only made tending the light much easier, eliminating the long night watches in the tower, but it also made life in the keepers' quarters much more pleasant. The introduction of indoor plumbing, appliances like refrigerators and washing machines, telephones, and radios enhanced the lives of the keepers and their families. Motorized boats made it easier to access the mainland.

Not all stations were provided with telephones. When installation of a telephone was requested at Portland Head Light Station in 1932, first district Superintendent C. E. Sherman replied,

It is not considered absolutely necessary that a telephone be installed at Portland Head Lighthouse for the purpose of communication, should an accident occur at that place, as in case of shipwreck or other accidents in the vicinity of this light, the keepers could get communication to the outside by the use of phone on Government reservation not far away. As a matter of fact, it is believed that if a telephone were installed at this station, and since it is visited by many people during the summer season, it would require the services of one of the personnel at this station to give the greater part of his time to answer same.[30]

In 1932 the *Courier-Gazette* asked lighthouse keepers to contribute to a

In 1898, the Rockland and Vinalhaven Telephone and Telegraph Company requested permission to install one of its instruments at the Whitehead Island Light Station.[31] One by one light stations were connected with the outside world. The keeper at Little River wrote the Courier-Gazette *on February 6, 1932, "There is a telephone here, with Libby Island and Cross Island coast guard station on the same line and it gives* great pleasure to exchange conversation with them and talk with the children that are away at school." In the same column, the keeper at Burnt Island wrote, "There is no telephone here but they hope that some day our big Uncle Sam will be rich enough to put telephones in all the lonely stations."

Photo of Little River Island Light Station. (Courtesy of U.S. Coast Guard)

Telephones on islands were not always dependable. Offshore stations relied on cables to connect them with the mainland. On February 28, 1932, the keeper at Matinicus Rock (below) wrote, "Another week of rough weather gone by, and with it the telephone cable, although it has lasted well this winter. That is sorry news, as it means a lot to the folks out here."[32] The cable was not fixed until June. On March 4, 1932, the Mount Desert keeper wrote, "Our telephone is out of commission at present and if it were not for our radios, we would be cut off from the outside world entirely."[33] (Courtesy of U.S. Coast Guard)

regular column. The January 23, 1932, issue announced that

Keeper R. W. Powers of Matinicus Rock Light, 25 miles from the mainland wrote that government telephones now connect all these stations with the outside world, and have greatly lessened their isolation. The radio too plays a big part in making lighthouse life far different from what it used to be.

February 20, 1932. Indian Island Keeper W. F. Reed. "There is no telephone so they cannot talk with neighbors, and as few boats pass at this time of year, it is very quiet. Someone goes to Rockport every day for the mail and once in a while the *Cornish* or a large steamer is seen going up or down the bay."

December 24, 1938. "The telephone cable [at Baker Island] is gone. It certainly is a dull place here at present. Its replacement would be a fine Christmas present."

August 5, 1939. "The telephone on Seguin connecting with the mainland has been out of order for the past week, making it inconvenient for communications with the mainland."[34]

Part V. Lighthouses under the Bureau of Lighthouses, 1911-1939

Gene Watts, keeper at Libby Island Light Station, wrote the Maine Coast Fisherman *in October 1949: "Upon my arrival the main light was an IOV, and kerosene lamps were used in the dwelling, but thanks to Bill Clark and his crew, all that has been changed. We now have 110-volt electricity all over the place, light tower and all. We have a modern bathroom with tile walls, also an up-to-date kitchen with all the conveniences. . . ." (Courtesy of U.S. Coast Guard)*

Discontinued lights

As lighting technology evolved after the turn of the nineteenth century, the duties of the traditional lighthouse keeper changed with it. The use of acetylene and electricity did not require the care of full-time keepers. In the 1930s several light stations were discontinued or replaced with automated beacons in nearby locations. These included Blue Hill Bay, Dice Head, Grindle Point, Hendricks Head, Indian Island, Narraguagus (Pond Island), Pumpkin Island, Tenants Harbor, and Winter Harbor. In most cases the station or merely the keeper's dwelling was sold off to private owners.

In the case of Dice Head, the light was moved to a skeletal tower and the old tower was acquired by the town of Castine. The Hendricks Head light was discontinued but reactivated in 1951 after electricity came to the station. Pumpkin Island received an acetylene light.

Deactivated in 1934, the light on Grindle Point was moved to a nearby skeletal tower. The lighthouse was acquired by the town of Islesboro and converted to the Sailor's Memorial Museum. In 1987, the citizens convinced the Coast Guard to move the light back into the old tower and the modern tower was removed.

In 1939, all active lighthouses were transferred to the jurisdiction of the U.S. Coast Guard, where they remain at the beginning of the twenty-first century. Maintaining aids to navigation was and continues to be only one of many missions of the Coast Guard. The administration of lighthouses has been very different under this quasi-military agency. Coast Guard personnel rotated among many types of duties, few became career lighthouse keepers.

Tenants Harbor Light Station (right) on Southern Island was established in 1857. The station has been in private hands since the 1930s, the bell tower on the right serves as an artist's studio. (1989 HABS/HAER photo by Richard Cheek)

In 1932 the Superintendent of Lights recommended that the station at Winter Harbor Light Station (left) be replaced with a lighted bell buoy, saving an estimated $1,660 in maintenance costs.[35] The property was later sold. (Courtesy of U.S. Coast Guard)

Part V. Lighthouses under the Bureau of Lighthouses, 1911-1939

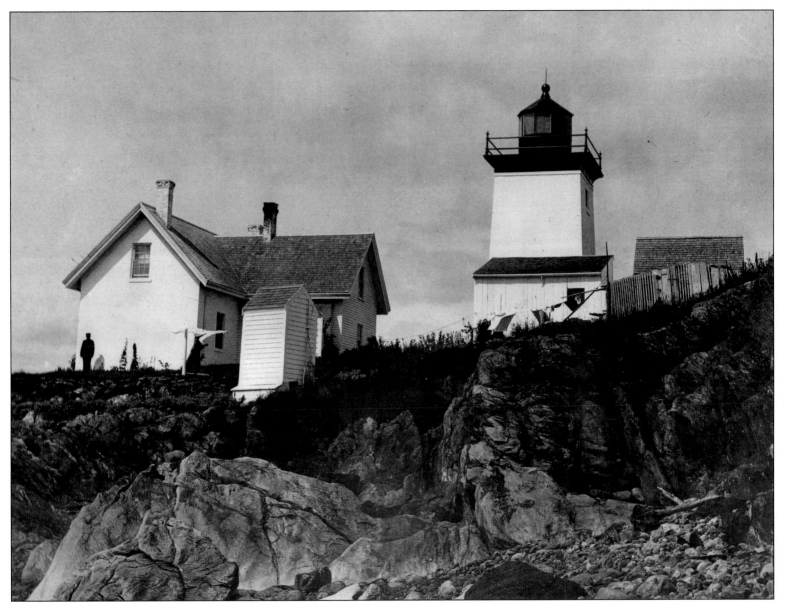

The lighthouse on Beauchomp Point on Indian Island at the entrance to Rockport Harbor was established in 1850 and discontinued in 1859 "on account of its nearness to Negro Island light-house, it is of no use to general navigation of the bay, and it is of but little use to the village near which it is situated, the commerce of which is small."[36] The light was re-established on January 15, 1875. Around 1934 the light was discontinued and sold at public auction. (National Archives photo # 26-LG-2-55)

Endnotes

[1] George R. Putnam, *Sentinels of the Coasts* (New York: W.W. Norton & Company, Inc., 1937), p. 156.

[2] *Annual Report of the Secretary of Commerce*, 1938, p. 127.

[3] Ibid., pp. 125, 127.

[4] Ibid., p. 130.

[5] Putnam, p. 207.

[6] Ibid., p. 200.

[7] Commissioner of Lighthouses to Superintendent of Lighthouses, Portland, Maine, January 12, 1925; Superintendent Sherman to Commissioner of Lighthouses, February 4, 1927 (NA, RG 26, E 50, File # 74B).

[8] Edward H. Carlson, "Portland Lightship Will Return to Station after Undergoing Repairs: Vessel Which Has Been in Continuous Service Off Cape Elizabeth 26 Years, Has Had Complete Overhauling in Preparation for Winter Gales," *Portland Press Herald*, October 12, 1928. Courtesy of Ken Black.

[9] "New Radio Beacon for Lonely Island on the Maine Coast," January 27, 1932, author and newspaper unknown, p. 99. Courtesy of Ken Black.

[10] "First Lighthouse District Now Has 3 Radio Beacons," from unknown newspaper dated May 8, 1932. Courtesy of Ken Black.

[11] "Manana Island Station Will Enable Vessels to Determine Distance from Land," author unknown, *Bar Harbor Times*, December 24, 1937. Courtesy of Ken Black.

[12] U.S. Commerce Department, *Annual Report of the Secretary of Commerce*, 1938, p. 125.

[13] U.S. Coast Guard, *Aids to Navigation, 1945* (Washington, D.C.: Government Printing Office, 1946), p. 1101.

[14] LORAN determines location through triangulation based on a string of radio stations. It also provides distance and bearing (direction) of other locations, which can be saved until needed. It gives speed of craft and rate of progress, continually adjusting for wind and current. Now being superseded by Global Positioning System (GPS), which uses satellites to determine exact location.

[15] Jeremy D'Entremont's history of Dice Head Light Station at <www.lighthouse.cc/dicehead/history.html> and Friends of Flying Santa website at <www.flyingsanta.com>.

[16] December 31, 1932, column of the *Courier-Gazette.* Reprinted with permission from the *Courier-Gazette*, Rockland, Maine.

[17] Brian Tague, *The Origins and History of the Flying Santa, 1929-2001*, at <www.flyingsanta.com/HistoryOrigins.html>.

[18] 1911 entry, Keeper's journal, Egg Rock Light Station (NA, RG 26, E 80).

[19] James Donohue, Maine Commissioner of Sea & Shore Fisheries, Rockland, to George M. Bowers, Commissioner of Fisheries, Washington, D.C., January 20, 1911 (NA, RG 26, E 50, File #524).

[20] Petition received by Bureau of Lighthouses, January 7, 1911 (NA, RG 26, E 50, File #524).

[21] McDonald to Bureau of Lighthouses, June 14, 1911 (NA, RG 26, E 50, File #524).

[22] Tapley to McDonald, February 4, 1911 (NA, RG 26, E 50, File #524).

[23] George R. Putnam to A. E. Wallace, June 17, 1911 (NA, RG 26, E 50, File #524).

[24] *Courier-Gazette*, February 4, 1933. Reprinted with permission from the *Courier-Gazette*, Rockland, Maine.

[25] Ibid.

[26] Ibid., February 4, 1933.

[27] Ibid., February 11, 1933.

[28] Ibid., February 18, 1933.

[29] Ibid., February 25, 1933.

[30] C. E. Sherman, December 13, 1932 (NA, RG 26, E 50, File # 665).

[31] Nichols to USLHB, July 29, 1898 (NA, RG 26 E 24 or Letterbook 1219).

[32] Reprinted with permission from the *Courier-Gazette*, Rockland, Maine.

[33] Ibid.

[34] Ibid.

[35] C. E. Sherman, Superintendent of Lighthouses, "Form 80: Recommendations as to Aids to Navigation," October 20, 1932 (NA, RG 26, E 50, File # 3910).

[36] 1857 *Annual Report.*

Epilogue

As technology changed in the twentieth century, so did the role of the traditional keeper. With the development of automated lights and fog signals, many keeper positions became obsolete. In the 1960s, the Coast Guard began a system of comprehensive automation. By the late 1980s, most stations in Maine had been automated. The last resident keeper, Karen McLean, was stationed at the Doubling Point Range Lights, and kept the lights at nearby Doubling Point and Squirrel Point. The last of those lights were automated in 1990, and McLean left a couple of years later.[1] The dwelling at the Doubling Point Range Station still serves as the quarters for Coast Guard Group Portland. Although many towers still retain a working optic, by the end of the twentieth century, sophisticated navigational equipment such as global positioning systems (GPS) had rendered lighthouses technologically obsolete.

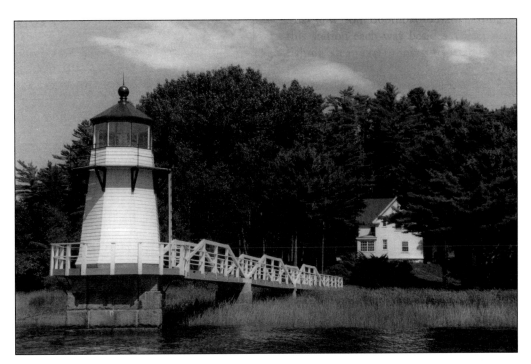

The tower originally built onshore at Doubling Point was moved offshore onto a pier around 1899.[2] In 1935 the keepers at neighboring Doubling Point Range Light Station took over the duties of the keeper at Doubling Point. The dwelling and grounds were sold to a private owner. In 1998 the Friends of Doubling Point acquired the tower and pier under the Maine Lights Program. Their first major task was to repair the granite-block foundation, which had been damaged by ice. (2002 photo by Candace Clifford)

As personnel left the light stations, the Coast Guard sometimes destroyed auxiliary buildings to cut down on maintenance costs and prevent vandalism. Some stations lost their keepers' quarters and other support structures no longer needed for aiding navigation. Not surprisingly, maintenance of traditional lighthouses was a low priority in budgeting the limited resources of the Coast Guard. In many cases the Coast Guard moved the light onto a steel pole to avoid the costly maintenance of a tower.

As some stations fell into neglect, concerned community groups and non-profit organizations began to pursue leasing arrangements with the Coast Guard to help maintain and preserve the treasured landmarks. In 1996 congressional legislation permitted the Coast Guard to transfer 36 Maine lights to the Island Institute of Rockland, Maine, under the Maine Lights Program so that the most appropriate steward could be chosen through an application process reviewed by a selection committee.

A variety of stewards now keep Maine's lighthouses: Baker Island and Bass Harbor Head Light Stations can be viewed within the boundaries of Acadia National Park. Egg Rock, Libby Island, Matinicus Rock, Petit Manan, and Two Bush Island are located within National

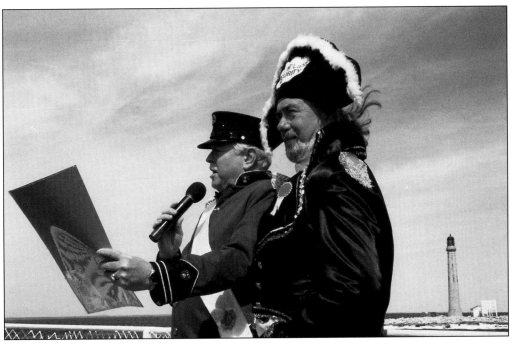

The U.S. Coast Guard burned the deteriorated keepers' dwelling at Boon Island (facing page) when maintaining it was no longer viable. (Photo courtesy of U.S. Coast Guard) Today the station is leased to the American Lighthouse Foundation, which developed a novel fund-raising and public relations scheme. On April 1, 2003, newspapers reported that the "Republic of Boon Island" had declared its independence. A special cruise commemorated the day, with Tim Harrison, Regent Lord Master of the Republic of Boon Island (and Chairman of the American Lighthouse Foundation), reading the Declaration of Boon Independence, Secretary General Ron Foster at his side (above). (Photo by Jeremy D'Entremont) Interested parties may pay for the privilege of becoming citizens and obtaining political office.

A retired Coast Guard officer and founder of the Shore Village Museum in Rockland, Maine, Ken Black (right) poses with the third-order fixed Fresnel lens from Whitehead Island Lighthouse. The museum boasts one of the country's largest collections of lighthouse artifacts, including lenses, fog signals, and lamps. Most of the equipment is in working condition so the visitor can see the functioning lights and hear the various fog signals. In 2005, the collection will be moved to a new location on the Rockland waterfront and the museum will be renamed Maine's Lighthouse Museum. (Photo by Candace Clifford, 2002)

Maine Lighthouses: Documentation of Their Past

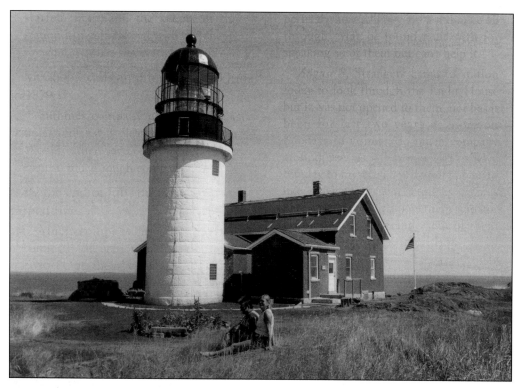

After Seguin Island Light Station was automated in 1985, local citizens concerned about its preservation and upkeep formed the Friends of Seguin. In 1989 they acquired a lease from the U.S. Coast Guard to maintain the station. In 1996, they applied for, and later received, full jurisdiction over the station through the Maine Lights Program, which transferred 28 stations to federal and state agencies, local municipalities, and non-profits. The original fixed, first-order Henry LePaute 1857 lens remains in the Seguin lantern as an active aid to navigation maintained by the Coast Guard. Friends of Seguin hire caretakers every summer to live on the island and provide access to the tower and museum housed in one side of the duplex keepers' quarters. Visitors must have a boat to transport them to the island; moorings are provided (there is no dock). The caretakers also cut the grass; maintain the four public trails on the 64-acre island; keep a log; clean the quarters, museum, and tower; and do needed repairs and painting. They host approximately 2,500 visitors each summer.[3] Anne Webster, former director of the Maine Lights Program and president of Friends of Seguin, relaxes with her husband, Troy Wallace, in front of the Seguin Lighthouse. (Photo by Candace Clifford, 2002)

Wildlife Refuges managed by the U.S. Fish and Wildlife Service. The State of Maine's Department of Marine Resources has restored Burnt Island Light Station and interprets it as it was in the 1950s. School groups visit the island on both day and overnight trips for programs in marine and maritime education.

The grounds of Fort Point and West Quoddy Head Light Stations are accessible in two state parks. The town of Vinalhaven uses the keeper's quarters at Browns Head as a residence for the town manager, while the towns of Cape Elizabeth, St. George, Bristol, and Islesboro have set up museums at Portland Head, Marshall Point, Pemaquid Point, and Grindle Point Light Stations. The College of the Atlantic owns and maintains the light stations at Great Duck Island and Mount Desert Rock as part of their educational programs in ecological research. The American Lighthouse Foundation, a national non-profit with multiple local chapters, is involved with the preservation of Boon Island, Cape Elizabeth, Halfway Rock, Little River Island, Pemaquid Point, Perkins Island, Prospect Harbor, Rockland Harbor Breakwater, and Wood Island Light Stations.

The Pine Island Camp, which already owned land on Whitehead Island, acquired Whitehead Island Light Station in 1998 through the Maine Lights Program. The Coast Guard still maintains a light and fog signal there. The camp's first major repair was a new roof for the surviving keeper's dwelling and whistle house. Interior restoration of the duplex keeper's dwelling was completed through the camp's "Whitehead lightkeepers" program for 15- and 16-year-old high school students who spend three weeks on the island during the summer. From 1999 through 2001, they spent a part of each day removing plaster and damaged woodwork, scraping paint, and painting while a professional crew replaced the walls. The dwelling will be used for camp housing.[4] (Photo by Candace Clifford, 2002)

The first step facing any new lighthouse steward is to repair and stabilize the property. Without the daily care and maintenance of resident keepers, the buildings quickly deteriorate in the harsh marine environment. Bringing these buildings back is a challenging task, especially on offshore stations. Taking a creative approach, the Friends of Seguin relied on National Guard helicopters to move materials for building a new roof. Volunteer manpower for other projects has come from the Coast Guard, the Navy, the Sheriff's Department, and the Eagle Scouts. Some stations with more established preservation programs have developed interpretive exhibits and displays, welcoming thousands of visitors. Deeded to the Town of Cape Elizabeth in 1990, Portland Head Lighthouse reportedly draws close to a million visitors annually.

Lighthouses were built for the simple utilitarian purpose of guiding mariners safely to their destination. With that essential function now obsolete, these structures today evoke a more rigorous era when Maine depended on the sea for its livelihood. The landscapes they dominate touch our hearts with memories of what aids to navigation meant to "those in peril on the sea." Dedicated groups and communities who cherish the strong emotions that lighthouses evoke have replaced the faithful keepers who kept the lights burning and the fog signals running through all the dark nights and foggy days. The task now is to preserve these landmarks so as to offer their rich histories to future generations.

Endnotes

[1]Personal communication from Anne Webster Wallace, Georgetown, Maine, November 23, 2003.
[2]1900 *Annual Report*.
[3]Interview with Anne Webster, President of Friends of Seguin, Inc., and former Director of the Maine Lights Program, September 2002.
[4]Interview with David Gamage, Whitehead Island resident and grandson of former lighthouse keeper Arthur Beal, September 2002.

Epilogue

Appendix: Maine's Light Stations

Avery Rock (site)
Location: Island in Machias Bay
Year station established: 1875
Year last existing tower lit: 1875
Is the light operational? No
Date deactivated: 1946 (tower destroyed in a storm)

Baker Island
Location: Cranberry Isles/Somes Sound Approach
Year station established: 1828
Year existing historic tower lit: 1855
Is the light operational? No
Date deactivated: 2002
Owner/manager:U.S. Coast Guard owns station/National Park Service owns island
Current use: Active aid to navigation in National Park
Open to the public? Yes, grounds open summers by National Park Service tour
Access: Offshore in Acadia National Park

Bass Harbor Head
Location: Mount Desert Island
Year station established: 1858
Year existing historic tower lit: 1858
Is the light operational? Yes
Owner/manager: U.S. Coast Guard
Current use: Active aid to navigation/ Coast Guard housing

Open to the public? Yes, grounds only
Access: Acadia National Park

Bear Island
Location: Bear Island/Northeast Harbor
Year station established: 1839
Year existing historic tower lit: 1889
Is the light operational? Yes
Dates deactivated: 1981-1989
Owner/manager: National Park Service
Current use: Leased to private party/ private aid to navigation
Open to the public? No

Blue Hill Bay
Location: On Green Island/Blue Hill Bay
Year station established: 1856
Year existing historic tower lit: 1856
Is the light operational? No
Date deactivated: 1933
Owner/manager: Private owner
Current use: Summer home
Open to the public? No

Boon Island
Location: Off York Beach
Year station established: 1812 (unlighted beacon in 1799)
Year existing historic tower lit: 1855
Is the light operational? Yes
Owner/manager: U.S. Coast Guard lease to American Lighthouse Foundation

Current use: Active aid to navigation
Open to the public? No

Browns Head
Location: Northwest end of Vinalhaven Island
Year station established: 1832
Year existing historic tower lit: 1857
Is the light operational? Yes
Owner/manager: Town of Vinalhaven
Current use: Active aid to navigation/ residence for town manager
Open to the public? Yes, grounds open year round
Access: Ferry from Rockland

Burnt Coat Harbor
Location: Hockamock Head/Swans Island
Year station established: 1872
Year existing historic tower lit: 1872
Is the light operational? Yes (front range discontinued in 1884 and removed)
Owner/manager: Town of Swans Island
Current use: Active aid to navigation
Open to the public? Yes, grounds only
Access: Ferry from Bass Harbor

Burnt Island
Location: West side of Boothbay Harbor entrance
Year station established: 1821
Year existing historic tower lit: 1821

Is the light operational? Yes
Owner/manager: Maine Department of
   Marine Resources
Current use: Active aid to navigation/
   educational facility
Open to the public? Yes, grounds open
   daily 10 a.m.-5 p.m. during spring,
   summer, and fall
Access: Boat

Cape Elizabeth
Location: Casco Bay entrance
Year station established: 1828
Year existing historic towers lit: 1874
Is the light operational? Yes (east tower)
Owner/manager: U.S. Coast Guard (east
   tower)/private owner (west tower)
Current use: Active aid to navigation in
   east tower/west tower is part of private
   residence
Open to the public? No
Access: East tower can be viewed from
   Twin Lights State Park

Cape Neddick "The Nubble"
Location: Off Cape Neddick/York Harbor
Year station established: 1879
Year existing historic tower lit: 1879
Is the light operational? Yes
Owner/manager: Town of York
Current use: Active aid to navigation
Open to the public? No
Access: Can be viewed from Sohier City
   Park

Crabtree Ledge (site)
Location: Frenchman Bay
Year station established: 1890
Year existing historic tower lit: 1890
Is the light operational? No
Date deactivated: 1934 (tower later
   destroyed in a storm)

(The) Cuckolds
Location: Cape Newagen/Booth Bay
   Approach
Year station established: 1892
Year existing historic tower lit: 1907
Is the light operational? Yes
Owner/manager: U.S. Coast Guard
Current use: Active aid to navigation
Open to the public? No

Curtis Island
Location: Camden Harbor entrance/
   Penobscot Bay
Year station established: 1835
Year existing historic tower lit: 1896
Is the light operational? Yes
Owner/manager: Town of Camden
Current use: Active aid to navigation in
   town park
Open to the public? Yes, grounds are park
Access: Boat

Deer Island Thorofare
Location: Mark Island/Deer Island
   Thorofare
Year station established: 1858
Year existing historic tower lit: 1858
Is the light operational? Yes
Owner/manager: Island Heritage Trust
Current use: Active aid to navigation in
   bird sanctuary
Open to the public? No

Dice Head (Old)
Location: Penobscot River mouth
Year station established: 1829
Year existing historic tower lit: 1829
Is the light operational? No
Date deactivated: 1937
Owner/manager: Town of Castine
Current use: Private residence
Open to the public? Yes, grounds only
Access: Car

Doubling Point Range
Location: Arrowsic Island/Kennebec River
Year station established: 1898
Year existing historic tower lit: 1898
Is the light operational? Yes
Owner/manager: Range Light Keepers
Current use: Active aid to navigation
Open to the public? Yes, grounds only
Access: Car

Doubling Point
Location: Arrowsic Island/Kennebec River
Year station established: 1899
Year existing historic tower lit: 1899
Is the light operational? Yes
Owner/manager: Friends of Doubling
   Point own tower; grounds and dwelling
   are privately owned
Current use: Active aid to navigation
Open to the public? No

Eagle Island
Location: East Penobscot Bay
Year station established: 1838
Year existing historic tower lit: 1838
Is the light operational? Yes
Owner/manager: Eagle Light Caretakers
   own tower
Current use: Active aid to navigation
Open to the public? No

Egg Rock
Location: Entrance to Frenchman Bay near
   Winter Harbor
Year station established: 1875
Year existing historic tower lit: 1875
Is the light operational? Yes
Owner/manager: U.S. Fish & Wildlife
   Service
Current use: Active aid to navigation
Open to the public? No

Fort Point

Location: Entrance to Penobscot River
Year station established: 1837
Year existing historic tower lit: 1857
Is the light operational? Yes
Owner/manager: State of Maine
Current use: Active aid to navigation in state park
Open to the public? Yes, grounds only
Access: Fort Point State Park

Fort Popham (site)

Location: Popham Beach/Kennebec River
Year station established: 1903
Year existing historic tower lit: 1903
Is the light operational? No
Date deactivated: 1949 (light moved onto fort)

Franklin Island

Location: Muscongus Bay
Year station established: 1807 (replaced 1805 daymark)
Year existing historic tower lit: 1855
Is the light operational? Yes
Owner/manager: U.S. Coast Guard
Current use: Active aid to navigation
Open to the public? No

Goat Island

Location: Cape Porpoise Harbor
Year station established: 1835
Year existing historic tower lit: 1859
Is the light operational? Yes
Owner/manager: Kennebunkport Conservation Trust
Current use: Active aid to navigation
Open to the public? Yes
Access: By private boat at high tide

Dice Head Light Station, deactivated in 1937, now serves as a private residence. The surrounding grounds are a public park. (National Archives photo # 26-LG-1-92)

Goose Rocks

Location: East entrance Fox Islands Thorofare
Year station established: 1890
Year existing historic tower lit: 1890
Is the light operational? Yes
Owner/manager: U.S. Coast Guard
Current use: Active aid to navigation
Open to the public? No

Great Duck Island

Location: Blue Hill Bay Approach
Year station established: 1890
Year existing historic tower lit: 1890
Is the light operational? Yes
Owner/manager: College of the Atlantic
Current use: Active aid to navigation/ ecological research
Open to the public? No

Grindle Point
Location: Gilkey Harbor
Year station established: 1850
Year existing historic tower lit: 1874
Is the light operational? Yes
Date deactivated: 1934-1987
Owner/manager: Town of Islesboro
Current use: Active aid to navigation/ museum in keeper's dwelling
Open to the public? Yes, summers by appointment
Access: Ferry from Lincolnville Beach

Halfway Rock
Location: Casco Bay off Bailey Island
Year station established: 1871
Year existing historic tower lit: 1871
Is the light operational? Yes
Owner/manager: U.S. Coast Guard lease to American Lighthouse Foundation
Current use: Active aid to navigation
Open to the public? No

Hendricks Head
Location: Sheepscot River Entrance
Year station established: 1829
Year existing historic tower lit: 1875
Is the light operational? Yes
Dates deactivated: 1935-1951
Owner/manager: Private owner
Current use: Active aid to navigation/ private residence
Open to the public? No

Heron Neck
Location: Green's Island
Year station established: 1854
Year existing historic tower lit: 1854
Is the light operational? Yes
Owner/manager: Island Institute
Current use: Active aid to navigation/ research & education facility
Open to the public? No

Indian Island
Location: Rockport Harbor
Year station established: 1850
Year existing historic tower lit: 1874
Is the light operational? No
Date deactivated: 1934
Owner/manager: Private owner
Current use: Private property
Open to the public? No

Isle au Haut
Location: Robinson Point
Year station established: 1907
Year existing historic tower lit: 1907
Is the light operational? Yes
Owner/manager: Town of Isle au Haut owns tower/private owner owns other buildings
Current use: Active aid to navigation/inn
Open to the public? Yes, tower open on special occasions
Access: Ferry from Stonington

Libby Island
Location: Machias Bay entrance
Year station established: 1822
Year existing historic tower lit: 1823
Is the light operational? Yes
Owner/manager: U.S. Fish & Wildlife Service
Current use: Active aid to navigation in National Wildlife Refuge
Open to the public? No

Little River Island
Location: Cutler Harbor
Year station established: 1847
Year existing historic tower lit: 1876
Is the light operational? No
Date deactivated: 1975
Owner/manager: American Lighthouse Foundation

Current use: Bird sanctuary/under restoration
Open to the public? Yes
Access: Boat

Lubec Channel
Location: Lubec Channel
Year station established: 1890
Year existing historic tower lit: 1890
Is the light operational? Yes
Owner/manager: U.S. Coast Guard
Current use: Active aid to navigation
Open to the public? No

Marshall Point
Location: Port Clyde Harbor entrance
Year station established: 1832
Year existing historic tower lit: 1857
Is the light operational? Yes
Owner/manager: Town of St. George/St. George Historical Society
Current use: Active aid to navigation/ museum
Open to the public? Yes, museum in keeper's dwelling
Access: Marshall Point Road

Matinicus Rock
Location: 6 miles south of Matinicus Island
Year station established: 1827
Year existing historic tower lit: 1857
Is the light operational? Yes
Owner/manager: U.S. Fish & Wildlife Service
Current use: Active aid to navigation in National Wildlife Refuge
Open to the public? Yes, grounds open daily and tower by appointment, September through March
Access: Boat

Monhegan Island

Location: Monhegan Island
Year station established: 1824
Year existing historic tower lit: 1850
Is the light operational? Yes
Owner/manager: Monhegan Historical & Cultural Museum
Current use: Active aid to navigation/museum in keeper's dwelling
Open to the public? Yes, museum open July 1 to September 30, 11:30 a.m. to 3:30 p.m.
Access: Ferry from Port Clyde

Moose Peak

Location: Mistake Island/Eastern Bay
Year station established: 1826
Year existing historic tower lit: 1851
Is the light operational? Yes
Owner/manager: U.S. Coast Guard lease to Nature Conservancy
Current use: Active aid to navigation in nature preserve
Open to the public? No

Mount Desert Rock

Location: South of Mount Desert Island
Year station established: 1830
Year existing historic tower lit: 1847
Is the light operational? Yes
Owner/manager: College of the Atlantic
Current use: Active aid to navigation/wildlife research
Open to the public? No

Narraguagus

Location: East side Pond Island/Narraguagus Bay
Year station established: 1853
Year existing historic tower lit: 1853
Is the light operational? No
Date deactivated: 1934
Owner/manager: Private owner

Current use: Resort
Open to the public? No

Nash Island

Location: Southeast mouth of Pleasant Bay
Year station established: 1838
Year existing historic tower lit: 1874
Is the light operational? No
Date deactivated: 1982
Owner/manager: Friends of Nash Island, Inc.
Current use: Under restoration
Open to the public? No

Owls Head

Location: West Penobscot Bay/Rockland Harbor
Year station established: 1825
Year existing historic tower lit: 1825
Is the light operational? Yes
Owner/manager: U.S. Coast Guard
Current use: Active aid to navigation/Coast Guard housing in keeper's dwelling
Open to the public? Yes, grounds only
Access: Knox County Lighthouse Park off Route 73

Pemaquid Point

Location: Entrance to Muscongus Bay
Year station established: 1827
Year existing historic tower lit: 1835
Is the light operational? Yes
Owner/manager: U.S. Coast Guard owns tower, which is licensed to the American Lighthouse Foundation/Town of Bristol owns remainder
Current use: Active aid to navigation/Fishermen's Museum in keeper's dwelling

Open to the public? Yes, grounds open daily, tower occasionally
Access: End of Route 130

Perkins Island

Location: Kennebec River
Year station established: 1898
Year existing historic tower lit: 1898
Is the light operational? Yes
Owner/manager: U.S. Coast Guard owns tower/State of Maine owns dwelling
Current use: Active aid to navigation
Open to the public? Yes, grounds only
Access: Boat

Petit Manan

Location: Off Petit Manan Point
Year station established: 1817
Year existing historic tower lit: 1855
Is the light operational? Yes
Owner/manager: U.S. Coast Guard owns tower/U.S. Fish & Wildlife Service owns remainder
Current use: Active aid to navigation in National Wildlife Refuge
Open to the public? Yes, grounds open September through March
Access: Private boat

Pond Island

Location: West Side Kennebec River entrance
Year station established: 1821
Year existing historic tower lit: 1855
Is the light operational? Yes
Owner/manager: U.S. Coast Guard
Current use: Active aid to navigation in bird refuge
Open to the public? No

Portland Breakwater
Location: Portland Harbor
Year station established: 1855
Year existing historic tower lit: 1875
Is the light operational? No
Date deactivated: 1942
Owner/manager: City of South Portland
Current use: Town park
Open to the public? Yes, grounds only
Access: Off Breakwater Drive at "Bug
    Light Park"

Portland Head
Location: Portland Harbor/Casco Bay
Year station established: 1791
Year existing historic tower lit: 1791
Is the light operational? Yes
Owner/manager: Town of Cape Elizabeth
Current use: Active aid to navigation/
    museum
Open to the public? Yes, grounds open
    daily
Access: Fort Williams Park, 1000 Shore
    Road

Prospect Harbor
Location: Prospect Harbor Point
Year station established: 1850
Year existing historic tower lit: 1891
Is the light operational? Yes
Dates deactivated: 1859-1870
Owner/manager: U.S. Coast Guard owns
    tower and leases it to American
    Lighthouse Foundation/U.S. Navy
    owns remaining property
Current use: Active aid to navigation/
    keeper's dwelling used as Navy guest
    house
Open to the public? No

Pumpkin Island
Location: Eggemoggin Reach/Penobscot
    Bay
Year station established: 1854
Year existing historic tower lit: 1854
Is the light operational? No
Date deactivated: 1933
Owner/manager: Private owner
Current use: Private property
Open to the public? No

Ram Island
Location: Boothbay Harbor
Year station established: 1883
Year existing historic tower lit: 1883
Is the light operational? Yes
Owner/manager: Grand Banks Schooner
    Trust
Current use: Active aid to navigation
Open to the public? No

Ram Island Ledge
Location: Portland Harbor/Casco Bay
Year station established: 1905
Year existing historic tower lit: 1905
Is the light operational? Yes
Owner/manager: U.S. Coast Guard
Current use: Active aid to navigation
Open to the public? No

Rockland Harbor Breakwater
Location: Jameson Point/Rockland Harbor
Year station established: 1902 (replaced
    earlier aids to navigation on breakwater)
Year existing historic tower lit: 1902
Is the light operational? Yes
Owner/manager: City of Rockland lease to
    Friends of Rockland Breakwater
    Lighthouse
Current use: Active aid to navigation
Open to the public? Yes, grounds only
Access: End of Breakwater/Waldo Avenue
    and Samoset Road

Saddleback Ledge
Location: Isle au Haut Bay
Year station established: 1839
Year existing historic tower lit: 1839
Is the light operational? Yes
Owner/manager: U.S. Coast Guard
Current use: Active aid to navigation
Open to the public? No

Seguin Island
Location: Off Kennebec River mouth
Year station established: 1796
Year existing historic tower lit: 1857
Is the light operational? Yes
Owner/manager: Friends of Seguin Island,
    Inc.
Current use: Active aid to navigation/
    museum/bird sanctuary
Open to the public? Yes, open Memorial
    Day through Labor Day
Access: Boat from Bath, Popham Beach, or
    Boothbay Harbor

Spring Point Ledge
Location: Portland Harbor
Year station established: 1897
Year existing historic tower lit: 1897
Is the light operational? Yes
Owner/manager: Spring Point Ledge
    Light Trust
Current use: Active aid to navigation
Open to the public? Yes, grounds only -
    breakwater open anytime; Spring Point
    Museum open May through September
Access: Fort Preble Area

Squirrel Point
Location: Arrowsic Island/Kennebec River
Year station established: 1898
Year existing historic tower lit: 1898
Is the light operational? Yes
Owner/manager: Squirrel Point
    Association, Inc.

Current use: Active aid to navigation
Open to the public? No

St. Croix River (site)
Location: St. Croix Island
Year station established: 1857
Year last existing tower lit: 1901
Is the light operational? No
Date deactivated: 1976 (destroyed by fire)

Tenants Harbor
Location: Southern Island
Year station established: 1857
Year existing historic tower lit: 1857
Is the light operational? No
Date deactivated: 1933
Owner/manager: Private owner
Current use: Private property
Open to the public? No

Two Bush Island
Location: Two Bush Channel/Penobscot
    Bay Approach
Year station established: 1897
Year existing historic tower lit: 1897
Is the light operational? Yes
Owner/manager: U.S. Fish & Wildlife
    Service
Current use: Active aid to navigation
Open to the public? No

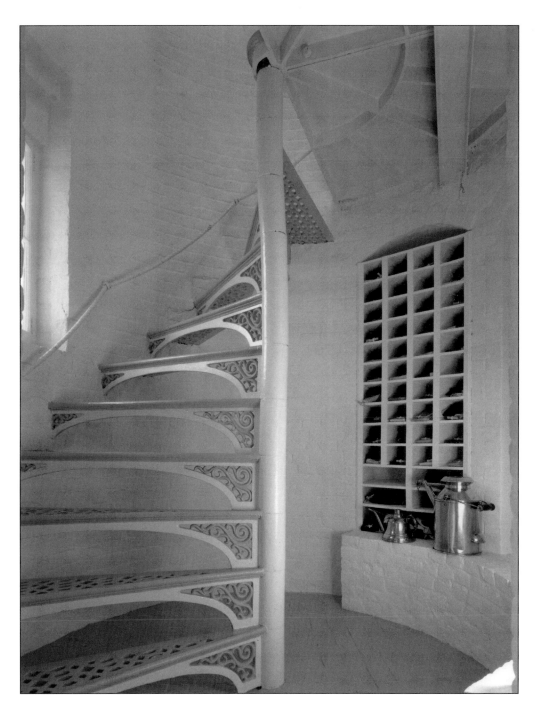

Stairway in privately owned Tenants Harbor Lighthouse. HABS/HAER photo by RIchard Clark, 1989.

West Quoddy Head
Location: Bay of Fundy
Year station established: 1808
Year existing historic tower lit: 1858
Is the light operational? Yes
Owner/manager: State of Maine Division of Natural Resources
Current use: Active aid to navigation in state park
Open to the public? Yes, grounds only 9 a.m. to sunset
Access: Quoddy Head State Park/Route 189

Whaleback Ledge
Location: Portsmouth Harbor/Piscataqua River
Year station established: 1820
Year existing historic tower lit: 1872
Is the light operational? Yes
Owner/manager: U.S. Coast Guard
Current use: Active aid to navigation
Open to the public? No

Whitehead Island
Location: Penobscot Bay southern entrance
Year station established: 1804
Year existing historic tower lit: 1852
Is the light operational? Yes
Owner/manager: Pine Island Camp
Current use: Active aid to navigation/ under restoration for educational programs and museum
Open to the public? No

Whitlocks Mill
Location: St. Croix River south bank
Year station established: 1892 (red lantern hung from a tree)
Year existing historic tower lit: 1910
Is the light operational? Yes
Owner/manager: St. Croix Historical Society owns tower/dwelling privately owned
Current use: Active aid to navigation
Open to the public? No

Winter Harbor
Location: Mark Island
Year station established: 1856
Year existing historic tower lit: 1856
Is the light operational? No
Date deactivated: 1933
Owner/manager: Private owner
Current use: Privately owned
Open to the public? No

Wood Island
Location: East side Wood Island/Saco River mouth
Year station established: 1807
Year existing historic tower lit: 1858
Is the light operational? Yes
Owner/manager: U.S. Coast Guard leases tower to Friends of Wood Island Lighthouse
Current use: Active aid to navigation in bird sanctuary
Open to the public? No

Note: These are stations that once had a resident keeper. "Year station established" refers to the year in which the tower was first lit. This appendix is based on the National Park Service's *Inventory of Historic Light Stations* available at <www.cr.nps.gov/maritime/light/me.htm>. Some of the material has been updated or revised by the author. Another good source for information on Maine lighthouses is Jeremy D'Entremont's web site at <www.lighthouse.cc/>.

Appendix: Maine's Light Stations

Bibliography

Bachelder, Peter Dow, *The Lighthouses & Lightships of Casco Bay* (Portland, Maine: The Breakwater Press, 1975)

A Biographical Directory of the U.S. Customs Service, 1771- 1989 (Washington, D.C.: U.S. Customs Service, Department of the Treasury, 1985)

Brown, Dona, *Inventing New England: Regional Tourism in the Nineteenth Century* (Washington: Smithsonian Institution Press, 1995)

Caldwell, Bill, *Lighthouses of Maine* (Camden, Maine: Down East Books, 1986)

Carse, Robert, *Keeper of the Lights: A History of American Lighthouses* (New York: Charles Scribners & Sons, 1968)

Clifford, Candace, editor, *1994 Inventory of Historic Light Stations*, National Park Service, National Maritime Initiative (Washington, D.C.: Government Printing Office, 1994). See web site at <www.cr.nps.gov/maritime/ltsum.htm>

_____, *U.S. Coast Guard Cutter Fir (WLM-212): A Lighthouse/Buoy Tender for the Pacific Northwest*, Historic American Engineering Record, National Park Service, 2001

Clifford, J. Candace and Mary Louise, *Nineteenth-Century Lights: Historic Images of American Lighthouses* (Alexandria, Virginia: Cypress Communications, 2000)

_____, *Women Who Kept the Lights: An Illustrated History of Female Lighthouse Keepers*, second edition (Alexandria, Virginia: Cypress Communications, 2001)

D'Entremont, Jeremy, "New England Lighthouses: A Virtual Guide," web site at <www.lighthouse.cc>

Hart, Frederick C., Jr., "Keepers of the Matinicus Light: Isaac H. and Abbie E. (Burgess) Grant and their Families" in *The New England Historical and Genealogical Register*, Volume 150, October 1996/Whole Number 600

Holland, Francis Ross, Jr., *America's Lighthouses: An Illustrated History* (New York: Dover Publications, Inc., 1972)

_____, *Great American Lighthouses* (Washington, D.C.: The Preservation Press, 1989)

Johnson, Arnold Burges, *Modern Light-House Service* (Washington, D.C.: Government Printing Office, 1890)

Marshall, Amy K., "A history of buoys and tenders," *Commandant's Bulletin*, November 1995

National Archives, Record Group 26 (Washington, D.C.):

Entry 6 (NC-31): "Annual Reports, 1820-53"

Entry 9 (NC-31): "Reports Submitted to the Board by Committees, 1874-1900"

Entry 16 (NC-31): "Miscellaneous Records, 1816-1929, 1918-36"

Entry 17A (NC-31): "Letters Received by the Treasury Department, 1785-1812"

Entry 17C (NC-31): "Letters Received from the Superintendents of Lights, 1803-52"

Entry 17D (NC-31): "Superintendent of Lighthouses Replies to Circulars, 1830-38"

Entry 17E (NC-31): "Letters Received from Winslow Lewis, 1811-44"

Entry 17F (NC-31): "Miscellaneous Letters Received (Alphabetical), 1801-52"

Entry 17G (NC-31): "Miscellaneous Letters Received (Numerical), 1801-52"

Entry 17H (NC-31): "Draft Copies of Letters Sent, 1813-52"

Entry 17J (NC-31): "Correspondence Relating to the Appointment of Keepers, 1801-52"

Entry 17K (NC-31): "Letters Received from the Secretary of the Treasury, 1830-52"

Entry 18 (NC-31): "Letters Sent Regarding the Light-House Service, 1792-1852"

Entry 23 (NC-31):"Letters Sent to District Inspectors and Engineers, 1852-1910"

Entry 24 (NC-31): "Letters Received from District Engineers and Inspectors, ca. 1853-1900"

Entry 25 (NC-31): "Correspondence of the Naval Committee, 1837-38"

Entry 35 (NC-31): "Lighthouse Letters, Series P, 1833-64"

Entry 45 (NC-31): "Miscellaneous Material Received by the Fifth Auditor, 1812-52"

Entry 46 (NC-31): "Correspondence of the Light-House Board, 1851-70"

Entry 48 (NC-31): "Correspondence of the Light-House Board, 1901-10"

Entry 50 (NC-31): "Correspondence of the Bureau of Light-Houses, 1911-39"

Entry 63 (NC-31)/Entry 6 (A-1): "Descriptive Lists of Lighthouse Stations, 1858-89, 1876-1939"

Entry 80 (NC-31): "Lighthouse Station Logs, 1872-1941"

Entry 98 (NC-31): "List of Light-House Keepers and Other Employees 1845-1912" (National Archives Microfilm Publication M1373)

Entry 111(NC-31): "Record of Reclassification of Light-House Keepers Salaries, 1922-28"

Entry 328 (A-1): "Buoy Tender Logs, 1873-1941"

National Archives, Record Group 26 (Waltham, Massachusetts)

Panayotoff, Ted, and Courtney Thompson. *The Lighthouse at Rockland Breakwater* (Rockland, Maine: The Friends of Rockland Breakwater, 2002)

Putnam, George R., *Sentinels of the Coasts* (New York: W.W. Norton & Company, Inc., 1937)

Rowe, William Hutchinson, *The Maritime History of Maine: Three Centuries of Shipbuilding and Seafaring* (New York: W.W. Norton & Company, 1948)

Shanks, Ralph, and Wick York, *The U.S. Life-Saving Service: Heroes, Rescues and Architecture of the Early Coast Guard* (Petaluma, California: Costano Books, 1996)

Sterling, Robert Thayer, *Lighthouses of the Maine Coast and the Men Who Kept Them* (Brattleboro, Vermont: Stephen Daye Press, 1935)

Small, Connie Scovill, *The Lighthouse Keeper's Wife* (Orono, Maine: The University of Maine Press, 1999)

Snow, Edward Rowe, *The Lighthouses of New England,* updated edition (Beverly, Massachusetts: Commonwealth Editions, 2002)

Thomas, Miriam Stover, *Come Hell or High Water* (Harpswell, Maine: 1970)

U.S. Coast Guard, *Aids to Navigation, 1945* (Washington, D.C.: Government Printing Office, 1946)

U.S. Coast Guard Historian's web site at <www.uscg.mil/hq/g-cp/history/collect.html>

U.S. Department of Commerce, *Annual Report of the Secretary of Commerce,* 1938

U.S. Light-House Board, Treasury Department, *Annual Reports of the Lighthouse Board* (Washington, D.C.)

U.S. Light-House Board, Treasury Department, *Instructions to Light-House Keepers, July 1881* (Washington, D.C.: Government Printing Office, 1881)

U.S. Light-House Board, Treasury Department, *Laws and Regulations Relating to the Light-House Establishment of the United States,* by authority of the Treasury Department (Washington, D.C.: Government Printing Office, 1880)

U.S. Light-House Board, Treasury Department, Various *Light Lists,* 1850s-1910

U.S. Light-House Board, Treasury Department, *Organization and Duties of the Light-house Board; and Regulations, Instructions, Circulars, and General Orders of the Light-house Establishment of the United States* (Washington, D.C.: Government Printing Office, 1871)

U.S. Light-House Establishment, *Public Documents and Extracts from Reports and Papers Relating to Light-Houses, Light-Vessels, and Illumination Apparatus, and to Beacons, Buoys, and Fog Signals, 1789-1871* (Washington, D.C.: Government Printing Office, 1871)

U.S. Lighthouse Society, *The Keeper's Log,* quarterly publication (San Francisco, California)

Updike, Richard W. , "Winslow Lewis and Lighthouses," in *The American Neptune,* January 1968

Interior of Spring Point Ledge Lighthouse in 1989. HABS/HAER photo by Richard Clark.

208

Index

Two Bush Island Light Station 66, 88–89, 108, 182, 192, 203

U

U.S. Army 61, 110, 167
U.S. Army Bureau of Topographical Engineers 24, 63
U.S. Board of Navy Commissioners. *See* Board of Navy Commissioners
U.S. Bureau of Lighthouses 62, 177–178
U.S. Coast Guard 110, 118, 181, 187, 191–196
U.S. Coast Guard cutters 110
U.S. Department of Commerce 177
U.S. Fish and Wildlife Service 194
U.S. Life-Saving Service 108, 118, 158, 167, 181
U.S. Light-House Board 56, 61–124, 127, 128, 132, 136, 149, 153, 159, 160, 169, 171, 173, 177; 1852 report 132; committees 61; duties of 61; members 61; personnel 128
U.S. Navy 61, 103, 156, 196
U.S. Revenue Cutter Service 2, 19, 37, 44, 49, 51, 53, 54, 103, 118, 119, 130
U.S. Secretary of the Treasury. *See* Secretary of the Treasury
U.S. Treasury Department 1, 12, 23, 118, 138
Upham, John 28

V

ventilation 10, 31, 40, 65, 89
ventilators. *See* lanterns
Vicksburgh, schooner 165
Vinalhaven, Maine 73, 88, 108, 194
Viola Brewer, schooner 109
visitors. *See* lighthouse visitors

W

W. H. Glover Co. 89
Wagner Mechanical Lamp 93
Waldo County Hospital 140
Walker, E. P. 88
War Department 74, 110, 146
War of 1812 13
Wasgatt, Ambrose J. 145
Wasgatt, Dr. 140
Wasgatt, William N. 138
Washington, George 1
Wassawinkeag Hotel 153
water collection 4, 11, 24, 28, 36, 56, 68, 85, 99, 136. *See also* cisterns
Watts, Gene 187
Wave, USLHT 103, 136
weather 127, 135, 138, 155, 178. *See also* storms
Webster, Anne 194
West Cuckholds 184
West Penobscot Bay 23, 142
West Quoddy Head Light Station 2, 12, 13, 23, 51, 65, 93, 95, 97–99, 101, 128, 160–161, 173, 178, 194, 203
Whaleback Ledge Light Station 38, 39, 58–59, 101, 203
wharf 110-111
Wheeler, Samuel 11
Whig party 46, 123
whistles. *See* fog signals: steam whistles
Whitehead Island 111, 195
Whitehead Island Lifesaving Station 167
Whitehead Island Light Station 11–13, 31, 89, 97, 101, 118, 126, 128, 134, 147, 149, 155, 165, 166, 185, 193, 195, 203
Whitlocks Mill Light Station 66, 112, 115–116, 203
Widow's Island 73
Wilde, George F. F. 118
Wiley, Henry 141–143; John F. 143
Williams, Charles S. 39; William C. 39–42

Wilson, Thomas 165
Wincapaw, Bill, Jr. 180
Wincapaw, Capt. William H. 180
Winter Harbor Light Station 65, 109, 187, 188, 204
Wiscasset Harbor 28
Witch Rock 113
Wm. Tibbetts, steamer 104
Wood Island Lifesaving Station 118
Wood Island Light Station 12, 14, 22, 194, 204
Woodbury, Levi 30, 130
wooden towers 3, 6, 8, 10–13, 28, 58, 65, 67, 76–79, 113, 125. *See also* lighthouse construction: materials
woodhouses 52, 53
Woodward, George 94, 126
World War II 180
Wrangel, USCGC 110

Y

York Beach, Maine 35, 155
York Harbor 42
York Nubble. *See* Cape Neddick Light Station

About the Authors

Candace Clifford, a lighthouse historian, served as consultant, to the National Park Service's Maritime Heritage Program (1988-2001) where she compiled and edited *1990 Inventory of Large Historic Vessels* and *1994 Inventory of Historic Light Stations*, produced *Historic Lighthouse Preservation Handbook*; created National Lighthouse Heritage website <www.cr.nps.gov/maritime/lt_index.htm>; coordinated U.S. Coast Guard cooperative projects; edited and finalized lighthouse nominations for the National Register of Historic Places and National Historic Landmarks program; and documented two Fresnel lens projects.

Currently an independent researcher, Candace does most of her work at the National Archives in Washington, D.C., documenting lighthouses and other maritime resources. Candace and Mary Louise Clifford are co-authors of *Women Who Kept the Lights: An Illustrated History of Female Lighthouse Keepers* and *Nineteenth-Century Lights: Historic Images of American Lighthouses.*

Mary Louise Clifford has published twelve other titles. Her fourth fiction title, published in 2005, is titled *Lonesome Road*—a young adult novel that involves a student at William and Mary seeking medical folklore from a Chickahominy Indian medicine woman, who lives in nearby Charles City County, Virginia. Her granddaughter Luney opens up a whole new world for Tom.